Praise for Thomas McGuane's

The Longest Silence

"It's vintage McGuane, the prose elegant and erudite."
—*The Denver Post*

"A meaty book, and an uplifting one, dazzlingly well-written. . . . As compelling a testimony to the power and mystery of obsession as I have ever read."
—Tom Fort, *Financial Times*

"Certain to entertain fellow enthusiasts and fans of his writing. . . . McGuane casts not only his fishing line, but also his magic at turning a precise phrase and evoking a delightful image."
—*Publishers Weekly* (starred review)

"An outlaw spirit moves through these fish stories. . . . Iconoclastic, unpredictable. . . . Audacious."
—*Kirkus Reviews*

"Readers will feel the strong, cold currents of fish-infested rivers at their legs." —*Booklist*

Thomas McGuane

The Longest Silence

Thomas McGuane lives on a ranch in McLeod,
Montana. He is the author of ten novels, three
works of nonfiction, and four collections of stories.

BOOKS BY THOMAS McGUANE

FICTION

The Sporting Club
The Bushwhacked Piano
Ninety-two in the Shade
Panama
Nobody's Angel
Something to Be Desired
To Skin a Cat
Keep the Change
Nothing but Blue Skies
The Cadence of Grass
Gallatin Canyon
Driving on the Rim
Crow Fair
Cloudbursts

NONFICTION

An Outside Chance
Some Horses

The Longest Silence

The Longest Silence

A LIFE IN FISHING

THOMAS MCGUANE

VINTAGE BOOKS
A Division of Penguin Random House LLC
New York

Several pieces that are newly collected in this edition originally
appeared in the following publications: "Sasha and the Salmon" (2013),
"Steelhead" (2011), "Black Squall" (2019), "Shrink to Fit" (2018) in
The Drake. "Trails of Tarpon" as "My Tarpon Addiction" in *Field & Stream*,
and subsequently in *Casting Quiet Waters*, edited by Jake MacDonald,
in 2014. "Seeing Snook" (1994) in *Sports Illustrated*.

The Library of Congress has cataloged the Knopf edition as follows:
Name: McGuane, Thomas.
Title: The longest silence : a life in fishing / Thomas McGuane.
Description: First edition | New York : Alfred A. Knopf, 1999.
Identifiers: LCCN 99027199
Subjects: | Fishing.
LCC: SH443 .M38 1999 | DDC 799.1—dc23
LC record available at https://lccn.loc.gov/99027199

Vintage Books Trade Paperback ISBN: 978-0-525-56530-7
eBook ISBN: 978-0-307-76391-4

Book design by Robert C. Olsson

www.vintagebooks.com

Printed in the United States of America
15 14 13 12 11 10

For Yvon Chouinard

Contents

Contents

Some Remarks

The sport of angling used to be a genteel business, at least in the world of ideals, a world of ladies and gentlemen. These have been replaced by a new set of paradigms: the bum, the addict, and the maniac. I'm afraid that this says much about the times we live in. The fisherman now is one who defies society, who rips lips, who drains the pool, who takes no prisoners, who is not to be confused with the sissy with the creel and the bamboo rod. Granted, he releases that which he catches, but in some cases, he strips the quarry of its perilous soul before tossing it back in the water. What was once a trout—cold, hard, spotted, and beautiful—becomes "number seven." Perhaps he's the winning run in the one-fly contest, or the fish that put the Czechoslovakians across the finish line ahead of the Americans in the world championship of fly-fishing.

Angling is a situation whose dramatic values are immediately charged by their context. The angler who, to the envy of his peers, has "gone fishin'" in that mythic sense that implies a non-return, soon finds himself alone in a leaden state of malaise and ennui. The spectacle of the angler gone native—that is in the miraculous event that he hasn't staved off a coma by giving up fishing—is a study in torpor at close range, practically in laboratory conditions.

Many fishing books by what are known as experts seem filled with the longueurs and repetitions that incite the clever reader to cry, "Get a life!" Worst of all are the lamentations of the angler who has given himself entirely to the sport and feels that sportsmen up for the week or the season or the run only to return to jobs and family *don't understand him.*

I'm afraid that the best angling is always a respite from burden. Good anglers should lead useful lives, and useful lives are marked by struggle, and difficulty, and even pain. Perhaps the agony of simple mortality should be enough. But probably it is not. As they say in South America, everyone knows that they are going to die; yet nobody believes it. Human lapses of this kind enable us to fish, fornicate, overeat, and bet on the horses.

Therefore, bow your back and fish when you can. When you get to the water you will be renewed. Leave as much behind as possible. Those motives to screw your boss or employees, cheat on your spouse, rob the state, or humiliate your companions will not serve you well if you expect to be restored in the eyes of God, fish, and the river, which will reward you with hollow waste if you don't behave. You may be cursed. You may be shriven. You may be drowned. At the very least, you may snap off your fly in the bushes.

We like to think of the idea of selective trout; it serves our anthropocentricity to believe that we are in a duel of wits with a fish, a sporting proposition. We would do well to understand that trout and other game fish are entirely lacking in sporting instincts. They would prefer to dine unmolested and without being eaten themselves.

In my view, a trout that is feeding selectively is doing the following: having ascertained that many of the objects going by his view are edible, he decides which ones he can eat efficiently and which will do him the most good. Then, in the interest of energy conservation, and if the chosen food item is in sufficient quantity, the trout gradually transfers the decision-making process to something like muscle memory, to thoughtless routine. If the fly we cast fails to trigger that recognition or is not in the rhythm in which the trout is feeding, we get a no-sale. The base of difficulty from the angler's point of view is the quantity of food items appearing before the trout. If he can key in and fill up, the angler may have a problem. That is why, even though it is full of fish, a bug soup like the Henry's Fork has brought so many to tears or aged them prematurely. It is also why one or two fish on the Fork can make such a satisfying day.

In this, the trout is like the interstate motorist who, having engaged the cruise control, sleepily notes at the mouth of an obscure off-ramp a sign that reads FREE BEER. Most motorists would conclude somewhat abstractly that there must be a catch. The paranoid motorist would conclude that it's an ambush. A few motorists, the dumb ones, might disengage the cruise control and pull off. Mike Lawson refers to slow-water smart trout as opposed to fast-water dumb trout. A dogged freestoner, I must prevaricate: the fast-water trout is an opportunist and his opportunities for observation are compressed by the turbulence of the conditions in which he lives. But even in faster water, the bigger fish dominate the feeding stations where a better look is possible: the long seams, the well-defined riffle corners with the isometrics of current well spaced, the luxury apartments of streambed hydrology. That's why they are bigger fish. These are masters of the perfect niche, one designed to keep herons, otters, mergansers, and you from raining on their parade. The perfect overhanging branch so hard on presentation, so cherished by trout, is sometimes removed, pruned away by riverkeepers who do not seem to realize that the fish leave with the offending branch and that while the sport may then luxuriate in unencumbered presentation, it is for naught. If a fish is there, he is smaller than the fish that used to be there.

I once fished a small spring creek in Gallatin County with George Anderson, a stickler for accurate casting. With George at my side, I was blazing away at a steady feeder, proud of every cast. When George said, "I see you've decided to go with the shotgun technique," I concluded I must improve. Since that day, many years ago, I have practiced. I keep a rod rigged and leaning against the house and I almost never doublehaul something into the weeping birch a hundred feet away. I frequently try to put the bit of red yarn in front of a robin's beak at thirty or forty feet. I have even had a couple of most satisfying takes. Perhaps things would pick up if I went to a San Juan worm. At the moment, takes per cast on robins are close to those for permit on a fly. They're not on long, but I've had some memorable moments where the robin backed doggedly, with the yarn, annoyed wings beating the grass, several feet, though not by any stretch of the imagination into the backing.

All salmonids must be saluted for bearing upon their collective shoulders the burden of generations of contradictory theorizing as to what they want to eat and how they are best persuaded to give up their lives and freedom.

These delights have sent me in search of second-class waters. I live near the great theme park of fly-fishing, the headwaters of the Missouri, but go there less and less. I spend more time on prairie rivers with their unstable banks and midsummer thermal problems. What do I find there besides a few fish who have been leading exceedingly private lives? I find solitude, which is not, take note, the same thing as loneliness.

We have reached the time in the life of the planet, and humanity's demands upon it, when every fisherman will have to be a riverkeeper, a steward of marine shallows, a watchman on the high seas. We are beyond having to put back what we have taken out. We must put back more than we take out. We must make holy war on the enemies of aquatic life as we have against gillnetters, polluters, and drainers of wetlands. Otherwise, as you have already learned, these creatures will continue to disappear at an accelerating rate. We will lose as much as we have lost already and there will be next to nothing, remnant populations, put-and-take, dim bulbs following the tank truck.

What happens to the chronic smeller of flowers, watcher of birds, listener to distant thunder? Certainly, he has lost efficiency as an angler. Has he become less of an angler? Perhaps. This is why fishermen are such liars. They are ashamed of their lollygagging and wastage of time. It's an understandable weakness. In some of today's brawny fish camps, flowers and birds can raise eyebrows.

I thought my father must have been a wonderful fisherman, but I wasn't sure. He taught me how to fish in a rather perfunctory way on the Pere Marquette River in Michigan. In later years, and to my great distress, he got away from fishing except in a ceremonial way, making an annual trip to Boca Grande or the River of Ponds or Piñas Bay. He had given up ordinary fishing and replaced it with extremely infrequent high-profile trips meant to substitute in intensity what he lacked in time. This in angling is a snare and delusion. Angling is extremely time consuming. That's sort of the whole point. That is why in our high-speed world anglers, as a kind of preemptive strike, call themselves bums, addicts, and maniacs. We're actually rather quiet people for the most part but our attitude toward time sets us at odds with our own society.

After my father died, I was invited to spend a day fishing with his oldest friend, my so-called uncle Ben, an excellent angler. We spent a satisfying day looking for bonefish in three feet of winter water in the Content Keys. At the end of the day, standing on the dock, I asked, with some trepidation:

"Uncle Ben, was my father a good fisherman?"

He smiled and said, "No, Tommy, he was not. But no one loved it more."

This to me is a conundrum. "No one loved it more." Isn't that enough? Who is the better angler, the patient bait soaker under the walls of the Seine, the black woman with the cane pole on Mobile Bay, the aging Russian bureaucrat on the River Volga, or the film producer on the Kharlovka or the flats of Ascension Bay? Let's be honest: it could be any of the above.

Last winter, I was fishing on a small steelhead river in Oregon. It was one of those rare times when fly-fishing was by far the most effective way to catch a fish. I was looking across the river in the shade of wintry alders at a pod of bright fish thirty feet long. I was looking success in the eye. As I approached the fish, I was watched by a gear fisherman in rubber barn boots and a worn-out mackinaw coat. I was able to hook a fish and slide it away from the school, land it down below, release it, resume my position, and hook another fish. The gear angler grew agitated. I released that fish and hooked a third. With this, he shot to my side holding a long-handled net at the ready. "If you don't want them, I'll take 'em," he said.

"I release my fish," I said. "That's just the way I like to fish."

"Mister," he said, "I've been trying to catch a fish for my old folks to eat for four days and I haven't even had a bite. Can't you let me have this one fish?"

Well, I thought about it. Most of these fish were of hatchery origin and it was quite legal to kill them. I didn't look forward to it but I said, "All right." A few minutes later the fish was in the net, a bright, wild, native male. My companion looked into the net and, before I could speak, said, "Oops, he ain't fin clipped. That's a native. Put him back."

I released the fish and the two of us watched him swim away. We shook hands and went our separate ways in an atmosphere of fellowship. He was a man we could all talk to, a brother in angling. A man like this could take our side against the dams and subdivisions. He knew which ones were wild. If fly fishermen have an edge in this elaboration of soul that we resent hearing called a sport but are too timid to call an art, it is in our willingness to deepen the experience at nearly any personal cost. That is the reason we tie flies, not to save money through bulk purchase of hooks and feathers. That is why some of us cannot live without that breath of varnish from the rod tube when we rig up for another holy day. The motto of every serious angler is "Nearer My God to Thee." Humans have suspected for thousands of years that angling and religion are connected. But if you can find no higher ideal than outfishing your buddies, catching something big enough to stuff or winning a trophy, you have a lot of work to do before you are what Izaak Walton would call an angler.

Recently I heard of an old friend saying that the two rules of life he followed were: don't even tell your mother your fishing spots, and other fishermen are the number-one enemy. It is embarrassing to note the ring of truth these rules seem to have. But I think we're going to have to rise above them. Sixty million disorganized fishermen are being hornswaggled by tightly organized and greedy elites. Last year, under the shadow of numerous environmental organizations locally headquartered, and against the wishes of 70 percent of its citizenry, Montana's legislature undermined the best water quality laws in the Rockies and made them the worst. This, in the epicenter of North American trout fishing. Still, we cast a mistrustful eye on one another, like worn-out, secretive prospectors of last century's gold camps. The world goes on without us, using our rivers for other than their original purposes. We really ought to get together.

I began remembering a time when my son and I were dropped at a small tundra pond in Alaska after a short ride in a beautiful Grumman Beaver that the owner had acquired from the Austrian forest service, which had owned it for thirty years and scarcely flown it. It was a zero-hours Beaver, the newest one in the world, an unimaginable prize in Alaska. Our short flight took us over the heroic spaciousness of the northern edge of the Katmai wildlife area, an area of truly fierce beauty. Nothing we'd ever seen prepared us for it. Our landing interrupted a bald eagle's attempt to ambush a flock of young harlequin ducks, and the eagle angrily wheeled around behind us. Picture a pond as small and intimate as Walden with hundreds of miles of visibility in all directions, ground that quivered, mountains that looked like they predated the world itself, a sky that was a record of the North Pacific's infinity of moods.

I didn't realize tundra was so interesting. We got out of the float plane and began walking on an endless flower- and moss-covered pudding that trembled under our feet at first and then, as we got away from the lake, firmed up to about the consistency of a mattress. In its intricacy of gold, green, pink, and yellow, an outburst of almost incomprehensible botanic creativity, we lamented every footstep. This was land that seemed to never have expected human passage, a place made for the vast spatial needs of Alaskan brown bears and arctic wolves. We used a small raft to get around. My son and I, along with Don and Dave, an eccentric piano duo from a foothills town in the West, sat on the sides of the raft, wadered legs dangling in the water, and coasted along the small river on our way to fishing spots. As we passed high banks, I saw claw marks ten feet off the ground where the bears had feasted on cliff swallow nestlings. With fly rods in our hands, we had dropped through time. Fishing had given us this.

Early on, I decided that fishing would be my way of looking at the world. First it taught me how to look at rivers. Lately it has been teaching me how to look at people, myself included. To the reader accustomed to the sort of instructional fishing writing which I myself enjoy, I must seem to have gotten very far afield. I simply feel that the frontier of angling is no longer either technical or geographical. The Bible tells us to watch and to listen. Something like this suggests what fishing ought to be about: using the ceremony of our sport and passion to arouse greater reverberations within ourselves.

The Longest Silence

Small Streams in Michigan

THE FIRST FLY ROD I ever owned was eight feet of carpet beater made by a company whose cork grips were supplied by my father. My father worked for a Portuguese cork company whose owners swam at Estoril and supplied our family with innumerable objects of cork, including cork shoes, cork boxes, cork purses, and unidentified flying cork objects that my brother and I threw at each other. In our living room we had large cut-glass decanters of Burgundy, long soured, and my brother and I would have a couple of hits of that vinegar and head for the cellar to throw cork.

Everyone in our family had a huge brown fly rod with a Portuguese cork handle and identical Pflueger Medalist reels of the size used for Atlantic salmon. As I look back, I am touched by my father's attempts to bring us to sport, *en famille*.

I remember when he and my mother canoed the Pere Marquette in that early phase. Passing underneath the branches of streamside trees, my mother seized one of them in terror. The branch flexed; the canoe turned sideways in the current and began to go under. My father bellowed to let go of the branch. My mother did and the branch shot across the canoe like a longbow, taking my father across the chest and knocking him overboard.

With his weight gone, one end of the canoe rose four feet out of the water and my mother twirled downstream until my father contrived to race along a footpath and make the rescue.

When it was done, two rods with Portuguese cork grips were gone. The canoe was saved until the time my brother and I used it as a toboggan in snow-filled streambeds and beat the bottom out of it.

At that time, we lived down on Lake Erie, where I conducted a mixed-bag sporting life, catching perch and rock bass on worms, some pike on Daredevils, some bass on a silver spoon. In the winter, I wandered around the lake on the ice and shot crows, a painful memory.

But when we went up north with our Portuguese cork handle fly rods, I knew the trout were there. And so I spurned worms, owned a fly box, and espoused purist attitudes in the traditional burst of posturing common to new fly fishers.

There was a lake near the cabin, and I would paddle out upon it trailing all my fly line and a Mickey Finn streamer. Then I would paddle around the lake, trolling that fly until I caught a trout. This is about the minimum, fly-wise. But I do remember, with a certain finality, what those trout looked like lying between the canoe's varnished ribs, and how it felt to put the trout and jackknife on the dock in the evening, pull the canoe up on the beach, and clean my catch.

I don't doubt that for many fine anglers the picture of what fishing could be begins with a vision of worm gobs lying in dark underwater holes, the perfect booby trap. The casters I used to see, throwing surface plugs in flat arcs up under the brushy banks, made that kind of fishing seem a myth. And once I could even see the point of fishing with outriggers. But now trout seem to be everything that is smart and perfect in fish, and their taking of a floating fly or free-drifting nymph is a culmination in sport comparable to anything. But what interests me is how I came to believe that.

I recall grouse hunting near the Pere Marquette when I was very young. It had just snowed, and I had killed one bird, which bulged warm in the back of my coat. I kicked out a few more birds in a forgotten orchard and couldn't get a shot, then walked down a wooded hill that ended in a very small stream, perhaps two feet wide, but cut rather deeply in mossy ground. A short distance above where I stood, the stream made a pool, clear and round as a lens. In the middle of that pool a nice brook trout held in the cold current. With a precision that still impresses me, it moved from one side to the other to intercept nymphs, always perfectly returning to its holding position in the little pool.

Not long after that, during trout season, I waded the Pere Marquette one hot day on which not a single rising fish was to be found. I plodded along, flicking wan, pointless casts along the bank.

The river at one point broke into channels, and one channel bulged up against a logjam, producing a kind of pool. I had always approached this place with care because trout soared around its upper parts and if a cast could be placed very quietly on the slick bulge of water, a take was often the result. I crept up, but no trout grazed under its surface waiting for my Lady Beaverkill to parachute in.

Salvation, though, was around the corner. The deep, shadowy color of the pool seemed to hold a new glint. I stood erect. There was nothing near the top of the pool for me to spook, but clearly trout were deep within it, moving enough to send up their glints.

I remembered the brooky in the minute fissure of stream when I'd been grouse shooting, and I recalled how steadily he had held except to intercept a free-swimming nymph in the icy water. It occurred to me that something like that sudden lateral movement and return must be what was sending these messages to me from this large pool in the Pere Marquette.

I tied on an indeterminately colored nymph and shot a cast up to the head of the pool. The nymph dropped and sank, and the point of my floating line began its retreat back toward me at current speed. About a third of the way back, the line point stopped. I lifted and felt the weight. A couple of minutes later, I trapped a nice brown trout against the gravel at the foot of the pool with my trembling hands.

This was before I had learned the thrill of the release, of a trout darting from your opening hands or resting its weight very slightly in your palms underwater, then easing off. So three nice trout went from the pool into my creel and then, after a decent interval, into my mouth.

Anyway, the connection was complete. And even if I couldn't always put it together, I saw how it was with nymphs. Years of casting and retrieving made it difficult to slackline a tumbling nymph— the forms of manipulation in trout fishing are always so remote—but

I realized that fishing a nymph invisible under the pools and runs on a tensionless line was not inferior in magic to fishing a dry-fly.

Later we found a long beaver pond covering many acres of ground in a dense mixed forest of pine and conifer. I had a hunch that good-size brook trout had migrated down from the stream and into the pond.

Beaver ponds are a mixed blessing, providing only a few years of good fishing. After that the standing water turns sour and the size of the average fish gets smaller as his head grows proportionately larger. But this pond was only a couple of years old, with a soft bottom covered with drowned leaves.

I had some trouble locating the pond but ended up tracking its source through the cedars. It was almost evening when I got there, and huge columns of light came down through the forest. There was a good hatch of mayflies in progress along the stream, with small trout rising to them and cedar waxwings overhead hovering in the swarm.

The pond was perfect. Some dead trees stood ghostlike in its middle, and the pond itself inundated small bays around the water-tolerant cedars. Best of all, big, easy rises were in numerous places, slow takes that produced an actual sucking noise.

I cautiously waded for position. The pond was so smooth that I anxiously anticipated the fall of line on its surface. I had a piece of inner tube in my shirt and I used it to thoroughly straighten my leader.

Every time I moved on the soft bottom, a huge cloud of mud arose, carried behind me and then filtered down through the beaver dam. It was a cool summer evening and I was wearing a flannel shirt; I shivered a little and tried to keep from looking up when one of the big rises opened on the pond.

I tied on my favorite fly, the Adams, a pattern that exemplifies my indecisive nature. The Adams looks a little like all bugs. It's gray and speckly and a great salesman. My fly box is mainly Adamses in about eight different sizes. In the future, I mean to be a fine streamside entomologist. I'm going to start on that when I am much too old to do any of the two thousand things I can think of that are more fun than screening insects in cold running water.

Making a first cast on delicate water can be a problem. You haven't warmed up and it may be your most important cast. I had the advantage on this glassy pond of being able to see a number of widely separated rises, and I felt that, at worst, I could blow off one fish and still keep my act alive for one or two more.

I looked around, trying to find a place for my backcast, stripped some line, and false-cast carefully until the instant a rise began to open on the surface. I threw and dropped the fly much closer than I deserved. I poised myself not to break the light tippet on the strike and held that attitude up to the descending moment I realized the fish wasn't going to take. Another fish rose and I covered him, waited, and got no take.

I let the line lie on the water and tried to calm down. My loop was turning over clean and quiet; the leader was popping out straight. The Adams sat cheerily on its good hackle points. I refused to believe the fish were that selective. Then I hung up a cast behind me, trying to cover a fish at too new an angle, and a lull set in.

You never know about lulls. You ask, Is it my fault? Do the trout know I'm here? Have they heard or felt my size-twelve tread on this boggy ground? Is my casting coarse and inaccurate? Where can I buy a drink at this hour?

It was getting dark. I didn't have a fish. The rises kept appearing. I kept casting and never got a take. There is a metallic loss of light one feels when it is all over. You press to the end but it's kaput. I left in blackness. A warm wind came up and gave the mosquitoes new hope. I lit a cigar to keep them out of my face and trudged through the forms of the big cedars along the stream, trying not to fall. I snagged my suspenders on a bramble and snapped myself. The moon was full and I was thinking about the TV.

The next evening I was back earlier. This time I crawled to the edge of the pond with the light at my back and had a good look. The first thing I saw was the rises, as many as the night before. I remembered how they had failed to materialize then and checked my excitement. As I watched, I caught a rise at the moment it opened, then saw the fish drop beneath the ring and continue cruising until it was beyond my view. The next rise I caught, I saw another cruiser, moving immediately away from the place of the rise and looking for another insect. I began to realize my error of the night before. These were cruising fish, waiting for something to pass through their observation lane. There were a good number of them traveling about the pond, hunting for food.

I retreated from my place beside the pond, circled around below the dam and waded into my position of the night before. I tied on another Adams, this time a rather large one. I cast it straight out into the middle of the pond and let it lie.

Rises continued to happen, picking up a little as evening advanced and the cedar waxwings returned to wait, like me, for the hatch. My Adams floated in place, clearly visible, and I could see the curves of my leader in the surface skin of the water. I waited for a trying length of time. I had to see my theory through because, like many a simpleminded sportsman, I see myself as a problem solver.

The fly dropped out of sight. I didn't respond until the ring had already started to spread, and I lifted the rod and felt the fish. The trout darted off in a half-dozen chugging didoes in the dark water over drowned leaves. I landed him a moment later, a brook trout of a solid pound. I studied him a moment and thought what a bright, lissome, perfect fish this little American char is.

Brook trout are cheerfully colored in deep reds, grays, and blues, with ivory leading edges and deep moony spots on their fins. They are called squaretails elsewhere, after the clear graphics of their profiles. I reached for my Adams and felt the small teeth roughen the first knuckles of my thumb and forefinger. Then I let him go. He sank to the leaves at my feet, thought for a minute, and made off.

I rinsed the fly carefully. That long float required a well-dried fly. Then I false-cast the fly a moment to dry it, applied some Mucilin dressing, which I kept smeared on the back of my left hand, and cast again. This time I stared at the fly for ten or fifteen minutes, long enough to notice the Adams changing its waterline. But then it sank suddenly and I had another fish.

Since casting was nearly eliminated from this episode, the fishing did not seem fast. But at the end of a couple of hours, I had taken seven fish. The takers were all solid, confident, and deep. I released all the fish, and by the time I'd hiked out of the boggy forest that night, I could feel glory all around me.

One might say, pragmatically, that in still or nearly still waters, feeding trout cruise; and that in streams and rivers they tend to take a feeding lane and watch a panel of moving water overhead, elevating to eat when something passes; and that the repeated rises of a holding trout in a stream are as unlike the disparate rises of my beaver pond as they are unlike the deep glintings of nymphing trout. But the fact is, these episodes are remembered as complete dramatic entities, whose real function, finally, is to be savored. It is fine, of course, to escalate them toward further successes. But in the end, angling has nothing whatsoever to do with success.

Nevertheless, by the time the aforementioned nymphing trout had been met and dealt with, I had come to think of myself as a pretty smart fisherman. I had a six-cylinder black Ford, a mahogany tackle box, two split-cane rods, and Adamses in eight sizes. I had cheap, clean lodgings within quick reach of the Pigeon, Black, and Sturgeon rivers, where I ate decently prepared food with the owner, one or two other fishermen, and perhaps a young salesman with a line of practical shoes and a Ford like mine.

From here, I'd pick a stretch of the Pigeon or the Black for the early fishing, wade the oxbow between the railroad bridges on the Sturgeon in the afternoon. Then, in the evening, I'd head for a wooden bridge over the Sturgeon near Wolverine.

Below the bridge was a large pool deeply surrounded by brush and inhabited by nearly nocturnal brown trout. A sandy bottom shelved off into the undercut banks and it was a rarity to find a feeding fish here in the daytime. But shortly after dinnertime in the summer, when the hatches seemed to come, the trout would venture out into the open pool and feed with greater boldness.

I stood on the bridge and rigged my rod with a relatively short, heavy leader. The fish were not leader-shy this late. I tied on a fly known locally as a "caddis," though it was anything but an actual caddis. This was a huge, four-winged fly with a crosshatched deerhair body. Lying in your open hand, it covered the palm, and when cast, its wings made a turbulent noise like the sound of a bat passing your ear.

The trout liked it real well. What I appreciated was that I could fish from this wooden bridge in the black of night without fear of falling in a hole, filling my waders, and passing on. I'd cast that big baby until two or three in the morning, guessing at the rate at which I should retrieve to keep up with the fly backing down on the current toward me. I had to strike by sound every rise I heard. Five out of six rises I struck would just snatch the fly and line into a heap at my feet. But that one out of six would be solid to a trout, and some of those trout were big by my small-stream standards.

Finally, something would end the fishing—an especially baleful frog in the swamp, a screech owl or a train a couple of miles away— and I'd reel up for the evening. I'd take my trout and lay them out in the headlights of the Ford and think how sweet it was. Then I'd clean them with my pocketknife, slitting them to the vent, separating the gills at the point of jaw and shucking those fastidious entrails. I'd run out the black blood along the spine with my thumbnail so it wouldn't change their flavor, restack them in the creel, and head back to my lodgings.

THE FIRST TIME I met my wife's grandfather I was twenty and a full-blown trout snob. Pomp, as he was called, was a gifted bait fisherman, and he took the position that I fly-fished because I didn't want to get worms on my hands.

Pomp and his wife lived near Kaleva, Michigan, which is one of the numerous Finnish communities in the state. They had a cabin overlooking Bear Creek on a small piece of ground next to a gradually approaching gravel pit, and they lived a through-the-looking-glass life, to which we all tried to annex ourselves.

My wife had a better line on the situation than I. She had summered in a jungle hammock with her grandparents, helped bake pies for the raccoons, been accidentally locked in the sauna of the neighbor's farm, now abandoned, with nothing inside but a moth-eaten Korean War infantry uniform. Moreover, she could report to me the kind of trout fishing Pomp was capable of—upstream bait-fishing, the deadliest in the right hands. He had great hands. Not only that, he belonged to the category of sportsmen who will stop at nothing.

Bear Creek ran through a large corrugated culvert under a country road. Pomp had located a very large trout living there, a spotted brute that finned forward in the evening to feed in the pool at the upstream end of the culvert. How he knew about that trout I can't say, but for sure he knew it by indirection. He had great instincts about trout, much envied by the locals. Pomp was from farther south in Michigan, and among the old-timers there was a competition over who was from farther north than who. Now it has become a perfect frenzy as the footloose Michigander wages the war of roots with fellow cottage builders.

Anyway, he crept up and hooked the thing and quickly discovered it was bigger than he expected. The trout fought its way down the culvert. At the far end it would be a lost cause, the line cut through by the culvert itself. I was a fly fisherman, new to Pomp's world, when I first heard this story, and I confess that I reached this point in the narrative without beginning to see how I would have landed the fish. But Pomp had a solution.

He had his wife lie across the far end of the culvert. He fought the fish to a standstill inside the pipe and landed it. As I say, this was early in our experience together, and the reader will remember that it was his opinion that I fished with flies in order to keep from touching worms.

Heretofore, I had hoped to outfish him in our already burgeoning, if covert, competition. But his emplacement of his wife at the far end of the culvert in order to beat that trout showed me what I was up against.

And in fact, as a bit of pleasant foreshortening, I ought to say that he consistently outfished me all along, right through the year of his death, the news of which came by telephone, as usual, in some pointless city.

I had accumulated some ways of taking trout above and below the surface. We would start at dawn with shots of bourbon from the refrigerator, cold to take away its edge in the morning. Next, trout, potatoes and eggs for breakfast, during which Pomp would describe to me and to my fly-fishing brother-in-law, Dan Crockett, the hopelessness of our plight and the cleanliness of worms. It has been several decades since Dan and I contemplated those words. This morning, after thousands of trout have fallen to his rod, Dan died of cancer.

Then on into the day, fishing, principally, the Betsey, the Bear, and the Little Manistee rivers. Usually, we ended on the Bear, below the cabin, and it was then, during the evening hatch, that I hoped to even my morbidly reduced score.

The day I'm thinking of was in August, when the trout were down deep where only Pomp could reason with them. I dutifully cast my flies up into the brilliant light hour after hour and had, for my pains, a few small fish. Pomp had a lot more. And his were bigger, having sent their smaller, more gullible friends to the surface for my flies.

But by late afternoon, summer rain clouds had begun to build higher and blacker, and finally startling cracks of thunder commenced. We were scattered along the banks of the Bear, and as the storm built, I knew Pomp would head for the cabin. I started that way, too, but as I passed the lower bridge pool, trout were rising everywhere. I stopped to make a cast and promptly caught one. By the time I'd landed it, the trees were bowing and surging, and casting was simply a question of rolling the line downwind onto the pool. The lightning was literally blasting into the forest, and I was suddenly cold from the wind-driven rain. But the trout were rising with still more intensity.

When I was a child, I heard that a man was killed by lightning that ran down the drainspout of a bus station. Ever since then, lightning has had a primordial power to scare me. I kept casting, struck, misstruck, and landed trout, while the electric demon raced around those Michigan woods.

I knew Pomp was up in the cabin. Probably had a cigar and was watching the water stream from the corner of the roof. Something was likely baking in the kitchen. But I meant to hang in there until I limited out. Well, I didn't. The storm stopped abruptly and the universe was full of ozone and new light and I was ready for the cabin.

Outside the cabin, there was a wooden table next to a continuously flowing well where we cleaned our trout. The overflow of the well ran down the hill to the Bear, and when we cleaned the trout, we chucked the insides down the hill for the raccoons. I laid my trout out on the table and went in to get Pomp.

Pomp came out and said, "What do you know about that!"

Back in Ireland

I'M FISHING THROUGH thirty years of unreliable memory, to a meandering trip through southern Ireland in a Morris Minor of ancient vintage. I have a few changes of clothes, a rubberized Irish raincoat; and the rest is my fishing gear. I have accepted driving on the other side of the road and shifting with my left hand, the delicate hum of the little motor, the alarming Third World driving habits of the locals.

I remember standing on the pilings at the mouth of the Galway river casting Blue Zulus for "white trout," the extremely strong little sea trout which are part of Ireland's fame. I also remember hanging over the old bridge in Galway City to watch the big, bright Atlantic salmon resting in the middle of town. I remember meeting and being taken in by a well-to-do American family who had purchased a beautiful Georgian home on the Blackwater river. An Irish girl built me a peat fire in the morning and told me that it was never necessary to eat anything but potatoes. I was comfortable and happy until I saw that my role would be to entertain the family's teenage son, a whining nitwit. I drove him around the countryside in the Morris and gave him casting lessons. Almost old enough to join the army, he sniveled on about "Mummy" until the arrangement lost all value. The Blackwater River itself was hedged in by endless rules and the Americans imitating the Anglo-Irish gentry were avid to obey what they took to be an ancient order. These were the Kennedy years and when JFK passed over a garden party in the compound where I stayed, ruffling aristocratic hairs with his helicopter, no one looked up.

Walking to the Blackwater one day, I met a local man home on furlough from his duties with a NATO peacekeeping force in the Middle East. He had a young pointer bitch with him, a lithe, speckled ballerina of a bird dog. While we talked, she soothed her impatience by leaping back and forth across a little brook, glancing anxiously at her owner, who had ruined her jaunt by talking to this American. Something about the sight of that beautiful and energetic dog made me anxious to leave my comforts, my peat fire, and my unspoken duties to the nitwit. Discomfort set in and I was once again on my way in the little Morris, clothes and the tools of my passion in back. I remember spotting the young puke cuddling Mummy in the doorway. Neither of them waved and I was aware of having made a bad impression. It was opportunism gone sour.

I think I was headed for the River Maigue, probably because I liked the name when I passed through Kilmallock, a small market town in County Limerick on the road to Rathluirc, a town which after numerous sackings by fun-loving Oliver Cromwell became "an abode of wolves." Four hundred years later, things had quieted down. There I spotted an establishment called Tom McGuane's Dry Goods. I stopped the car and went in. The store was of the marginal type then common in southern Ireland, where no light was turned on until it was firmly established that a customer was present. A man walked past me, pulled the string. I introduced myself. Without any special reaction, he replied, "How do you do, Tom. I'm Tom McGuane." I met Mrs. McGuane and her two beautiful daughters. All lived in the back of the store in immaculate austerity and that air of an impending joke that is many people's favorite part of Irish life. I explained to my hosts that I was looking for a place to fish. We had already decided that we were unrelated.

"Get a room at Mrs. D'Arcy's pub across the way. We'll send someone round for you after supper."

I got a white, breezy, comfortable room on the second story for about the price of an American hamburger. I spread out my books and tackle while watching the street below, anxious about the vagueness of my arrangements. There was a high overcast sky and the ancient street below me and the sight of the ruins of a medieval abbey in an empty pasture added to the sense, critical to fishing, that time no longer mattered. I was at that blissful stage in my life when my services were sought by no one. I didn't know how good I had it.

A man appeared below, Ned Noonan was his name, already in his hip boots, carrying a long-handled net and a trout rod. He had been sent to see me by the other Tom McGuane. He wore an old tweed cap and a gray suitcoat with a shoulder that bore the permanent scar of his creel strap and with pockets slung open at the top from years of duty. I went downstairs and we met.

"Shall we start at the Morning Star?" he inquired politely, "or the Loobagh?"

"I am afraid I don't know one from another."

"Morning Star it is then. I understand you have an automobile?"

"I do."

Ned gazed around the inside of my Morris with enormous approval. To an Irish dairyman who liked to fish, it was a very tangible luxury. Later, I could reconstruct the glee with which Ned imagined new territories. He'd had a fly rod in his hand all his life and a matchbox of homemade flies: sedges, rusty spinners, Bloody Butchers, grouse-and-orange, grouse and anything you could name. I remember first noticing his high straight backcast as he knelt before a wall of haw-thorns to present his fly to a feeding fish. He fished to eat and for the love of it. He had made the rod, made the net, made the flies and his wife had woven the creel. He was a blood-and-bone trout fisherman with a Pioneer's pin in his lapel, declaring that he abjured spiritous drink.

We fished that first evening, paralyzed by reciprocal politeness, on a small stream that wandered lazily through cow pastures. We would have better things to do once Ned absorbed the full power and implications of the 1951 Morris, parked like a black gumdrop beside the hedge.

It was very pleasant under the great clouds of swallows and may-flies, despite the thin population of fish. The scattering of ancient ruins, the long, mysterious Irish summer evening, the small trout whose ancestors swam this water when the ruins were full of people—all lent a gravity to our proceedings that I was to feel throughout my stay. Too, it was the company of anglers like Ned Noonan who could never recall when they began fishing, so undivided was it from the thread of their lives.

When I came in that evening, I returned the wave of an ardent and heavily made-up young woman with unnatural blond hair, rather a beauty but profoundly influenced by the latest Carnaby Street fashions. From time to time, she appeared in a burst of enthusiasm and ill-concealed carnality while her neighbors either stared at their shoes or moved off a short way to bless themselves. I saw her waving from the tops of buildings, from various windows and from the nave of the thirteenth-century church of Saints Peter and Paul, in ruins but the final resting place of Gaelic poets. Finally, I saw her cavorting with an entire hurley team in Blossom's Gate, the last remaining of four medieval gates. These strong, raucous men from Cork City made me realize I was more in my own depth with my shelf of books and tin box of flies upstairs at Mrs. D'Arcy's.

Blessing themselves was something the local people did many times a day. When we drove out past the parish church, Ned and my other companions would elevate the thumb and first two fingers in front of themselves and in a space smaller than a dime, make a sign of the cross, a rakish bit of muscle memory that I found myself imitating. It seemed to help before a difficult presentation to a large fish such as the listless slob of a brown trout, curd fattened at the outlet of a small creamery on the Loobagh River, where it took my grouse-and-orange.

In the water meadows whose edges I strolled awaiting the evening fishing, cranes stood alongside the half-submerged and ruined bits of fence or shot out of the hedge like arrows. Strangers wandered from other towns in black rubber boots, waterproofs, and tweed caps. Some were stockmen, driving a handful of cattle by the road, "farming the long mile." When the sky cleared, the great traveling clouds seemed to belong to the ocean. I often thought of the wild girl who turned every cornice into a parapet from which to display her international plumage—learned from magazines—directed at me, at the drifting farm men and tinkers of the road, at the hurley team from Cork. I abashedly made mention of her to Ned, who shyly informed me that the "poor thing was mad." This latter is less condemning than one might first suppose. When I wanted a sweater, we sent for the wool which arrived by train in a week, a lovely greenish-gray I had selected. Then we took it to a woman whose grown daughter was also "mad." The mother took my measurements while the haunted, tall daughter stood in the shadows. In a week the mad daughter made me a beautiful sweater. At Sunday Mass, I sat and watched a priest genuflecting against the stone flags, cracking one knee over and over until my pewmate turned to me and said, "The poor thing's mad." That only made my bottle blonde more interesting, though a sudden image of myself riding a madwoman through the moonlit streets of a tiny, poor, devoutly Catholic town where I had neither credit nor credibility (the townspeople had arbitrarily decided that I was from New Zealand) seemed frightening. Better to remain a quiet-spoken mock Kiwi with a fly rod and a Morris than risk it with someone who more and more often crooked a finger at me in demented invitation as I slipped back to my room above Mrs. D'Arcy's.

One night I read a copy of the *Dublin Times* about a month old. The Beatles had seized the English-speaking world and would soon have the rest. There was an upstart band from London, the Rolling Stones, who would soon play Dublin. A large advertisement suggested this band was going places. I looked at their pictures in astonishment. Only the English cities, I thought, could come up with these drooling imbeciles whose stippled and wolfish jaws and pusspocket eyes indicated a genetic impasse. A decade later, I tried and failed to get tickets to their concert at Altamont, where with their retinue of Hell's Angels, a rock 'n' roll ceremony of murder was performed for our guitar-ridden new world. I didn't even see it coming.

In my room, I had set out my books—my onionskin Keats, Borrow's *The Bible in Spain* and *Lavengro*, my Thoreau and Walton, my battered Yeats—and my notebook with its hopeful scratchings and imitations, my pencils, and my knife. Downstairs in the pub I ate what I was given, and it was remarkably good with a bottle of black stout to see it on its way. A black-and-white photograph I took at the time has a notation that indicates that I was going native: "A brace of fine trout

taken in the gloaming" (!). Another photograph shows me lugubri-
ously standing beside Yeats's grave, not revealing that my attitude
is much the product of being stared at by local Protestants on their
way to church, indignant at my tourism. I recall gazing at an eighth-
century high cross in the town from which my mother's family origi-
nated, staring at the stone monks, headless corpses, Daniel in the
lion's den, the peculiarly repeated faces and Celtic spirals.

Now, cheerfully ensconced in a medieval trout town, I was ready to
do battle with my bamboo rod. I had discovered that I held no advantage over the locals' cast of three wet flies with my single nymphs and
dries. Indeed, on evidence, I was quick to turn to their ways. Years
later, Americans would "discover" this soft-hackle revolution. At an
ancient monastery outside Dublin accessed by a stone causeway over
fast water, pierced by a circular opening for the angling convenience
of the friars, I imagined they sought the trout and salmon with the
down-winged, bright fly that was born in early times on the spate rivers of the Celtic world, in Wales, Scotland, Ireland, and perhaps Corn-
wall. A thousand years later, it pops up in American fly shops as a
novelty. Constant discovery is the eternal joy of the ahistorical.

My new friend Ned informed me that we would advance upon the
River Maigue by Morris Minor on the morrow. We had the usual array
of grouse-and-anythings as well as his great proof against failure, the
rusty spinner. I looked forward to the trip with enthusiasm tempered
by the conviction that Ned knew where every drop of water in Ireland
was headed. He was beyond being a presentationist, reading not only
the thought of the trout but the next thought which the trout had not
yet thought. As a result, my frequent cautious dragless drifts were
set against the backdrop of Ned's brief presentations and the hiss of
his taut leader at an angle to the current. While I did the customary
North American deep-sea wading, he knelt on the bank in his worn-
out hip boots. If brush was behind him, he turned to look quickly for
a hole in it and then, without looking again, sent the tight bow of his
backcast into it without a hitch.

Because of Ned's membership in a teetotaling society, I led a
very quiet life in Kilmallock. When we headed out into the six-hour
evening the roisterers were aligned in the pub, and they were there

when we returned home in the dark with fish to clean and supper to get. I like both lives but they really don't intersect.

Ned's wife was a sharp-minded realist who made me the occasional meal. She had a tusklike tooth that kept her mouth slightly ajar: a drunken dentist, attempting to cure her toothache by extraction, had had the tooth halfway out when he fell into a stupor on the floor. The tooth recovered, as did Mrs. Noonan, but it compromised her dentition forever. And under no circumstances, she told me, would she ever go to a dentist again.

The blond sports girl left with the hurley team never to be further seen. Across from my room, I became aware of a gloomy figure smoking cigarettes in a second-floor window, an older man in a dark tweed coat, never without a cigarette, watching the street indifferently throughout the daylight hours. I learned that he was a "returned Yank," that is, a Kilmallock local who had emigrated to America, spent his working life as a policeman, and returned to his hometown with a vast Detroit automobile to impress the locals. The car was undrivable in the local streets and was somehow disposed of. I gathered that on learning his return was not to be a triumph, the old cop sank into the gloom in which I discovered him: cigarettes, the passing scene, and the conviction he made a huge mistake leaving Boston.

One night as I dined downstairs, a modest country couple in middle age came by to present their son to Mrs. D'Arcy, who was tough and efficient, something of an authority figure if not in the town, at least on this street. The son had recently joined the Irish coast guard, and by some bureaucratic gyration he'd been sent, without ever seeing any settlement other than his native borough, straight to New York City. What an astonishment this must have provided, I thought. Butting in, I asked the young man what he thought of New York. His mother answered for him proudly, "Agh, he took no notice of it."

This, I have since decided, is the war cry of the provincial. The proprietor of a bookshop in Montana, where I live, once said to me, "Piss on Europe. I'd rather be in Livingston." And an old gentleman who worked for me on the ranch sometimes boasted that he had lived here all his life and had never been to Billings, eighty miles distant. Personally, I like the young African who made his way to the North

Pole after having been enchanted by a photograph of the icebergs. Or the father of Beryl Markham, who at about the age we go on social security decided to leave Africa and homestead again in Argentina. There's no substitute for courage.

When we fished the Morning Star and the Loobagh, I remarked to my companions on the handsome, ruined, once fine houses we saw from time to time, roofless, with fire-blackened windows. The lack of answers suggested hard days with the Fenians, of whom my great-grandfather was one, a violent rascal who was killed later in Cuba while covertly serving the United States. My grandmother told me it had never been explained why he was buried in an army cemetery in Lexington, Kentucky. He had been a specialist in violence, which even in the early part of our century made all places home. I was increasingly aware during our evening forays in my Morris across a sometimes vacant landscape that its history had been a melancholy one, and that if the small towns seemed weary, they were entitled to.

We were heading for the Maigue. In back were our rods, reels, creels, long bamboo-handled nets which hang crossways from left shoulder to right hip, various arcana like the top part of a Morris turn signal *pace* Oliver Kite, the perfect spoon for inspecting the stomach contents of a trout, waders and waterproofs, a Genoa salami, soda bread, and a knife. We planned to go nearly to Adare, situated at the top of the River Maigue's tideway, a forest and pasture gallery of intimate trout stream.

Much of the water near Adare was preserved both by the Dunraven Hotel and local fisheries societies. I relied upon Ned to find us an opening. We went up past Croom, a market town once the resort of poets and now a place of ruined abbeys, ring forts, and crumbling round towers. You would have to be born not only among these lanes to find our aperture of unguarded water but also among its rumors, which seeped details of farmsteads and leases into the local collective consciousness.

We wandered down through a pasture and there flowed the Maigue like a woodland spring creek, where the rings of already feeding trout traveled thirty yards on the silken current before disappearing. Ned went upstream a way, only occasionally revealing himself through the steady motions of his rod.

I got myself in place to fish the spinner fall. Before I caught my first fish, a troupe of black-and-white cows gathered on the bank to watch me. After suspicion at the movements of my rod passed, they begin to cogitate on my activity, shifting their lower jaws and gazing from under long eyelashes, straight through me to some larger knowledge of human antics.

The fish I caught were all around two pounds apiece. I don't remember ever catching stronger, wilder, more violent or wanton fighters than these fish. They were vividly leopard-marked with short, hard bodies. They wore me out with their valor.

I have thought of that evening for thirty years. Then, in Montana, I ran into a man married to an Irish woman, a fly fisher who knew the Maigue. Don't go back, he said, they've drained the bogs and ruined it. Could this be? I knew how to find out. I wrote Ned Noonan in his tiny ancient town. I got the letter back: "Addressee unknown."

And yet, and yet. A letter arrived this summer from the other Tom McGuane's youngest daughter, Antonia. The blooming adolescent I remembered described herself as a divorced mother, a painter in Nova Scotia, and the director of a gallery for Inuit art. Ireland, she said, was prospering at last. And Kilmallock, where my old Morris had been a shining phaeton, was full of cars.

Sakonnet

B ECAUSE THIS WAS a visit and a return, I might have had the nerve, right at the beginning, to call it "Sakonnet Point Revisited" and take my lumps on the Victorianism and sentimentality counts, though half a page of murder and sex at the end would bail that out. If you are to cultivate a universal irony, as Edmund Wilson told Scott Fitzgerald to do, you must never visit anything in your works, much less revisit, ever.

But when you go back to a place where you spent many hours of childhood, you find that some of it has become important, if not actually numinous, and that universal irony might just have to eat hot lead for the moment, because there is no way of suppressing that importance. Also, there is the fact of its being no secret anyway. A Midwestern childhood is going to show, for instance, even after you have retired from the ad agency and are a simple crab fisherman by the sea, grave with Winslow Homer marineland wisdom. Sooner or later someone looks into your eyes and sees a flash of corn and automobiles, possibly even the chemical plant at Wyandotte, Michigan. You can't hide it.

Still, there was one thing certainly to be avoided: to wit, the notion when you go back to the summer place everything seems so small. You protest: "But when I got there, everything did seem small. . . ."

Don't say it! The smallness of that which is revisited is one of the touchstones of an underground literature in which the heart is constantly wrung by the artifacts of childhood. Undermining it would be like shooting Barbie.

I had neared Sakonnet Point thinking, This place is loaded with pitfalls, and I had visualized a perfect beach of distant memory now glittering with mercury, oiled ducks, aluminum, and maybe one defunct-but-glowing nuclear submarine. And I met my expectations at my first meal in the area: "the Down East Clam Special." The cook's budget had evidently been diverted into the tourist effluvium inspired by the American Revolution that I'd seen in the lobby. The clams in my chowder and fritters and fried clams were mere shadows of their former selves, calling into question whether they had ever been clams at all.

On my plate was universal irony in parable form, come to haunt me. I knew at that moment that I had my imaginative rights. As a result, I actually returned to Sakonnet Point half thinking to see the whalers of the *Pequod* striding up from their dories to welcome me. And, truly, when I saw the old houses on the rocky peninsula, they fitted the spangled Atlantic around them at exactly the equipoise that seems one of the harmonics of childhood.

I had my bass rod in the car and drove straight to Warren's Point. There was a nice shore-break surf and plenty of boiling whitewater that I could reach with a plug. Nevertheless, I didn't rush it. I needed a little breakthrough to make the pursuit plausible. When fishing on foot, you have none of the reassurances that the big accoutrements of the sport offer. No one riding a fighting chair on a John Rybovich sportfisherman thinks about not getting one in quite the same terms as the man on foot.

Before I began, I could see on the horizon the spectator boats from the last day of the America's Cup heading home. The Goodyear blimp seemed as stately in the pale sky as the striped bass I had visualized as my evening's reward.

I began to cast, dropping the big surface plug, an Atom Popper, into the whitewater around boulders and into the tumbling backwash of waves. I watched the boats heading home and wondered if *Gretel* had managed a comeback. During the day I had learned that an old friend of the family was in Fall River recovering from a heart attack and that his lobster pots still lay inside the course of the cup race. I wondered about that and cast until I began to have those first insidious notions that I had miscalculated the situation.

But suddenly, right in front of me, bait was in the air and the striped green-and-black backs of bass coursed through it. It is hard to convey this surprise: bait breaking like a small rainstorm and, bolting through the frantic minnows, perhaps a dozen striped bass. They went down at the moment I made my cast and reappeared thirty feet away. I picked up and cast again, and the same thing happened. Then the fish vanished.

I had missed the chance by not contriving an interception. I stood on my rock and rather forlornly hoped the surprise would happen again. To my immediate right, baitfish were splashing out of the water, throwing themselves up against the side of a sea-washed boulder. It occurred to me, slowly, that they were not doing this out of their own personal sense of sport. So I lobbed my plug over, made one turn on the handle, hooked a striper, and was tight to the fish in a magical burst of spray. The bass raced around among the rocks and seaweed, made one dogged run toward open water, then came my way. When he was within twenty feet, I let him hang in the trough until another wave formed, then glided the fish in on it and beached him.

The ocean swells and flattens, stripes itself abstractly with foam and changes color under the clouds. Sometimes a dense flock of gulls hangs overhead and their snowy shadows sink into the green, translucent sea.

Standing on a boulder amid breaking surf that is forming offshore, accelerating and rolling toward you is, after awhile, like looking into a fire. It is mesmeric.

All the time I was here I thought of my uncle Bill, who had died the previous year and in whose Sakonnet house I was staying, as I had in the past. He was a man of local fame as a gentleman and a wit. And he had a confidence and a sense of moral precision that amounted to a mild form of tyranny. But for me his probity was based almost more on his comic sense than on his morality, though the latter was considerable.

He was a judge in Massachusetts. I have heard that in his court one day two college students were convicted of having performed a panty raid on a girls' dormitory. My uncle sentenced them to take his charge card to Filene's department store in Boston and there "exhaust their interest in ladies' underwear," before reporting back to the court.

He exacted terrific cautions of my cousin Fred, my brother John, and me, and would never, when I fished here as a boy, have allowed me to get out on the exposed rocks I fished from now. His son Fred and I were not allowed to swim unguarded, carry pocketknives, or go to any potentially dangerous promontory to fish, a restriction that eliminated all the good places.

And he had small blindnesses that may have been infuriating to his family, for all I know. To me they simply made him more singular. By today's standards or even those of the time, he was rather unreconstructed, yet this renders him an infinitely more palpable individual in my memory than the adaptable nullities who have replaced men like him.

His discomfiture will be perceived in the following: One day he invited Fred and me to his court in Fall River. To his horrified surprise, the first case before him was that of a three-hundred-pound lady, the star of an all-night episode of *le sexe multiple*, and included a parade of abashed sailors who passed before Fred's and my astounded eyes at the behest of the prosecution. Unrepentant, the lady greeted the sailors with a heartiness they could not return.

After the session for the day, my uncle spirited us to Sakonnet to reflect upon the verities of nature. For us, at the time, nature was largely striped bass and how to get them. But the verity of a fat lady and eleven sailors trapped in the bell jar of my uncle Bill's court fought for our attention on equal footing.

I hooked another bass at the end of a long cast. Handsome to see them blast a plug out at the end of your best throw. I landed the fish as the sun fell, reaching through foam to seize the vigorous creature.

I was here during the 1954 hurricane that made the surf break in the horse pasture across the road from the house. Shingles lifted slowly from the garage roof and exploded into the sky. The house became an airplane; unimaginable plants and objects shot past its windows. The surf took out farm fences and drove pirouettes of foam into the sky. My cousins and I treated it as an adventure. Uncle Bill was our guarantee against the utter feasibility of the house going underwater. And if it flooded, we knew he would bring a suitable boat to an upstairs window.

Late that day the hurricane was over, having produced delirium and chaos: lobster pots in the streets, commercial fishing boats splintered all over the rocks, yards denuded of trees and bushes, vegetation burned and killed by wind-driven salt water.

Fred and I stole out and headed for the shore, titillated by rumors of looting. The rocky beach was better than we dreamed: burst tackle chests with more bass plugs than we could use, swordfish harpoons, ship-to-shore radios, marine engines, the works.

Picking through this lovely rubble like a pair of crows, we were approached by the special kind of histrionic New England lady (not Irish Catholic like us, we knew) who has a lot of change tied up in antiques and heirlooms that point to her great familial depth in this part of the world. At a glance, she called us "vile little ghouls," which rather queered it for us, neither of us knowing what ghouls were.

I kept fishing after dark, standing on a single rock and feeling disoriented by the foam swirling around me. I was getting sore from casting and jigging the plug. Moreover, casting in the dark is like smoking in the dark; something is missing. You see neither the trajectory nor the splash, nor the surface plug spouting and spoiling for trouble. But shortly I hooked a fish. It moved very little. I began to think it was possibly a deadhead rolling in the wash. I waited, just trying to keep everything together. The steady, unexcited quality of whatever this was prompted me to think it was not a fish. I lifted the rod sharply in hopes of eliciting some characteristic movement. And I got it. The fish burned off fifty or sixty yards, sulked, let me get half of it back, then began to run again, not fast or hysterical, but with the solid, irresistible motion of a Euclid bulldozer easing itself into a phosphate mine. It mixed up its plays, bulling, running, stopping, shaking. And then it was gone.

When I reeled up, I was surprised that I still had the plug, though its hooks were mangled beyond use. I'd been cleaned out. Nevertheless, with two good bass for the night, I felt resigned to my loss.

No I didn't.

I took two more fish the next day. There was a powerful sense of activity on the shore. Pollock were chasing minnows right up against the beach. And at one sublime moment at sundown, tuna were assailing the bait, dozens of the powerful fish in the air at once, trying to nail the smaller fish from above.

Then it was over and quiet. I looked out to sea in the last light, the white rollers coming in around me. The clearest item of civilization from my perspective was a small tanker heading north. Offshore, a few rocky shoals boiled whitely. The air was chilly. The beach where I had sunned myself as a child looked lonely and cold.

But from behind me came intimate noises: the door of a house closing, voices, a lawn mower. And, to a great extent, this is the character of bass fishing from the shore. In very civilized times it is reassuring to know that wild fish will run so close that a man on foot and within earshot of lawn mowers can touch their wildness with a fishing rod.

I hooked a bass after dark, blind-casting in the surf, a good fish that presented some landing difficulties; there were numerous rocks in front of me, hard to see in the dark. I held the flashlight in my mouth, shining it first along the curve of the rod out to the line and along it to the spot among the rocks where the line met the water, foaming very brightly in the beam. The surf was heavier now, booming into the boulders around me.

In a few moments I could see the thrashing bass, the plug in its mouth, a good fish. In the backwash, it looked radically striped and impressive.

I guided the tired striper through the rocks, beached him, removed the plug, and put him gently into a protected pool. He righted himself and I watched him breathe and fin, more vivid in my light than in any aquarium. Then abruptly he shot back into the foam and out to sea. I walked into the surf again, looking for the position, the exact placement of feet and tension of rod while casting, that had produced the strike.

One of my earliest trips to Sakonnet included a tour of The Breakers, the Vanderbilt summer palazzo. My grandmother was with us. Before raising her large family she had been among the child labor force in the Fall River mills, the kind of person who had helped make really fun things like palazzos at Newport possible.

Safe on first by two generations, I darted around the lugubrious mound, determined to live like that one day. Over the fireplace was an agate only slightly smaller than a fire hydrant. Here I would evaluate the preparation of the bass I had taken under the cliffs by the severest methods: eleven-foot Calcutta casting rod and handmade block-tin squid. The bass was to be brought in by the fireplace, *garni*, don't you know; and there would be days when the noble fish was to be consumed in bed. Many, many comic books would be spread about on the counterpane.

We went on to Sakonnet. As we drove I viewed every empty corn or potato field as a possible site for the mansion. The Rolls Silver Cloud would be parked to one side, its leather backseat slimy from hauling stripers. There was no end to my foppish longings.

The sun came up on a crystalline fall day; blue sky and delicate glaze. I hiked down the point beach, along the red ridge of rock, the dense beach scrub with its underledge of absolute shadow. As I walked I drove speeding clusters of sanderlings before me. If I didn't watch out, there might be the problem of sentiment.

When I got to the end and could see the islands with their ruins, I could observe the narrow, glittering tidal rip like an oceanic continuation of the rocky ridge of the point itself.

A few days before, the water had been cloudy and full of kelp and weed, especially the puffs of iodine-colored stuff that clung tenaciously to my plug. Today, though, the water was clear and green, with waves rising translucent before whitening onto the hard beach. I stuck the butt of my rod into the sand and sat down. From here, beautiful houses could be seen along the headlands. A small farm ran down the knolls, with black-and-white cattle grazing along its tilts. More than two hundred years ago, an American spy was killed by the British in the farm's driveway.

Fred came that evening from Fall River and we fished. The surf was heavier and I hooked and lost a bass very early on. Other fishermen were out, bad ones mostly. They trudged up and down the shore with their new rods, not casting but waiting for an irresistible sign to begin.

When it was dark, Fred, who had waded out to a far rock and periodically vanished from my view in the spray, hooked a fine bass. After some time, he landed it and made his way through the breakers with the fish in one hand, the rod in the other.

At the end of a fishing trip you're inclined to summarize things in your mind. A tally is needed for the quick description you will be asked for: so many fish at such-and-such weights and the method employed. Inevitably, what actually happened is indescribable.

It is assumed that the salient events of childhood are inordinate. During one of my first trips to Sakonnet, a trap boat caught an enormous oceanic sunfish, many hundred pounds in weight. A waterfront entrepreneur who usually sold crabs and tarred handlines bought the sunfish and towed it to the beach in an enclosed wooden wagon, where he charged ten cents admission for a view of it. I was an early sucker—and a repeater. In some way the sight seems to have taken like a vaccination. I remember very clearly ascending the wooden steps into the wagon, whose windows let water-reflected light play over the ceiling.

One by one we children goggled past the enormous animal laid out on a field of ice. The huge lolling discus of the temperate and tropical seas met our stares with a cold eye that was no less soulful for being the size of a hubcap.

Many years later I went back to Sakonnet on a December afternoon as a specific against the torpor of university. I was walking along the cove beach when I saw the wagon, not in significantly worse repair than when I had paid to enter it. Though to be honest, I didn't realize it was the wagon of my childhood until I stepped inside.

There, on a dry, iceless wooden table, lay the skeleton of the ocean sunfish.

It seemed safe to conclude in the face of this utterly astounding occasion that I was to be haunted. Accommodating myself to the fish's reappearance, I adjusted to the unforeseeable in a final way. If ever I opened an elevator door and found that skeleton on its floor, I would step in without comment, finding room for my feet between its ribs, and press the button of my destination.

Twilight on the Buffalo Paddock

D AWN: A CURIOUS MIXTURE of noises. Birds, ocean, trees soughing in a breeze off the Pacific; then, in the foreground, the steady cropping of buffaloes.

They are massing peacefully, feeding and nuzzling and ignoring the traffic. They are fat, happy, numerous beasts, and all around them are the gentle, primordial hills of Golden Gate Park, San Francisco, U.S.A. It is dawn on the buffalo paddock. It is 1966, the Summer of Love, and though I may well have spent the night listening to the Charlatans at one of the psychedelic ballrooms, I am doggedly trying to remember that I am an angler.

By midmorning in buffalo country things get a little more active at street level. Out of the passing string of health nuts, ordinary pedestrians, policemen, and twenty-first-century transcendental visionaries with electro-frizz hairdos that look more like spiral nebulae than anything out here in Vitalis Central—from this passing string, then, a citizen occasionally detaches himself, avoids the buffalo paddock by a few yards, and enters the grounds of the Golden Gate Angling and Casting Club. The club is the successor of an earlier organization, the San Francisco Fly Casting Club, which was founded in 1894. It has been located in Golden Gate Park only since the 1930s, when its facilities were constructed by the City of San Francisco.

The grounds of the club are not so prepossessing as its seventy-six-year history would lead one to expect. The clubhouse and casting pools are on an elevation that is shaped like a small mesa. It is a single story, dark and plain, and faces pools surrounded and overhung by immense, fragrant eucalyptus trees. The clubhouse is thoroughly grown in with laurel and rhododendron, and after street-level Golden Gate—the effect is distinctly otherworldly.

Today, as a man rehearses the ancient motions of casting a fly on the elegant green surfaces of the practice pools, he may even hear one of the stern invocations of our century: "Stick 'em up!" and be relieved, perhaps even decorously, of his belongings. It wouldn't be the first time. But that could only happen in midweek. On a weekend many of his fellow members will be there. Stickup artists will go to the beach and it will be feasible to watch your backcast instead of the underbrush.

This particular Sunday has been especially well attended. The men are wandering out of the clubhouse, where you can smell bacon, eggs, and pancakes, just as you might in the cook tent of one of the imperial steelhead camps these same anglers frequent in the Northwest. They pick up fly rods and make their way out along the casting pools, false-casting as they walk and trying occasional preliminary throws before really getting down to business. At the middle pool a man is casting with a tournament rod, a real magnum smokepole, and two or three people watch as he casts a 500-grain shooting head 180 feet.

Between him and the clubhouse, casting for accuracy with a conventional dry-fly rod, is a boy of thirteen. Later, this boy, Steve Rajeff, will be the world's champion caster. At this point he is a lifelong habitué and he tournament-casts as another city boy might fly remote-control airplanes, and he casts with uncommon elegance—a high, slow backcast, perfect timing, and a forecast that straightens with precision. He seems to overpower very slightly so that the line turns over and hangs an instant in the air to let the leader touch first. He regulates the width of the loop in his line to the inch and at will. When a headwind comes up, he tightens the loop into a perfectly formed, almost beveled, little wind cheater. It is quite beautiful.

Standing beside him, an older man supports his chin with one hand, hangs his fist in one discolored pocket of a cardigan, and looks concerned. From time to time he makes a suggestion; the boy listens, nods, and does differently. Like most who offer advice here, the older man has been a world casting champion. When he takes the rod, you see why. The slowness of the backcast approaches mannerism but the bluff is never called; the man's straightening, perfect cast never betrays gravity with shock waves or a sag.

So the two of them take turns, more or less. The boy does most of the casting, and while one casts facing the pool, the other is turned at right angles to him, watching his style, the angles, loft, timing, and speed of his cast.

At this point the boy is already more accurate than his elder and from time to time he lets his backcast drop a little so he can fire a tight bow in, and score—the technical proof of his bravura. But the older man has a way of letting the backcast carry and hang that has moment, or something akin to it. Anyway, the boy sees what it is and when the older man goes inside for breakfast the boy will try that, too, even though it crosses him up and brings the cast down around his ears. Embarrassed, he looks around, clears the line, fires it out with an impetuous roll cast and goes back to what he knows.

By this time a good many people are scattered along the sides of the pools. The group is not quite heterogeneous, and though its members seem less inclined to dressing up than many of San Francisco's populace, they are not the Silent Majority's wall of flannel, either. To be exact, sartorially, there is no shortage of really thick white socks here, sleeveless V-neck sweaters, or brown oxfords. The impression, you suppose, is vaguely up-country. My companion is widely known as a superb angler. He is not a member of the club and is inclined to bridle around tournament casters. They remind him of something more housebroken than fishing, and he doesn't like it. He thinks their equipment is too good, and of course it is, largely. When they talk about fly lines and shooting heads, getting fussy over fractions of grains of weight, he instinctively feels the tail's wagging the dog. Nevertheless, the fisherman has something to be grateful for. Shooting-head lines, now standard steelhead gear, modern techniques of power-

casting, and, in fact, much contemporary thinking about rod design—
actions and tapers—have arisen at this small, circumscribed anglers'
enclave. Still, it is difficult to imagine a tournament caster who would
confess to having no interest at all in fishing, though that is exactly
the case with some of them. Ritualistically, they continue to refer
their activities to practical streamcraft.

My companion typifies something, too, something anti-imperial in
style. Frayed lines and throwaway tackle, a reel with a crude painting
on the side of it, brutalized from being dropped on riverside rocks. His
rod is missing guides and has been reinforced at butt and ferrule with
electricians' tape that, in turn, has achieved a greenish corruption of
its own. He is a powerful caster whose special effects are all toward
fishing in bad wind and weather. He admits few fishermen into his
angling pantheon and, without mercy, divides the duffers into "bait
soakers," "yucks," and other categories of opprobrium. Good anglers
are "red-hots." His solutions to the problems of deteriorating fishing
habitat incline toward the clean gestures of the assassin.

I sit on one of the spectators' benches and chat with a steelhead
fisherman about the Skeena drainage in British Columbia. He's been
all over that country, caught summer-run fish miles inland that were
still bright from salt water. The conversation lags. Another member sits on the bench. "Was anybody ever really held up here?" I ask
rather warily.

"Sure was," says the man next to me, and turns to the new fellow
on the end of the bench. "Who was that?"

"Guy that got stuck up?"

"Yeah, who was that?"

"There were three of them, at different times."

The man next to me turns to me. "It was this guy from Oakland."

The man at the end of the bench isn't interested. The fellow next
to me asks him, "Didn't he get pistol-whipped or something?"

"Who's this?"

"The guy from Oakland."

"I don't know. I don't know. I don't know."

The man next to me turns to me again. "I'm not positive," he says with exaggerated care, "but the dry-fly man from Oakland got pistol-whipped unless I've got my signals real crossed."

"Did they take his rod?" I ask somewhat aimlessly.

"No."

"His reel or anything?"

"No," he says, "just glommed the wallet and cleared out. It was pretty crummy."

I excuse myself. With a new Winston tarpon and billfish fly rod I'm anxious to try, I go down to the last pool, where a handful of members are casting. I am a little sleepy from the gigantic breakfast they've given me. The elevation of the club drops off abruptly behind this last pool and a path leads down through the heavy tree roots to a little space that looks like the banks of a streambed. As I strip line from my reel, I notice that three people are undulating beneath the trees down there. One is a girl wearing Levi's and an Esther Williams total sun-block hat with mirrors hanging from its edges on strings. One of the men seems to be a Lapp. The other is dressed as Buffalo Bill and is more frenzied than his companions. Occasionally he adjusts his enormous cowboy hat with one hand, somehow finding the hat as it goes by on a weird parabolic course of its own. I wonder if he has seen the buffalo paddock.

Presently a girl in ballet costume leads an attractive pony into the clearing, followed by a young man carrying a light meter and a viewing lens hanging around his neck and wielding an enormous Bolex movie camera. He walks right past the girl and heads for us. I can see the huge coated surface of his telephoto lens, blue even at this distance, the shoulder stock of his camera, and the knurled turrets that seem to be all over it. His approach becomes imposing. He looks put out.

"We're trying to make a movie," he says. None of us knows what to reply. "The thing is, we're trying to make a movie."

The man next to me inquires, "Would you like us to get out of the way?"

"That's right. I'd like you out of the way."

All of the casters get out of the way. They hadn't known, apparently, that when it's a movie, you get out of the way.

At the end of the pool is The Pit. You can climb down into it and you are chest level to the water. This is a very realistic approximation of the actual situation when you are fishing, and any fancy ideas you might develop about your casting on the platforms can be quickly weeded out here. My new rod is very powerful and after a couple of hundred casts the epidermis of my thumb slips and a watery blister forms.

I return to the bench on which sits one of the club officials. I decide to find out if the Golden Gate outfit is merely exclusive. "It's funny," I say disingenuously, "with as many hippies as this city has, that there aren't any in the club. How's that?"

"They don't ask to join."

Inside the clubhouse, I chat with the membership. They're talking about casting tournaments and fishing—fishing generally and the vanishing fishing of California in particular. They know the problems. These are anglers in an epoch when an American river can be a fire hazard. The older men remember the California fishery when it was the best of them all, the most labyrinthine, the most beautiful. A great river system initiating in purling high-country streams, the whole thing substantiated by an enormous and stable watershed. Now the long, feathery river systems are stubs.

Many of the men standing here today used to haunt the High Sierra and Cascade ranges, overcoming altitude headaches to catch golden trout in the ultraviolet zone. Probably most of them have been primarily steelhead fishermen, though some fish for stripers in San Francisco Bay.

In view of the fact that the movement of people to California over the last five decades may be the biggest population shift in the history of the world, it is amazing the fishery held up so long. But in the last ten years it has gone off fast. Ironically, it is the greatness of the fishing lost that probably accounts for the distinction of the Golden Gate Club: it has bred a school of casters who are without any doubt the finest there has ever been.

Fishing for sport is itself an act of racial memory, and in places like the Golden Gate Club it moves toward the purer symbolism of tournaments. The old river-spawned fish have been replaced by pellet-fed and planted simulacra of themselves. Now even the latter seem to be vanishing in favor of plastic target rings and lines depicting increments of distance. It's very cerebral.

There has begun to be a feeling among the membership that, like music without the dance, casting without fishing lacks a certain something. And so they are fanatically concerned with the dubious California Water Plan and the rodent ethics and activities of the Army Corps of Engineers and the Bureau of Reclamation. The men sit around a table in the lodge and break out a bottle or two. They seem to be talking about some secret society, and when listening in I discover they mean those who have bought fishing licenses in the state of California. The men propose to rouse this sleeping giant of two million individuals to keep their ocean rivers from being converted into outdoor water-ski pavilions. But an air of anachronism hovers over them. The Now Generation seems to substantiate the claims of the high-dam builders, and it appears to be true that people really would rather water-ski on unmoving water than take in all the complexity of a river. Maybe some of them will see, way down beneath their skis, the drowned forests of California and the long, stony stripes of old riverbeds.

At any rate, they won't be dropping in today at the Golden Gate Club. Handmade split-cane rods and tapered lines seem a trifle dull. The Eel, the Trinity, the Russian, the Klamath, begin to seem, in the conversation of these men, rivers of the mind. Some imagine the anglers as sadists who want to hurt the little fish with sharp hooks hidden in chicken feathers. In the park I talk with a futurist who wants to know what difference it makes if the fish are lost since we can already synthesize food anyway, and I think of the high-protein gruel rock climbers carry in plastic tubes as our cuisine of tomorrow.

"Well," I tell the futurist, "I don't know what to say!"

The members begin to drift out of the lodge and head for the parking lot.

It's sundown in buffalo country.

If you're casting at the far pool you are inclined to switch your eye from time to time toward the underbrush. Did someone move in there?

Why go into it. This is too agreeable. I put on a sweater in the evening and watch the diehards. The pools have gone silver. The emptiness around the few members who remain seems to make their casting more singular, more eloquent.

The whole place is surrounded by trees. Nobody knows we're in here. I pick up my rod and cast.

Angling Versus Acts of God

THIS WAS ONE of the ways a fishing trip could begin. The airline smashed my tackle, and less than twenty-four hours after starting I lay in bed at our hotel in Victoria, food-poisoned and no longer able to imagine the wild rainbow trout I had set out for.

Frank, my companion, was speaking to the house physician. "It came on him very suddenly," he said. "He didn't even finish his drink."

At that moment our itinerary seemed to lie heavy upon the land. We were going up into the Skeena drainage, and I realized that if I could stop vomiting (and ruing the prawn dinner that had precipitated this eventuality), I would see matchless country and have angling to justify all the trouble. It would be the perfect antidote to food poisoning and all the other dark things.

As it was, the trip seemed a trifle askew. Coming in from Seattle, I had inadvertently been thrust among the members of an Ohio travel group; a mixed bag, coming from all parts of the country. "We're with Hiram Tours," one man said to our stewardess as we flew north from Seattle. "Is that Alaska down there? Or Oregon?"

The stewardess began a spontaneous rundown of the glories of Our Neighbor to the North. "There is a mountain in Banff," she explained momentously, "that they've named Mount Eisenhower." She paused to look first at the blank faces, then at the sullen Pacific beneath us. She exhaled audibly. "After your former president, that would be."

We flew on for some time in silence.

One of the tour group looked up beaming from the map on his lap. "Strait of Juan de Fuca!" he cried.

I could take it. I was ready for this kind of thing. I was going to virgin country and I still hadn't got food poisoning and my companion hadn't yet had to call the house physician to say, "He didn't even finish his drink."

They had been to San Francisco and were now doing the résumé. "Filthah hippahs!" said a lady from Little Rock. Then a young man bound for Vietnam announced, "Well, I'm off to defend my country!" in tones that seemed less than totally sincere. So the tour group, for this and other reasons, grew restive and was ready to pile off the plane by the time we arrived at Victoria.

I registered at the Empress Hotel, a stupendous Victorian edifice where the bellhops scurry and the waiters in the dining room murmur the most caring hopes about your meal, exactly the place to sport an RAF mustache. Frank arrived and we talked about our trip north. Then early to bed, with glimpses of the curious Victoria skyline, a pastiche of the high-rise and the venerable.

Every traveler here soon discovers the considerable reverence for the British connection. If the queen ever gets run out of England, this is where you'll find her holed up; the Victoria Chamber of Commerce will have drawn its wagons in a circle around her.

In addition to such good transpositions as the unmatched gardens of the city or its numerous bookstores, you get double-decker buses imported from London, coats of arms in woolen-store windows and tea and crumpets available everywhere from the Empress itself to the Rexall drugstore.

But to emphasize the town's studied dowdiness is unfair. It is obvious that Victoria is a town of what used to be called graciousness, and any ride around its perimeter will put the traveler's back to those unparalleled gardens and his face to the headlands of the San Juan Islands.

There had been heavy weather immediately prior to our arrival, and long, golden log booms, the shape and color of egg yolks, had been towed inside the bays for protection. Beyond, handsome trawlers were moored under clouds of gulls. If you squinted, it looked like Anchorage or Seattle or San Francisco or Monterey or—squinting tighter—Mazatlán: the Pacific community seemed continuous.

That first morning I picked up the menu downstairs in the hotel. A number of breakfasts were described: "the Charlotte," "the Windsor," "the Albert," "the Edward," "the Victoria," and "the Mountbatten."

"I'll have the Mountbatten," I said, "over lightly."

Frank made a number of order changes to his Edward.

"If you're going to substitute oatmeal and add an extra egg on your Edward," said the waitress, "you might just as well order á la carte."

I was hungry and abruptly ate my Mountbatten.

We spent the day driving as far up the coast as Saltspring Island. At one of the ferry crossings, watching the wind-striped water and high, beautiful fjords, I innocently poisoned myself with a prawn.

A local prawn? I don't know.

Within hours I had failed to finish my drink. My companion was on the phone to the house doctor. My vision was contracting. My gorge was rising for the tenth time. The Canadian Pacific, so recently thrilling, was now the scene of hopelessness and abandonment.

WE WERE GOING NORTH to Smithers by way of Williams Lake. The fellow passengers were more promising than the tour group—a few swells like ourselves, some surveyors, timber cruisers, a geologist. The minute the aircraft had elevation, a country revealed itself that was so tortuous, folded, and empty that some trick of time seemed to have been performed.

The sky came down to a jagged horizon of snow, and for 360 degrees a coastal forest, baleful and empty, rose to the mountains. Past the bright riveted wing, the ranges succeeded each other to the north in a blue eternity.

We landed at Williams Lake on the Fraser River, dropped off passengers, taxied, flew a few yards, landed again, taxied again, took off again, and landed. The pilot came out of the cockpit with his shirt unbuttoned and remarked with appalling candor that the plane felt like a Model A.

They sent us into Williams Lake to eat while they fixed the plane. In the cab we learned the airline we were using was bankrupt, and so it had come to seem. But at the restaurant they told us to return to the plane immediately.

When we boarded, the pilot said, "I hope it goes this time. Occasionally you're not lucky."

So we flew over the increasingly remote wilderness, hoping that we would be lucky and that the plane would work and be better in all ways than a Model A.

At Smithers, the seaplanes rested very high on their pontoons beside floating docks. A mechanic tapped away at a workbench nearby as we boarded a De Havilland Beaver.

Within a short time we hung precariously over a long, gravelly mountain ridge. The pilot craned around looking for mountain goats, while Frank and I exchanged nervous glances and judged the drop.

On either side of us stood implacable-looking peaks and ridges while underneath, blue-and-green lakes hung in saddles and rock-walled cirques. Occasionally the entire groundscape shone amid delicate water meadows, and in a short time we had landed and were taxiing toward our fishing camp. I thought of the trout under our gliding pontoons.

"How is the fishing?" Frank inquired routinely of Ejnar Madsen, the camp's co-owner.

"Extremely poor," said Ejnar.

"Really!"

We put our luggage down on the dock as it began to rain. There had been an Act of God and we could not be philosophical about it. I asked what had happened. The biggest summer rain in many years had raised the lake and turned the river almost black with runoff.

Next day we floated disconsolately down the slow, ineffably northern river in a twenty-five-foot, First Nations–built, spruce riverboat. The rain poured off our foul-weather gear and made puddles in our laps.

Between long spells of silence we burst into absurd conversations:

"Neighbor's cat crawls under the hood of the car. Next morning the neighbor starts the car. The fan does a job on the cat."

"Apropos of what?"

"Wait a minute. They take the cat to the vet. He shaves the cat's whole tail except for the end. The cat looks like a lion. Pretty soon the cat thinks he's a lion."

"In what way?"

"Forget it."

Now the rain was going sideways. You'd cast a fly and it would vanish long before it got to the water. We knew gloom.

Some very small, very stupid trout came upon our flies and ate them. We caught those trout. Of the large smart trout known to live in the lake, we took none. Some hours later we sat around the Air-Tight heater, for all purposes blanked.

We were fishing for rainbows in their original watershed. In such a situation they can be expected to be magnificent fish, quite unlike the hatchery imitations, which have, in effect, besmirched the species. They are strong and fast, and rise freely to a dry-fly. We were, moreover, in an area that produces fish of a rather large average size.

In the spring and early summer the fish here herd and pursue sockeye fry, including the sluggish little alevins, the very young fry, tadpole-shaped, with their still-unconsumed egg sacs. Ideally, the big rainbows are to be found chasing the bait on top, where they can be cast to, rather like pelagic fish. We liked this image. We would cast, fight, land, and release until our arms were tired. The rainbows could also be taken on dry-flies. There were mayflies and grasshoppers to imitate and in the lower stretch, stoneflies.

Though we hadn't made much of a beginning, our hopes were still running high. The next morning we were fishing by six, hunting feeding rainbows. It is "hunting" if you find something. If you do not, it is driving around the lake in an outboard.

"We should've brought the water skis."

"Oh, come on."

We continued hunting, as it were. And we didn't find anything, not one thing. When more of the unseasonable rain blew in from the exaggerated sky, we sat, fly rods in hand, like drowned rats. I began to take an interest in the details of the bilge.

Later, when it had cleared a little, we headed down the lake to a First Nations village inhabited by a branch of the Carrier tribe, so named because its widows once carried the charred bones of their husbands around on their backs. The village is situated prettily on a high series of hills and looks out on the lake and river where the two are joined. There are a couple of dozen buildings along a wooden walk and a small Hudson's Bay store.

When we passed the upper part of the town, a man worked on his outboard while a girl in an aniline-blue miniskirt pulled sockeye salmon from a net. Ravens and gulls screamed and circled overhead, waiting for a chance at the offal from the gutted salmon. There were a hundred thousand or more sockeyes in the river now. Many of them came up out of the wilderness with bearclaw marks on their flanks.

We docked at the lower end in a pounding rain and hurried up the hill to get under the eaves of the wooden schoolhouse. A notice in the window read:

> To Whom It May Concern:
> During the absence of the schoolteacher, this school building must be closed. It therefore cannot be used for dances, bingo games, or any other social gatherings. Anyone asking permission to use the school will be refused.
>
> R. M. McIntyre,
> Superintendent,
> Burns Lake Indian Agency

In two or three places on the walls of this wilderness school were dabbed the letters *LSD*, which did not stand for League of Spiritual Discovery. The letters were put there, doubtless, by someone who spoke English as a second language.

When the weather relented a little, we hiked up the hill to the old cemetery, which was mostly overgrown. The epitaphs were intriguing: "To the sacred memory of our brother killed by a gunshot wound." I found two old headmen's graves, "Chief William" and "Chief Agusa," whose titles were purely titular; the Carriers gave their chiefs little power. The cultural overlay seemed rather bald on the last stone I looked at. Beneath a conventional crucifix it read, "In memory of Ah Whagus. Died 1906. Age 86." Imagine the fishing when Ah Whagus was a boy.

We walked around the village. The shy people smiled at the ground or stayed inside when we passed. On the boardwalk someone had written "Big Fat Sally Do Your Stuff." Beyond the LSD graffiti and the noise of a transistor radio playing Dolly Parton—"I'm a lady mule skinner from down ol' Tennessee way"—black-shawled First Nations women were taking the salmon down the river to a lower island and smoking them against a winter that was probably more imminent to them than to us. The older people were locked in some intense dejection, but the children played with familiar, maniacal energy in the deep wet grass with their salmon-fattened dogs.

It had rained enough that our simple cabin with its Air-Tight heater acquired a special and luxurious glamour. When we got good and cold, usually the result of running the boat in one direction while the wind took the rain in another, we would head for the cabin, put some wood in the heater, douse it with coal oil, and throw in the magic match that made everything all better. This was the romance of the heater. We played with the flue, adjusted the draft, and while the logs rumbled and roared inside we tuned the thing like a violin. One afternoon, when a view through any of the windows would have suggested that the cabin was Captain Nemo's vessel and that we were at the bottom of the sea, Frank leapt to his feet with an expensive Japanese camera in his hands and began to take picture after picture of the tin heater rumbling peacefully, our wet laundry hanging around it in homage.

One of the exhilarations of fishing new places lies in rendering advice into some kind of obtained reality. Cast the fly, you are told, right along the bank and the trout will rise to it. So you cast and you cast until presently you are blue in the face and the appealing syllogism you started with is not always finished. When it does not work, you bring your vanquished person back to the dock, where there is no way to weigh or measure the long face you have brought instead of fish. At the first whiskey, you announce that it has been a trying day. Then someone else says that it is nice just to get out. Irrationally, you wonder how you can get even for that remark.

But once, when the British Columbia sky made one of those spectacular partings we associate with the paintings of Turner or the handing down of stone tablets, we saw what had been described to us in the beginning.

Large fish, their fins showing above the water, were working schools of salmon fry: a setup. We started the engine and ran upwind of them, cut the engine, and started to drift down. We had the goods on them. When in range I false-cast a few times, made a long cast beyond them, and gently retrieved into their midst.

I hooked a fish instantly. After a strong first run, it mysteriously flagged. As I reeled, it came obediently to the boat, where Frank netted it.

"What is that?" he asked. In the net was some kind of giant minnow.

"It looks like Martha Raye," I said bitterly. Later we learned that it was a squawfish. No one ever caught one on purpose.

Not until almost our last day did the river begin to disclose itself. We made a pass along the First Nations village, where we were seeing occasional rises. The problem was a river so clouded that the fish were unable to see the fly, a condition blamed on a nearby stump desert the loggers left in their wake.

We began to drift, blind-casting large Wulff flies ahead of us, mending the line to keep the river from bellying it and dragging the fly. In very short order, a bright band appeared beneath my fly, moved downstream with it and inhaled. I lifted and was solid to a very good fish, which was netted some minutes later. It bumped heavily in the bottom of the boat until I could get the fly out and release it.

We were startled. A short time later another came, boiling the fly under with a positive, deep take, and was released. There were no rises to be seen any longer, though fish rose fairly well to our own flies, until we had six. Then the whole factory shut down and nothing would persuade a trout to rise again. While it had lasted, all of British Columbia that existed had been the few square inches around my dry-fly. With the rise over, the world began to reappear: trees, lake, river, village, wet clothes.

It is this sort of possession you look for when angling. To watch the river flowing, the insects landing and hatching, the places where trout hold, and to insinuate the supple, binding movement of tapered line until, when the combination is right, the line becomes rigid and many of its motions are conceived at the other end. That stage continues for a time dictated by the size of the trout and the skill of the angler. When the initiative changes hands, the trout is soon in the net, without an idea in his head until you release him. Then you see him go off, looking for a spot, and thinking.

Twenty-Fish Days

O N A WARM DAY in mid-October at Sakonnet Point, I was stay-ing again at my uncle Bill's old house, with its view over the low weathered roofs to the harbor and the cove where we swam as children. My feelings of excited anticpation were unchanged after half a century. Roses still bloomed along the stone fences and the air was full of swallows and gulls. When I was growing up, we often visited family along the Massachusetts and Rhode Island shore where great importance was placed on the benefits of "salt air." As I recall, it was believed to contribute not only to good health but to salutary morals as well.

I sat on the wide, wooden porch with my morning coffee, waiting to go fishing once again with my cousin Fred, and vividly pictured, really saw before me, scenes from long ago: my aunts and uncles, brother and sister, cousins and parents, gathered on that damp and fragrant grass in sight of the sea and blue skies.

The harbor was an active commercial fishing place in those days, with a number of swordfish boats from whose pulpits swordfish and white marlin, called "skillygallee," were harpooned. The swordfisher-men were our heroes. We made model swordfish boats with needles and thread for harpoon and line, tied "choggy" minnows across their decks for a triumphant return to port. I remember my businessman father heading out in his long-billed cap for a day of swordfishing with the great Gus Benakes aboard the beautiful Nova Scotia boat, the

Bessie B. Those people are almost all gone. But much else has stayed the same. Even the old harbor tender, the *Nasaluga*, is still there.

As if to bless my fishing, a gold-crowned kinglet (probably dazed) landed on my shoulder while I drank my coffee and contemplated the striped bass fishing ahead. When Fred came we set out across the lawn just as we'd done forty-five years ago, carrying handlines and fiddler crabs. Now we bore graphite fly rods and bar-stock aluminum fly reels. Still, it felt the same. More to the point, we had arranged to fish with Fred's friend Dave Cornell, who guides these waters he knows so well.

I had come from across the country and we were making a late start. The wind was already blowing hard. Nevertheless, we quickly headed out through the harbor around the breakwater and were running between granite ledges past the ruins of the West Island Club, where sports of the Gilded Age cast baby lobsters for tackle-smashing striped bass. Club logs reveal their astounding catches followed by a rapid decline, paralleling the industrial pollution of their spawning rivers. Where once stood their fishing stations, grande-luxe living quarters and kitchen gardens, there remained only gull-whitened rocks and the nervous attendance of the green Atlantic.

The sea was rough. We made a few stabs at schooling albacore and worked our way east toward Westport, finally tying off to a mooring buoy and eating our lunch. Dave was thinking in defensive terms, based on uncooperative weather and the gentlemanly hours of his guests. He untied us from the buoy and we headed up a saltwater river, turning into a fairly busy marina. He positioned us just outside the pilings of some empty slips along a finger pier. In a very short time, I could hear bass popping along the seawall. We caught several small fish before facing that our options that day were sharply limited. We headed back to Sakonnet.

The next day, Fred and I were better behaved and we set out at daybreak, with Dave far more optimistic. We rounded Warren's Point and looked east toward the Massachusetts shore. The wooded land looked remarkably unpopulated except for a church steeple sticking up above the trees. Among those trees once lived Awashonks, the female chief of the Sakonnets during King Phillip's War. Between the green landmass and the Atlantic was a pure white line of low surf, sparkling with sea birds.

The ocean looked as wide and level as a snooker table. At a number of places, birds were diving into schools of bait pushed by predatorial fish underneath. There would be a patch of rough water with a stream of birds trailing from it like drifting white smoke. This looked suspiciously like the good old days.

We skirmished with a couple of schools of false albacore without success, casting from the drifting boat into the bait, the albacore cutting through like fighter planes in the clear water, succeeding through speed rather than maneuverability. With little opportunity to tease them into taking, it was hit or miss. We missed.

Dave Cornell fishes like a prowler. Even when he's in fish he's looking for more fish. I, most often confined by riverbanks, was fascinated by this wide-angled view. I soon was made comfortable by our fishing along the rocks, the ocean gulping and foaming around their bases. It looked right when a big green-and-white Deceiver dropped into this turmoil and was drawn into the fishy darkness. No dice.

Dave spotted a school of stripers. By the time we reached them they had strung out in a line and one of Dave's friends was already fishing the far end of it. This was suddenly not difficult fishing. To say that it was like taking candy from a baby would be to defame the baby. We had tied on Clouser Minnows, a pattern of nearly universal effectiveness, and striped bass see them as a tremendous opportunity.

Every once in a while, angling provides an episode one can keep for life. It is not necessarily about big fish, though it sometimes is, nor about great difficulty overcome. Rather, it's a kind of poetic singularity. Sometimes you're even aware of it as it's happening.

This was such an event. We drifted along the school of feeding stripers, my cousin in one end of the boat, me in the other, Dave Cornell making such adjustments as were needed to keep us lined up to the drift.

The feeding of this big school of bass was creating what looked like a low breaker traveling steadily over the surface. A dark mass of bait like a shadow full of silver flashes moved ahead of the disturbance.

Along the entire front of the wave, the length of it, were . . . mouths. Above and all down its length hovered the terns whose forked tails touched the water when they sighted bait, caught it and swept away.

We hooked and released bass continuously. Stripers were so hard to come by when Fred and I were kids that I looked at each of these handsome native fish as though I'd never seen one before.

Dave radioed to his colleague at the other end of the school and asked how he was doing. His friend said he thought they'd put the rods away and "just lip them from the boat."

When the sun came up fully, a beautiful sea haze spread across the land to the north. We poked around for a while, had lunch off Goose Wing Beach at Little Compton, then headed for the Elizabeth Islands, walking along the beach and into the beautiful stands of hardwoods, just beginning to turn color.

Dave ran us through Quicks' Hole between Pasque and Nashawena and pulled us into a beautiful, quiet bay on the north side of Nashawena. False albacore were finning around but they were ultra-alert and we found no takers.

We headed back to Sakonnet Point and put the boat on the trailer. Fred and I changed clothes, then followed Dave to his house in South Dartmouth, where we loaded his canoe on top of his car. Through judicious use of sandy roads, car, and canoe, we found ourselves in a remarkable world illuminated by sea light. Through a long bank of dunes, the ocean had made a hidden inlet. Once inside, the tidal channel formed a salt marsh. On the high ground encircling the marsh, old houses looked on, their windows shining in the late sun.

The channel made its serpentine way through the cattails and was the size of a trout stream, which it resembled in other ways, except for the blue crabs that backed away from us and the stone-heavy quahogs revealed by our sinking feet.

We spread out along the stream, finding places where sandbars faced the deep flowing water on the outside of bends and their undercut banks: easy casting in an absorbing world. That from beneath those banks, oceangoing striped bass took our streamers and fought the good fight seems a matter for wonder. Looking across the cattails and spartina, I could see Dave, then Fred, with deep bows in their rods.

I slept well that night, with all the windows open so the fog could creep around my bedclothes and I could better hear the sonorities of the sea buoy. All night long I received cheerful visits from family ghosts and remembered how I once longed for a single striped bass. I wondered how my life would have gone had I known at age twelve that at fifty-five I'd have a twenty-fish day. Perhaps Fred can tell me.

Henry's Fork

I WENT TO IDAHO to fish the Henry's Fork of the Snake River. I had heard grave reports about its present condition and the impact of dewatering on a great resource whose natural values have little standing in local law. I had the feeling that the Henry's Fork was managed with a sharp eye on potato production, the modern equivalent of killing buffalo for their tongues.

I spent a couple of days, fishing and driving around with Mike Lawson, a guide and operator of the fly shop, Last Chance on the Henry's Fork. He and his wife, Sheralee, have lived in the area all their lives. Mike grew up in Sugar City, one of the sacrificial hamlets in the pathway of the Teton Dam, a dubious waterworks that not only swindled the American taxpayer with an indisputably lousy cost-ratio but was also built in such a bad place that, upon bursting, it killed people as predictably as Uzis in the hands of crack dealers.

Mike took me to a small tailwater fishery downriver on the Fork, where it is less like a spring creek than a real, if small, river. As we passed the farms and ranches on our way, well kept by an industrious people, Mike said with real feeling, "I grew up with these folks. I don't want anything bad to happen to a single one of them. But if they don't learn to negotiate and compromise, they're going to lose it all." Mike is right in the middle of it, as an angler, as a conservationist, as a native son, and as a Mormon. Mike is serious about his faith, an elder in his church, a great fisherman, and a perfect angling companion, relaxed and persistent, informed about his immediate natural world. That he is also an active conservationist on behalf of his beloved rivers has put him in direct conflict with many people in these same communities. One would need to have spent substantial time in these closely knit western farm and ranch towns to understand what personal strength this requires. Mike Lawson's ability to temper this toughness with his love of the native people is absolutely remarkable.

One of the unpleasant subcurrents of the conservation movement is a general loathing of Mormons as dam builders and irrigators and subverters of the Bureau of Reclamation. It is naive not to understand that Mormons are the irrigation pioneers of the arid West, or to fail to see a certain heroism in their survival against persecution and the poor gambler's odds of desert life. But the appropriateness of some of their water practices is now dimming. The slogan on Idaho license plates, "Famous Potatoes," has come to seem like some obsolete farmer joke instead of what it is, the merest insinuation of the power of Idaho's all-powerful water lobbies as well as her many nature-hating politicians with their zero ratings from the League of Conservation Voters.

At the spot where we encountered the river, there were several rapid channels deflected by a narrow, wooded island. Though the crossing Mike chose looked difficult to me, this was Mike's river, so we locked arms and set out. I soon felt the strength of the river and erosion of gravel under my feet as the current sped by. "I'm going," Mike said, a remark which at first seemed obvious until he was swept into a crablike grasp over the top of a submerged boulder. By then I was already floundering downstream myself. We wallowed back to shore, reconsidered, started out again, and this time we made it.

Now we could look around from the gravelly, mid-river shallows. "All kinds of birds winter in here," Mike said. "Some of them stay the whole winter. I've seen a great gray owl here." The little canyonlike enclosure did seem protected in every direction with its tall, stately rock walls and floor of twisting river currents.

We caught a few trout and then, fishing upstream, I hooked a fish on a nymph, a most delicate take and a rather measured reaction as I set the hook. When the fish eased out of the current to the slack water, it rolled once and I saw that it was an enormous rainbow. At first it fought, as large trout sometimes do, like an annoyed dog, shaking its head in the current, and planing off at a leisurely angle to turn and shake once again. I had enough sense of the fish's size to resist making him mad. Then, with one sand-filled boil, he turned and ran downstream. At the point where the channels rejoined each other, the river deepened too much for me to wade after him, so I pushed my fingers through the arbor of the reel and tried to slow the spool down. I got nowhere. As the line peeled off and the diameter of the spooled line decreased, everything got faster. The reel's click ran together in a little screech as the hog trout roared off.

By now, Mike had passed me and was trying to find a path downstream to follow the fish. Thirty yards below me, the backing passed over his head, parallel to the riverbank. Watching the hundred yards of line shrink, the last look I'd had of the fish—its dull red stripe wider than my hand—seemed to hang before me as I acknowledged that this was the largest resident trout I'd ever hooked. I thought of the fish I'd stared at on restaurant walls in northern Michigan as a boy. Most of them would have seemed like *cuisine minceur* to this beast.

Then the trout stopped. A single turn of backing remained on the spindle at the center of my empty reel. Yet the fish had stopped right then and there! It was like literature! He paused long enough for me to consider how wonderful life could be when it had great literature-style items, such as coincidence and fate and elegant ironies. Then, in that moment of anti-magic, when literature is converted to the far more familiar aspects of the land in which we actually live and breathe and spend our days, the great trout turned and straightened my hook. I had so much line downstream that there was still a substantial bow in my rod. I had to reel it all in. I had to salute the now-absent great fish who had made such short shrift of me. The more line I reeled in, the less bow there was in my rod, and finally, with nothing to commemorate the fish except the whispering river around my knees, my rod was nothing but a straight, dead stick. But there was a terrific, evangelical silence. It is a fact that we are made almost entirely of river water, but the flesh that remains organizes this spectral borrowing from riparian valleys and, rod in hand, blesses our origins by counting coups.

The next day, I fished the slower water upstream to see the outcome of the severe drawdowns, and to see which of the diversity of values represented by the Henry's Fork had been honored. The Bureau of Reclamation, now world-famous as a welfare program for corporate and millionaire irrigation farmers, had taken a strict constructionist view of its duties and announced that its only responsibility in the management of Island Park Dam was the supply of irrigation water. Indeed, for years its flow regimes have been dead wrong for wildlife. Idaho Fish and Game, pointing to their limited rotenone budget in a proposed trash fish kill, collaborated in the draw-down of the reservoir pool to catastrophic levels. The sediment bed was invaded and over fifty thousand tons of silt headed into the finest piece of trout water in the nation. It poured through the Box Canyon and upper Last Chance area. When it reached Harriman State Park, the august Railroad Ranch, the water slowed down and the silt dropped to the bottom. Fifteen years after I last fished here, I returned and saw that it had gone badly downhill. The silt was bermed up around boulders on the bottom while huge, vague clouds of muck spread out before me in the priceless waters the Harriman family had entrusted to the State of Idaho. Where were those hundreds of big, surface-feeding rainbows of not so long ago? Grossly reduced, to put it mildly. The corpse of the old Railroad Ranch was a fitting monument to the short memories and hit-and-run management techniques of several public agencies.

So, the slug of silt headed downstream. The resident trout of the lake were captured, more or less, and replanted into the Henry's Fork where, by the time of my visit, they were silvery and gaunt and not at all the vaunted river fish of yore. The trash fish were offed, the poison dispersed, the pool refilled and replanted with hatchery rainbows. Given the important genetic differences within trout species, this approach often results in populations of fish-mutts, such as the Skamania strain of steelhead that have seemed such a panacea to fishery agencies throughout the Northwest. Many people around the Henry's Fork thought that more thoughtful criteria might have been employed in so important an area.

IT OUGHT TO BE ENOUGH to say that the Idaho Department of Fish and Game had so disgraced itself that I bought the shortest-term license, three days, that they could force me to own. Blame for the steep decline of this great fishery must be shared by the supervisor and staff of the Targhee National Forest who have abetted the clear-cutting of this fragile region. Only the state's high rate of unemployment explains Targhee's ongoing ability to recruit qualified young people.

At present, the Nature Conservancy is trying to buy a ranch on the Henry's Fork above Island Park reservoir, and one would hope they will use the water to help with critical winter flows. But in this part of the West, the prior appropriation concept's doctrinal heartland, the subject of instream flow is both controversial and ambiguous. The "use it or lose it" approach to water seems to invade even the sacred precincts of private property, an astonishing lapse in an area obsessed with individual rights. The owner of a decreed water right can neither sell it nor give it to the stream itself. His rights as an owner are restricted.

Parts of the West, dominated by the church of irrigated farming, seem willing to accept this abrogation of individual rights, as opportunistic as that may seem to outsiders. State or federal property condemnations to accommodate motor vehicles and new roads are acceptable to most Westerners, but they consider the same practice "unconstitutional" when it's deployed to protect the natural world.

This spell of fishing, rambling, and philosophizing with Mike Lawson took place in the Island Park caldera, the mouth of an ancient volcano, one of the largest and oldest in the world. The impression on the ground is of a broad, level, circular area with a surrounding rim of low mountains, quite low really when viewed against the Tetons to the east—for me the most impressive way to see them. Bubbling through the porous and mineral-rich basalt of the old lava floor, substantial volumes of water form streams and rivers that are eyed sharply by farmers and trout fishermen alike. They're eyed perhaps even more sharply by migratory creatures like the trumpeter swan, who staged an eleventh-hour comeback from extinction in this glorious place.

Not completely discouraged by the condition of the Railroad Ranch, Mike and I traveled along the river and were soon so submerged in its glories that I began to forget its troubles. At Upper Mesa Falls, a curtain of vertically dropping mountain water, wonderfully tall, plunged between steep forest walls. A plume of mist climbed high into the blue Idaho sky, striped with rainbows. Mike pointed to a place far below us where nearly invisible water raced across slabs of basalt. In high school, he and his friends used to work their way out on the rock to catch wild trout at the base of the falls. Once, he was swept away toward Cardiac Canyon and lost his father's watch. I began to suspect that this river-lover, probably like most others, had been swept away often.

That evening we floated the Box Canyon through bird-filled shafts of declining light, the cold, clear water racing through a gallery of boulders where trout took up their stations for passing food. When we pulled our boat out at the bottom of the canyon, Mike related how as a baby, guarded by an inattentive aunt, he was, you guessed it, swept away by the Henry's Fork, then recaptured by the heroic effort of his mother as he bobbed among the rocks.

I was happy to think that the rivers that first carried me, literally and figuratively, off my feet—the Pere Marquette, the Pine, the Black, the Manistee—were now in the Wild and Scenic Rivers system and receiving its imperfect benediction. As we looked down into the canyon where the trackbed wound around above the Henry's Fork, Mike told me how his railroader father had taken him along the tracks in the inspector's motorcar and dropped him here and there to fish. I thought Mike's river ought to have that kind of care, too.

Above all, it ought to have some water. The first thing I wished was for the Nature Conservancy to acquire the upper Henry's Fork and find a way to keep that water in the river, not only through Island Park reservoir but through the crooked channel of western water law as well.

Tying Flies

I T SEEMS TO ME there are several schools of fly-tying: traditional, imitative, defiant, and autobiographical. Traditional tying produces a fly that is usually a generalist pattern and has a greater pure aesthetic component than those of my other arbitrarily named categories. Some of these high-concept flies, like other aesthetic ideas of their day, have gone into appropriate eclipse: the Parmachene Belle, Queen of Waters, even the Royal Coachman, as well as the elaborate salmon flies of the past that are now enjoying a resurgence but only as objects for display. In their prime, with ingredients drawn from the most recondite corners of the British Empire, they were the equivalent of Victorian architectural follies, far removed from their origins in utility. Other traditional flies have a restraint and beauty that makes them undiscardable: the Adams, the Quill Gordon, the Hendricksons, the Cahills, all remain useful and pretty. They remind us of the poetic history of our passion as well as its deficiencies. They don't much look like the flies they imitate except in the most basic way, and they encapsulate certain preconceptions about fish which are aesthetic at base, such as the notion that trout really prefer beautiful mayflies to such tiresome things as caddises, stoneflies, midges, and worms.

Some great fishermen–fly-tyers have been generalists, including the French anglers who supply restaurants from hard-fished public rivers. Most flies for anadromous fish, like steelhead and salmon, are generalizations. The convinced generalist is often one who knows his water intimately and professes a great belief in sharp casting and good overall streamcraft.

The imitative school is looking for truth and often overshoots the mark. Fish are suspicious of perfect imitations of the naturals. This quest to copy, to some anglers like me, is not an interesting idea and may remind one of those superior grade-school companions whose model airplanes made one's own efforts such objects of ridicule. Nevertheless, there is a passionate coven of fly-tyers using all the material the space age offers to make astonishing replicas of the things fish eat. It would seem to me that if some canny manufacturer succeeded in making plastic copies of blue-winged olives, pale morning duns, callibaetis spinners—and if they can make such nice outfits for Barbie, what's to stop them?—that something has been lost.

The defiant and autobiographical fly-tyer is ofen the same person. Not awed by custom, they name their flies Chernobyl Ants, Egg-Sucking Leeches, Yuk Bugs, or name flies after themselves, in the manner of knot inventors, a modest and understandable quest for immortality. These tyers try to convey themselves as they wish to be perceived in their creations: the gonzo type, the bum, the aggressively unpretentious (brown fly) type. One brilliant steelheader refuses to play these games and only fishes with flies he finds or is given. Another hangs a strip of deerhide on a Gamakatsu Octopus hook and fishes it on a floating line. Among the innovators are those who design a whole genre of artificial flies, a nearly impossible thing to do, and let the individual tyers flesh out the idea with their own refinements. Such are the Wulff flies, Lefty's Deceivers, Crazy Charlies, Clouser Minnows, and the Comparaduns. Others take such a degree of experience and sophistication to cross into a new innocence, reinventing fly-tying to produce a series of flies that seem as creative as the naturals. I'm thinking of Darrell Martin and Ken Iwamasa, who suggest fresh ways of looking at water, light, and insects as well as the materials we use.

One of the most difficult accomplishments in fly-tying is to reexamine an established category and do it better and more simply. One of the best instances of this is the Elk Hair Caddis, which combines indigenous materials and rapidity of execution, appeals equally to imitation and generalization, and produces a fly that if fished well will catch well. The Adams is another superb example; purportedly tied to imitate a fluttering caddis, it is so full of Catskill-style mayfly traits and general earthiness as to be an outstanding choice for the dry-fly fisherman who relies on casting and streamcraft instead of encyclopedic fly boxes. And in its downwinged version, it's not a bad caddis. Frank Sawyer's Pheasant Tail nymphs, or the Gold-Ribbed Hare's Ears, create a poetic economy from limited materials. But there are times when these flies will be badly outfished by more specific imitations. Those who believe that steadiness and acuity in presentation, the avoidance of lost motion and indecision, produce a better bag are drawn to such flies. The stalkers of difficult individual trout think more in terms of the fly that is perfect both in time and place.

Many of us are inclined to fish with flies we think are beautiful. Happily, some of the flies I find practical are, when crisply tied, beautiful. I think the Adams is beautiful. The jauntiness and efficacity of the Royal Wulff has a western, freestoner kind of beauty; it works so well that a whole school of sophisticated anglers will do anything to keep from using it. A. K. Best's quill-bodied flies make me shiver. The defiant bugginess of Dave's Hopper is beautiful for its go-ahead-eat-me legs and general profile. The fragile and austere quill-winged and hackleless duns of René Harrop, simple yet madly difficult to tie, make a silhouette on the surface of the water that causes a predator's heart to pound. There's an old pattern called the Borcher's Special that gives me a heightened sense of empowerment, and a fly from the Dan Bailey catalog of thirty years ago, the Meloche, that makes me feel equal to the emergence of pale morning duns. Of course it's all in my head; that's the point. Any sustained perusal of the fly books of the world should demonstrate that fish have been remarkably tolerant of our follies. I'm afraid the exercise has made a presentationist out of me. Clearly, it is not *what* those long-gone or far-flung anglers offered the fish, it's *how* they offered it.

The trouble is, you can't properly present something you don't believe in. There is a sort of infatuation when an angler looks at flies. We look through pictures of flies much as we search through our old high school yearbooks, a kind of a scanning process until something stops the eye. The same feeling is obtained when looking in the compartments of a fly shop or fly box. An odd transference occurs in the imagination. One holds up the fly and *thinks* both like a fish and like a fisherman, and perhaps as a species of prey, all at once; though maybe it is not thinking. A convergence of emotion is sought, the unknowable conviction of a sorcerer, the feeling that, yes, this will do nicely, a feeling that enlarges as the fly is knotted to the tippet, held again to the light to further charge one's conviction, then off it goes at the end of a cast. If it catches fish, a wider smile opens within. If it fails utterly, it is subjected once more to the gaze at close range, the sorcerer feeling rueful. You ask yourself, How did I fall for this one? Though you return it to your fly box, you really want to throw it away. I once lit one with a match.

Very slowly over my life I have become a fly-tyer. There was a time when I was contemptuous of it, on the grounds that it took time away from fishing, which is not entirely untrue. Then, grudgingly, I tied some simple saltwater patterns, and finally, expendable freshwater streamers, leeches, simple down-wing patterns. While tying has grown on me enormously, my numerous deficiencies will probably never be overcome. If a fly has too many steps, I either simplify it or tie something else. I will never tie good feather wings, especially the no-hackle duns I so admire but will never successfully imitate. I get red-faced doing legs for the hoppers; mine look like dogs pissing on a fire hydrant. Instead, I have tried to do a cleaner and crisper job on the flies that give me confidence: hairwing and parachute Adamses, Royal Wulffs, Dave Hughes's little parachute olives, pheasant tail nymphs, Prince nymphs, Gold-Ribbed Hare's Ears, Pale Morning Duns, Stimulators, light and dark Spruce flies, tiny green Crazy Charlies for bonefish, various versions of the classic Cockroach for tarpon, simple yarn crabs for permit, mylar-and-white Deceivers for snook, and so on. My real loves are trout flies, steelhead flies, and salmon flies. The latter are probably interchangeable but, since they express different cultures, are rarely mixed. I have been crossing the line in using Allee Shrimps for steelhead, though not the other way around, as the deep voodoo of salmon is something I am unready to disturb. I tie Rusty Rats, Blue Charms, Monroe Killers, Willie Gunns, and the fly with which I am most confident, the Black Bear Green Butt, awfully close to the steelheaders' classic, the Green Butt Skunk. For steelhead, I vastly prefer the McVey Ugly, a knockoff of the classic McLeod Ugly, hatched by Peter McVey, the great chef, angler, and cane-rod builder of British Columbia.

I still have many friends who prefer leaving this to the experts, as I once did. But now that I know that the object is to please myself, that the machinelike finish possible for the professional who ties a hundred-dozen of the same pattern doesn't matter much to the fish, nor does it necessarily subject the tyer to repetitive motion diseases or dark hours at the county nut farm. I try to tie flies that will make me fish better, to fish more often, to dream of fish when I can't fish, to remind myself to do what I can to make the world more accommodating to fish and, in short, to take further steps toward actually becoming a fish myself.

Spring

IN SPRING, warm wind comes to Montana before anything turns green, though not quite before some birds—owls and juncos for example—nest and even begin to hatch their young. The tiny ground-hugging phlox displays its chaste white flowers; the harrier begins to lose his winter white and the red-tailed hawks haul all manner of junk, including the hot-orange twine we use to bind haybales, to build their messy nests in the black cottonwoods along the creek. The creek itself is some days pellucid, throwing the shadows of trout on its graveled bottom, and on others milky with low country runoff. On the cliffs, rock marmots aggressively pull up the bunch grass and take it under ledges and down holes to build nests. All the birds are particularly loud and indelicate just now; but the red-shafted flickers screeching from the tops of the tallest, barest cottonwoods seem the most brazen, Brewer's blackbirds the busiest in this bright sun that encourages their iridescence. In the summer pasture north of our house the teal pause in the water-filled buffalo wallows of ancient times; the magpies tumble and mob in the clumped junipers. The meadowlark stands on the stones of the Native American grave east of the Charlie Wild draw and sings her heart out.

When I hike, I frequently come up on groups of mule deer feeding, as though I were a great stalker, but the deer are so close to their physical limits at this edge between winter and spring that they are not very alert. When the shadow of a marsh hawk flickers through them, they don't jump as they would later on, and the ears of some hang down as they do on sick calves. When they flee, the inverted rowing motion of their synchronized legs doesn't send such a shudder of power through their trunks as it will in another month.

The sagebrush buttercup is the brightest thing in the landscape, a buttercup so early that it follows the retreating snow in a yellow haze. This is the first flower the grizzly sees when he wakes up from his nap. Cousin to the cursed crowfoot, a poisonous, blistering, inflaming flower, sagebrush buttercup is an important spring food to the blue grouse. I stood in a field of this beautiful flower, feeling the strap of my binoculars cut into my neck and sensing in the vault of tremendous sky an uncertain skirmish between the winds of winter and those of spring. To the north, the Crazy Mountains looked starved for restoration, and it was good to remember that their slaggish forms would soon burst into something I always think I can imagine but never quite do.

In the cottonwoods below the house stands a crooked giant whose top is splayed into a garish, surrendering shape. At the crotch of these upper branches, a great horned owl has raised a single baby. And when the sun comes out, she encourages him to advance along the dead branch on the north side of his nest. Nearly her height, his downy looseness gives him away. He doesn't seem to know what is expected of him. He stares at me amazed, while the wind takes bits of his down and sails them off toward the banks of wild roses. His mother, glaring from above with her yellow eyes, looks like the wife of Satan. As many times as I have seen her, I've never seen her first. She is always watching from her tree as though she weighed a plan for me.

Over the sere landscape, creatures are chasing one another just like the children at the local junior high. The kingfishers scream and the meadowlark sings as cascadingly and melodiously on the wind as she does standing on a strand of barbed wire. Some of our calves are buoyant; in others the rains have brought on scours, their backs humped, their ears down, and their legs scalded with diarrhea. The cows have begun to "ride" one another, and our five bulls holler from their segregated pasture south of the county road. The long, cold rains have given two calves pneumonia. One runs a high fever and stares at the ground, the other has compacted her lungs and will never do well. The vet said, "She'd be just as well off if she died." In the corral where the sick calves stand, mating barn swallows chase each other, fall to the ground, and breed.

I saddle a horse to tour the pastures in search of spring grass. Everything is late this year. We're two weeks behind town, only fifteen miles away. There's a yearling buck dead by the first spring, nearly devoured by coyotes who have seized intestines and backed several yards from the carcass. This is merely a boon to the coyotes, who have come by this meal as honestly as did the Pennsylvania wolves who devoured the bodies of Braddock's soldiers after the battle of Monongahela. The face of creation takes in everything with a level stare. When I was younger these manifestations of life's fury were comfortably free of premonition. Now they bear a gravity that dignifies the one-day lives of insects, the terrible slaughterhouse journey of livestock, and, of course, ourselves and our double handful of borrowed minerals. The old man I see staring from his porch rocker when I go to town is staring into a tremendous distance. As surely as homeowners pride themselves on property that fronts the beach, the lake, or the golf course, we all enjoy abyss frontage; and some, like the fellow in his rocker, seem absorbed by the view.

The obsessive busy-ness Thoreau complained of is rooted in fear; fear: of mortality, and then of the pain of loss and separation. Only in the observation of nature can we recover that view of eternity that consoled our forebears. The remains of the young buck dead at the spring are sounded in the cliffs above our house in the calls of young coyotes, testing the future with their brand-new voices, under the stars of outer space.

The rivers stayed high for longer than I could remember seeing. And finding fishable water wasn't easy. I went to West Yellowstone, which sits high in several watersheds. Every year, the fly shops there boast some new fly that is certain to cancel blank days for all time. This year it was a tiny doodad that resembled a little bristling worm. When I bought a few of them, another angler, a hay farmer in a colorful "Spawn 'Til You Die" T-shirt just looked at them in my palm and swung his head from side to side as he remembered the shoals of trout suicides this inoffensive little thing had produced. Either that or he was wondering how anyone could fall for this one at all.

I drove into Yellowstone Park, headed for the Firehole River. The tourists paused at everything, stopping in the middle of the highway with a heedlessness so uncharacteristic of Americans that it was pleasantly maddening. I parked on a high bank overlooking the river and rigged up, then picked my way through grazing buffalo to reach the bank of this beautiful stream. Steam from hot springs and geysers and fumaroles drifted weirdly over the classic waters of the Firehole and several buffalo fed all the way down to the marshy edge of the river, where a few bank feeders sucked down emerging mayflies. I ought to have had good success with pale morning duns but the gusting wind out of the canyon had suppressed the hatch.

There were plenty of fishermen, some disconsolate and making halfhearted casts, some pressing on with a higher view, some extraordinarily costumed in the new predatorial style, camouflaged and fishing like New Zealanders with dark-dyed lines. All these solicitations were being declined by the trout. The few mayflies to appear were tumbled along the surface by the wind, unprofitable for fish to run down.

So I drove on to the upper Madison, which was not exactly quiet either. Deciding to enjoy the uproar, I stopped at a general store and bought some bubble gum, read the cartoon, and rigged my tackle. A young boy came up and showed me his round, plastic fly box and asked why he hadn't caught a fish all day. I gave him three of the mysterious, bristling worms. Without saying much, I communicated the idea that I had long relied on this remarkable fly. I could see hope renew itself in his face as he considered the logic of this irrational new shape wound on a small hook. But I was already violating my foremost rule for catching more fish: keep the fly in the water.

Clearly, the Madison was too high. But I was going forward with this thing by hook or by crook because no other options were currently available to me. I started at the top of a long braided channel, casting the new fly into the flow and studying the point of my line as it came back to me. Except for some bottom tapping, nothing enlivened the drift of the nymph, and a good spell passed with my arm starting to tire from keeping the rod high and the line out of the water. I pushed through willows at the gravel bar and started down another channel with the same results. I felt guilty for giving the three useless flies to the youngster. I continued through three channels, two hours, and five fly changes: Peeking Caddis, Gold-Ribbed Hare's Ear, Prince Nymph, Squirrel Tail, and finally, the venerable English Pheasant Tail Nymph, size #16. I tried to keep the leader slicing deep into the water without drag, while the end of the fly line eased along behind, telegraphing the movements of the nymph drifting below. No dice; the river was too high.

I drove on to a small tributary of the upper Missouri. It lay in a high country with such long winters and high moisture that it had a peatish, muskeglike feel in places. The word "creek" seemed right for it and suggested its crumbling banks and easy meanders. The moose and colorful reed birds correctly implied a brief, damp summer. But the amount of water in it was exactly right, not too low and not too high. Here we would have an encounter.

I walked the level, rich-smelling pastures where sandhill cranes croaked out their love to each other. In sloughs off the river, the eared grebe swam daintily and rolled for a dive like a tiny, crested loon. Where irrigation drawdown had exposed luscious, wormy mud, the elegant Wilson's phalarope stepped carefully in search of a meal. Along the ranch road that passed a small impoundment of water, a fertilizer truck sailed through clouds of drifting mayflies. This country was swollen with a sparkling exhalation of life: wild grass and bright yellow patches of balsamroot flowers, water igniting in spring light. As I stood on a bank over the river, drawing the tapered line through the guides of my rod and looking off toward the wild hills of new sagebrush to the east, I realized evening was coming on and I had forgotten to eat.

The water curled around boulders with a bulge and moved in a nervous rush against my legs as I fished upstream. Here and there were small glassy panels of undisturbed water, and in one of these panels the end of the line stopped. I lifted the rod tip and felt the weight that to an angler is not just weight.

A rainbow trout ripped straight downstream and with the full strength of the river on his tail, prepared to defeat me and my tackle-fueled pyramid scheme. All the pressure of slow fishing rested on the solid shoulders of the fish and I stumbled and wallowed along behind, underplaying him, trying to remember if the leader had any wind knots and knowing that the tiny, barbless hook was but a faint connection. Still, I had managed to detain this fish, and for the moment we were living in each other's lives.

When the trout held in a bar of current, his pink stripe shone up through the cold green water of springtime. And that's where it stops in memory, so that such things may be accumulated and produce a renewable happiness. I led him into the slower water at the river's edge, supported his cool belly in the water with my hand, and let him go.

The cafe in town had homemade soup, a jukebox, a telephone, and enough light in the booths to read the newspaper. It all seemed very complete.

Runoff

THE FISHING LIFE in Montana produces a particular apprehension that affects fishermen like a circadian rhythm: irrational dread of runoff. Early spring is capable of balmy days, and though the water is cold, the rivers are as benign as brooks in dreams, their pools and channels bright and perfect. But year-round experience shows that in short order they will be buried in snowmelt and irrigation waste, their babied low-water contours disappearing under a hoggish brown rush. Once runoff commences, the weather is often wonderful. The canopies of cottonwood will open like green umbrellas. But it can be a long wait before the rivers clear, a lull so long it seems possible to lose track of the whole idea of fishing.

In early spring, it is time to begin when friends say, "I know I should get out. I just haven't had the time." Here is the chance to steal a march, to exercise those fish whose memory has been dulled by the long winter. Crazy experiments can be undertaken, such as photographing a trout held in your left hand with a camera held in your right hand. Before-the-runoff is time out of time, the opportunity to steal fishing from an impudent year.

You know you've started early enough when the first landowner whose permission you ask stares at you with xenophobic eyes. His first thought is that you are there to pilfer or abuse his family. Let him examine your rod and scrutinize your eyes. Those of a fisherman are often not so good, so keep them moving. Spot a bit of natural history and describe it for him: "Isn't that our first curlew?" Above all, don't say that your dad and your granddad before you fished this same stretch at their pleasure. The landowner of today is unlikely to appreciate any surprising seniority; he's having hell holding onto the place. Turn and walk calmly to your vehicle. Don't back to it.

I wandered around the various forks of my home river separated by many miles of rolling hills. One would be running off, the other clear, depending upon the exact kind of country it drained. I clambered down slick or snowy rocks to dangle my thermometer in the water. But in the spring there was, even on a snowy day, a new quality of light, as if the light had acquired a palpable richness that trees, grass, and animals could also feel, a nutritious light coming through falling snow. There had come a turning point and now spring was more inexorable than the blizzards. I knew the minute this snow quit there would be someplace I could fish.

The next morning was still and everything was melting. I went to a small river out in the foothills north of where I live. This early in the year, when I drive down through a ranch yard or walk across a pasture toward the stream, my heart pounds for a glimpse of moving water. Yet moving water has, all my life, been the most constant passion I've had. It can be current or it can be tide, though it can't be a lake and it can't be mid-ocean, where I have spent baffled days and weeks more or less scratching my head. Today the river was in perfect shape, with enough water that most of its braided channels were full. There were geese on the banks and they talked at me in a state of high alarm as they lifted and replaced their feet with weird deliberation.

As soon as I got in the river, I felt how very cold the water was. Nevertheless, a few caddises skittered on top. An hour later, some big gray drakes came off like a heavenly message sent on coded insects, a message that there would indeed be dry-fly fishing on earth again. I'm always saying, though it's hardly my idea, that the natural state of the universe is cold. But cold-blooded trout and cold-blooded mayflies are indications of the world's retained heat, as is the angler, wading upstream in a cold spring wind in search of delight. Nevertheless, the day had opened a few F-stops at the aperture of sky, a promise and a beginning. I caught one of the mayflies and had a long look: about a

No. 12; olive, brown, and gray the operative colors; two-part tail. I had something pretty close in my fly box, having rejected the Red Quill and the Quill Gordon as close but no cigar.

A couple of brilliant male mergansers passed overhead. They are hard on fish and despised, but their beauty is undisputed. In a short time they would migrate out of here, though I didn't know where they went. They were referred to in Lewis and Clark's journals as the "red-headed fishing duck," a better name.

The river combined in a single channel, where the volume of water produced a steady riffle of two or three feet in depth. I started where it tailed out and worked my way up to where slick water fell off into the rapids. The mayflies were not in great numbers but they were carried down this slick and over the lip into the riffle. My staring magnified their plight into postcards of Niagara Falls, a bit of sympathetic fancy canceled by the sight of swirls in the first fast water. I cast my fly straight into this activity and instantly hooked a good rainbow. It must have been the long winter's wait or the knowledge that the day could end at any minute, but I desperately wanted to land this fish. I backed down out of the fast water while the fish ran and jumped, then I sort of cruised him into the shallows and got a hand on him. He was a brilliant-looking fish, and I thought I could detect distress in his eyes as he looked, gulping, out into midair. I slipped the barbless hook out and eased him back into the shallows. Two sharp angles and he was gone in deep green water.

It started to cloud up and grow blustery. The temperature plummeted. I went back to my truck, stripped off my waders, put up my gear and started home, passing the old black tires hung on fenceposts with messages painted on them about cafes and no hunting. I kept thinking that the sort of sporadic hatch that had begun to occur was perfect for leisurely dry-fly fishing, if only the weather had held. By the time I got to the house it was winter again and I was trying to look up that dun, concluding for all the good it would do me that it was *Ephemerella compar*. Even as I write this, I visualize a trout scholar in pince-nez rising up out of a Livingston spring creek to correct my findings.

When you have stopped work to go fishing and then been weathered out, your sense of idleness knows no bounds. You wander around the house and watch the sky from various windows. From my bedroom I could see great gusts of snow, big plumes and curtains marching across the pasture. Did I really catch a rainbow on a dry-fly this morning?

The next day broke off still and sunny, and spring was sucking that snow up and taking it to Yucatán. At the post office I ran into a friend of mine who'd seen a young male gyrfalcon—a gyrfalcon!—hunting partridges on my place. Within an hour I was standing with my fly rod in the middle of a bunch of loose horses, looking off a bank into a deep, green-black pool where swam a number of hog rainbows. I had been there before, of course, and you couldn't approach this spot except to stand below where the slow-moving pool tailed out rather rapidly. The trouble was you had to stay far enough away from the pool that it was hard to keep your line off the tailwater, which otherwise produced instantaneous drag. You needed a seven-foot rod to make the cast and a twenty-foot rod to handle the slack. They hadn't built this model yet; it would need to be a two-piece rod with a spring-loaded hinge driven by a cartridge in the handle, further equipped with a flash suppressor. Many of us had been to this pool to learn why the rainbows had grown to be hogs who would never be dragged onto a gravel bar. They were going to stay where they were, with their backs up and their bellies down, eating whenever they felt like it. I had to try it anyway and floated one up onto the pool. I got a drag-free drift of around three-eighths of an inch and then went looking for another spot.

Geese and mallards flew up ahead of me as I waded, circling for altitude in the high bare tops of the cottonwoods. The air was so still and transparent you could hear everything. When the mallards circled over my head, their wingtips touched in a tense flutter and made a popping sound.

In a little back eddy, caddises were being carried down a line of three feeding fish. I arranged for my fly to be among them and got a drift I couldn't begin to improve upon, so a nice brown sucked it down. I moved up the edge of the bar to other feeding fish. The geese on the bar who'd been ignoring me now began to watch and pace around. I noted one of the fish was of good size and feeding in a steady rhythm. I made a kind of measuring cast from my knees. The geese were getting more nervous. I made a final cast and it dropped right in the slot and started floating back to the good fish. I looked over to see what the geese were doing. The trout grabbed the fly. I looked back and missed the strike. I delivered an oath. The geese ran awkwardly into graceful flight and banked on around to the north.

This was a wonderful time to find yourself astream. You didn't bump into experts. You didn't bump into anybody. You could own this place in your thoughts as completely as a Hudson Bay trapper. The strangely human killdeer were all over the place, human in that their breeding activities were accompanied by screaming fights and continuous loud bickering. When they came in for a landing, their wings set in a quiet glide while their legs ran frantically in midair. The trees in the slower bends were in a state of pickup-sticks destruction from the activity of beavers. A kingfisher flew over my head with a trout hanging from its bill. I came around a bend without alerting three more geese, floating in a backwater, sound asleep with their heads under their wings. I decided not to wake them. I ended my day right there. When I drove up out of the river bottom in my car, I looked back to see a blue heron fishing the back eddy where I'd just caught a trout. On the radio were predictions of high temperatures and I knew what that low-country meltoff would mean to my days on the river.

Spring was here and it was hot. In one day it shot up to the eighties. I could feel the purling melt coming out from under the snowbanks. Runoff was going to drop me in midstride.

I drove away from the places I thought would get the first dirty water, away from the disturbed ground. At daybreak out on the interstate I found myself in a formation of Montana Pioneers driving Model-Ts. This piquancy didn't hold me up long and I soon made my way to a wonderful little district where various grasses, burgeoning brush, wildflowers, and blue-green strips of fragrant sage had all somehow got the news that spring had sprung. The cover was so deep in places that deer moving through it revealed only their ears, which flipped up and disappeared. An old pry bar lay lost in the grass, polished smooth by use. Ranchers never had the help they needed and they were all masters of prying. These bars had the poetry of any old tool, whether a dental instrument, or old greasy hammers, or screwdrivers around a man's workshop, especially when the tool owner is not in immediate evidence, or is dead.

The river whispered past this spot in a kind of secretive hurry. I got in and waded upstream, then sat on a small logjam to tie on a fly. The logs under me groaned with the movement of current. I was suddenly so extremely happy, the sight of this water was throwing me into such a rapturous state, that I began to wonder what it could mean. I sometimes wondered if there wasn't something misanthropic in this passion for solitude.

I put my thermometer into the river, knowing already it was going to come out in the forties. Taking the river's temperature is like taking your own temperature, with all the drama of the secret darkness of the interior of your mouth; you wait and wait and try to wait long enough. Is it 98.6 or am I right in thinking I don't feel too good? The water was 49 degrees, fairly acceptable for now.

Across from my seat was an old cabin. These old structures along Montana trout rivers are part of their provenance, part of what comes back to you, like the wooded elevations that shape and bend and push and pull each river so that as you try to re-create one in your mind the next winter, there is a point where you get lost, always an oxbow or meander where a certain memory whiteout occurs. I am always anxious to return to such a stretch and rescue it from amnesia.

To reach my pool, I had to wade across the riffle above the logjam and then work my way around a humongous dead cow inflated to a height of five feet at the ribcage. The smell was overpowering but I needed to get to that pool. A mule deer doe was back in the trees watching me with her twin yearling fawns. One was already getting little velvet antlers.

For some reason I was thinking how many angry people, angry faces, you saw in these romantic landscapes, as though the dream had backfired in isolation. There were the enraged visages behind pickup truck windshields with rifles in the back window at all seasons of the year. I remembered an old rancher telling me about a rape that had just occurred in Gardiner, and in his eyes was the most extraordinary mixture of lust and rage I have ever seen. He lived off by himself in a beautiful canyon and this was the sort of thing he came up with. A friend of mine from the Midwest looked at the chairs in a restaurant covered with all the local cattle brands and cried out in despair, "Why are these people always tooling everything?" The pleasures of being seduced by the daily flux of the masses were not available. All the information about the world had failed to produce the feeling of the global village; the information had only exaggerated the feeling of isolation. I had in my own heart the usual modicum of loneliness, annoyance, and desire for revenge, but it never seemed to make it to the river. Isolation always held out the opportunity of solitude: the rivers kept coming down from the hills.

Having reached my pool, having forded the vast stench of the cow, I was rewarded with a sparse hatch of sulfur mayflies with mottled gray wings. I caught three nice browns in a row before it shut off. I knew this would happen. A man once told me, after I'd asked when you could assume a horse would ground-tie and you could go off and leave him knowing he'd be there when you got back: "The horse will tell you." When I asked an old man in Alabama how he knew a dog was staunch enough to break it to stand to shot, he said: "The dog will tell you." There are times for every angler when he catches fish because the fish told him he could, and times when the trout announce they are through for the day.

Two of the most interesting fish of the next little while were ones I couldn't catch. One was on the far edge of a current that ran alongside a log. The trout was making a slow porpoising rise. I managed to reach him and he managed to rise, but drag got the fly and carried it away an instant before he took. The next fish, another steady feeder, rose to a Light Cahill. The dinner bell at a nearby ranch house rang sharply. I looked up, the fish struck, and I missed it.

I caught a nice rainbow by accident, which is the river's way of telling you that you've been misreading it. And then thunder and lightning commenced. I got out of the river. Bolting rain foretold the flood. I went up and sat under the trunk lid of my car, quite comfortably, and ate my lunch, setting a Granny Smith apple on the spare tire. The thermos of coffee seemed a boon almost comparable to the oranges we kept on ice during the hot early weeks of bird season. The rain steadied down and I could watch two or three bends of the river and eat in a state of deep contentment. I didn't know of a better feeling than to be fishing and having enough time; you weren't so pressured that if you got a bad bank you couldn't wait until the good bank turned your way and the riffles were in the right corners. The meal next to a stream was transforming, too, so that in addition to the magic apple there was the magic peanut-butter-and-jelly sandwich.

The rain stopped and I went down to where an irrigation ditch took out along a rip-rapped bank. I had a very nice Honduran cigar to smoke while I watched a heron fish the shallows. The air was still. When I puffed a great cloud of smoke and it drifted across the little river, I imagined it was the ghost of my grandfather, who loved to fish. The ghost glided past the heron, who politely ignored him.

I just knew something was going on. There was a readiness; the rain had barely withdrawn. The sky looked so heavy you felt if you scratched it you'd drown. This was the storm that would loosen the mountain snows, and the glistening fingers of this small river system would turn as brown as a farmer's hand. Time, in its most famous configuration, was running out. This could be my last day on the stream for a good while. Having broken out of the pattern of home life and work, you might as well keep going.

I crawled down into a canyon made by the river. It was not far from where I had been fishing and the canyon was not that deep. But I needed both hands to make the descent, lowering myself from projecting roots and points of rock, and I had to throw the rod down in front of me because there was no good way to carry it. I found myself between tall cream-and-gray rock walls. The river flowed straight into dissolved chimneys, rock scours, solution holes and fanciful stone bridges.

The sky overhead was reduced to a narrow band over which the storm had re-formed. More killdeer conducted their crazed, weeping, wing-dragging drama around my feet. The storm became ugly and I looked all around the bottom of the small canyon for a safe place to be. Lightning jumped close overhead with a roaring crack. The rain poured down, periodically lit up by the lightning. What little I knew about electricity made me think that bushes were a poor connection, so I burrowed into a thick clump of laurels, became mighty small, and studied the laurel: round, serrated leaf, brownish yellow bark, a kind of silvery brightness from afar. It had become very gloomy. By looking at the dark mouths of the caves in the far canyon wall, I could monitor the heaviness of the rain while the steady rattle on the hood of my parka filled in the blanks. I spotted a lightning-killed tree at about my level on the far side. The river had seemed so cheerful and full of green-blue pools. Now it was all pounded white by rain and only the darker V's of current indicated that it was anything but standing water.

Then the air pressure lightened. The dark sky broke wide open in blue. An owl crossed the river, avoiding the return of light. The rain stopped and the surface of river was miraculously refinished as a trout stream. I looked at the drops of water hanging from my fly rod. I thought of the windows of the trout opening onto a new world and how appropriate it would be if one of them could see my fly.

The standing water along roadsides in spring is a wonderful thing. On the way home, I saw a flight of northern shoveler ducks, eccentric creatures in mahogany and green, and off in a pasture stock pond, teal flew and circled like butterflies unable to decide whether to land. I wondered what it was about the edges of things that is so vital, the edges of habitat, the edges of seasons, always in the form of an advent. Spring in Montana is a kind of pandemonium of release. Certainly there are more sophisticated ways of taking it in than mine. But going afield with my fishing rod seemed not so intrusive, and the ceremony helped, quickening my memory back through an entire life spent fishing. Besides, like "military intelligence" and "airline cuisine," "sophisticated angler" is an oxymoron. And if it wasn't, it would be nothing to strive for. Angling is where the child, if not the infant, gets to go on living.

It was ten minutes to five. There was absolutely no wind. I could see the corners of a few irrigation dams sticking up out of the ditches. The cottonwoods were in a blush of green. I was ready for high water.

The Big Hole

I FISH ALL THE TIME when I'm at home, so when I get a chance to go on a vacation, I make sure to get in plenty of fishing. I live in south-central Montana, and because of drought and fires this year it resembles one of the man-made hells such as the Los Angeles basin. I make a trip every summer to fish the Big Hole River, and this year, knowing it was somewhat out of the range of smoke and ash and heat, I particularly looked forward to it. My friends Craig and Peggy Fellin have a small fishing lodge, with a capacity of eight, and I was perhaps their most regular annual guest.

Montana is so large and contains such a diversity of distinct regions that a trip from where I live to the southwesternmost corner, the Big Hole, provides a tremendous transition of environment, change of weather, change of terrain, and culture. The Big Hole ranchers are different from others in the state, and many of their farming and stock management practices also differ. The age of that district is seen in the old ranch headquarters, the hoary barns, the places founded by Frenchmen and fur traders, the stables that once held famous racehorses and, one valley over in the Bitterroot, the old mission churches.

But to head across Montana this year is alarming. With limited annual rainfall, much of its appearance is desertic to begin with. But this year the yellow desiccation of midsummer crawled closer to the green shapes of mountains, until finally the wooded high country stood in ghastly attendance over what looked to be a dying landscape. Then all the fires began, first in Yellowstone, then in the Scapegoat and Bob Marshall areas. Inspired by this festivity, Missoula arsonists began to have at it until the feeling began to be that, generally speaking, Montana was on fire.

Water had become fascinating. It was fascinating to water the lawn. It was fascinating to direct a fine mist at a flowerpot. It was fascinating to take a bucket and measure the flow that filled the tank that watered my cows. It was fascinating to watch the saddle horses dip their muzzles in a spring. Suddenly other things in the landscape were not interesting. Wind generators were not interesting. Electricity was not interesting. Power lines were not interesting. Telephones were not interesting, and all the wires and relays over the prairie that laced this largely empty region to the fervid nation were not so very interesting anymore. Water had become the only interesting thing. It had rained one-quarter of an inch in three months. I had watched water-laden clouds go overhead at terrific speed without losing a drop. Montana was getting less rain than the Mojave Desert. The little clouds that look like the clouds on a baby's crib were the sort of thing you wanted to shout at. Wind beat the ground on the rumor of water. Stockmen hauled water to battered, unusable pastures for their cows and calves. Forest springs remembered by generations suddenly evaporated.

I drove west on the interstate along the Yellowstone River. A long Burlington Northern train came around a curve in the river in the dry air, approached in silence, then was alongside me at once in a whirring rush of metal and movement. Astonishingly, the air was filled with a train smell, an industrial odor that stood out sharply in the drought-stricken air. But the ash in the air was from the fires, and the smoke that poured out from the valley of the upper Yellowstone had the inappropriately sentimental tang of autumn leaf-burning. Still, the train rolled on, and the first thing one wondered was whether or not it was a machine for starting fires.

As I climbed toward the Continental Divide, things did seem a little greener. Some of the hay meadows actually looked like they might be producing hay instead of emergency pasture. Passing through the round red rocks of Homestake Pass, wadded together like enormous pencil erasers, I descended toward Butte and stopped to refill my tank. While the attendant cleaned the windshield, I stood inside the cool gas station and looked at pictures of Our Lady of the Rockies, now under construction. Great cranes brought workers and their equipment to her vast robes. A helicopter arrived with her head. No other town in Montana felt so strongly about the Virgin Mary, and it brought to her memory a mighty effort.

As I headed south toward Idaho and the Missouri headwaters that I love to fish, I entertained some nervous thoughts. I knew that sections of the Jefferson, the Red Rock, and the Big Hole itself had dried up because of irrigation. Montana has no provision for decreed instream use of water; in a bad year, agriculture can take it all without regard to fish or the fishermen who spend more than a hundred million annually. Montana farmers and ranchers make thousands of new enemies each year over this issue, and those enemies are becoming a political force that would like to review not only the efficiency of their water use but other subjects as well, such as the constitutionality of their grazing-lease arrangements on public land. Vestigial rivers flowing out of the smoke only make the plight more emphatic.

I took the turnoff toward the Divide and saw the Big Hole for the first time in a year. The extremely low water merely percolated through rubble rock. Nevertheless, the beauty of the river's narrow valley, the sage-covered walls, and the slit of railroad bed on the far bank seemed quite intact.

I turned up the Wise River from the town of that name. The river headed into the Pioneer Mountains, and as I started up its valley I eyed its floor with but one thing in mind: Any water? A short time later I unpacked in my wonderfully comfortable little cabin by the side of the river. Water raced by! Irrigation water went overhead on a trestlelike affair. Standing underneath it on my way to dinner, I could smell the cold runoff dripping down the timbers that held it up. I was starting to feel encouraged that my fly rod might not have been a purely comic utensil. There wasn't even any smoke in the air.

I had a beautifully prepared meal with the Fellins and their guests. This small lodge seems to attract fairly serious fishermen. So the gloomy enthusiasms, the bursts of ill-directed sexuality, the unwelcome appearance of the alter ego, the showdowns between couples, and the displays of minor violence that one associates with high-powered sporting lodges are absent here. One dines well and sleeps contentedly, storing maximum energy for the rivers.

I headed for my cabin early and the Fellins' big Labrador male accompanied me partway. He didn't stray far, because in the nearby bush were moose who chased him back to the house. It is a great pleasure for a family man to sleep in some building by himself once in a while; I slept the night away in a kind of mock-bachelor bliss, the windows wide open and the chilly mountain air pouring over my lofty comforter. My first home was made of logs, and the smell and solidity of those structures restored my highly eroded sense of well-being. I began to think of sallying forth with fly rod in hand to tune and sample the universe in the name of trout. This has been an issue of consequence since my bowlegged early childhood, and the feeling has grown stronger.

The morning of a beautiful summer day in Montana. What more could be asked? Hawks threw their cries against tall red cliffs along the Big Hole, then soared into transparency against the brilliant blue sky. The peculiar sluicing movement of the dewatered but still beautiful river at the base of the cliffs and railroad bed, the powerful sage smell, the bright yellow clusters of drought-resistant resinweed, and here and there the slowly opening rings of feeding trout brought me on point. I suddenly longed to see the loop of my line stretch over moving water. The float, the gulp: This way, please.

We went to a portion of the river that split into two channels, one of which slowed down considerably and presented an ideal place to ambush fish feeding on tricorythodes, better known as "tricos." These are minute, clear-winged mayflies as beautiful as all the mayflies whose poetic forms have found their way into the imagination of sportsmen, certain of whom have taken pen to paper.

By the time we reached the stream the duns were hatching and the forms of rising trout, variously called "sipping," "slurping," and "gulping," opened upon the water. Duns are the immature forms of mayflies, recently transmuted from the nymphal stage, and they are reasonably easy targets for trout. The tricos are unlike other mayflies in that they complete their cycle in a matter of hours instead of days. To the angler this means that good fishing is to be had while the duns are on the water. A few hours later there commences an even better stage, the spinner fall. Duns that flew up above the riffles molt to achieve sexual maturity in a whirlwind of sparkling mayfly turbulence, then return to the surface of the streams to lay their eggs. At this point they are duck soup for feeding trout, and the alert angler may now slip up and still manage to catch a few.

During the emergence of the duns, I managed to catch several small but handsome and always mythologically perfect and wonderful brown trout. Trico fishing is never easy, because the flies are so small, size 22, and they're hard to see, especially if one uses a truly imitative pattern. I ended up using a small Adams, which says "bug" to the trout in a general yet friendly and duplicitous way. I was swept by the perfection of things: the glorious shape of each trout, the angelic miniature perfection of mayflies, and by the pure wild silk of the Big Hole River. For such things are we placed on this careening mudball.

Overhead, the duns had accumulated in a glittering, transparent mass. We awaited the spinner fall. The duns gradually stopped emerging. The trout that had been feeding in the riffles tailed back into the slick water. We watched and waited for thousands of these sparkling creatures to fall to the hungry trout. Then the wind came up and blew them all away.

We were able to float one section of the Big Hole, though the long riffles were shallow and noisy under the boat. Floating is a fine way to fish western rivers, where the slow and careful dissection of pools is less appropriate than it is in the trout streams of the East. Though drift boats have proliferated beyond reason, it is also a terrific way to see the country while maintaining an air of purpose. As you float, the all-important bank unrolls before you through the course of the day like a variegated ribbon of earth and water.

It is also the fastest way to get the feel of a new river. On the Big Hole are elbows and back eddies and turning pools of white foam. There are dropping chutes of long bubble trails that hold trout. I've always thought the Big Hole had more midstream trout lies than any other river I know. Pockets behind boulders are favorite spots, as are places where bottom structures cause angular turns of current where trout can shelter yet enjoy a steady procession of foods.

The wind followed us to the Beaverhead River that evening. With its brushy banks and downed trees sweeping the undercut banks, it looks almost like a Michigan or Wisconsin trout river. It also has the largest trout in the state, and when conditions are difficult, as they were that evening, it's easy to see how they got to be so big. Almost as soon as the fly is presented in one of the holes and notches along the bank, it's time to pick it up and look for another place to cast. To lose your fly in the brush in front of you on the Beaverhead or in the obstructions behind you is equally easy. The wind really defeated us that evening. Craig rowed heroically, trying to keep the johnboat in position. At dusk we stopped to fish a small run during an intense hatch of caddis, and in the cloud of insects seethed myriad bats. It seemed impossible to cast through the swarm without snagging a bat. I managed to catch a few of what Craig called the smallest fish ever to be caught out of the Beaverhead. But it had been a sixteen-hour fishing day, and my thoughts lay entirely with the down pillow on my bed in the cabin on the gurgling bank of the Wise River.

The next day, another banquet breakfast: baked eggs with asparagus spears, oatmeal pancakes, sausages, honeydew melon, homemade cinnamon rolls, coffee, and the kind of sleepy, merry conversation I associate with the beginning of a day astream. Then we were off on a different kind of junket. This time we drove awhile, parked the truck, and took off on a cross-country hike. I noticed that many of the wildflowers that had disappeared in my drought-ridden region still bloomed here. We had a leisurely walk along an abandoned railroad bed and along the pine-covered slopes of foothills. An old Confederate whose plantation had been burned during the War Between the States had first run cattle here. Then gold-mining ventures, real ones and swindles, found an agreeable setting in the little valley. Now it was ghost towns and trackless railroad bed, sagebrush reclaiming it all into marginal pasture. I picked up an ancient rail spike and slipped it in my vest to take home for a paperweight.

We traversed a high slope above a river too small and fragile to be named, and descended to begin fishing. The water looked plain and shoally, inconsequential and dimensionless from above, but like so many things in the West that seem flattened by distance and separation, this little river was a detailed paradise at close range. Rufous and calliope hummingbirds were feeding in the Indian paintbrush along the bank, and the thin-water stretches were separated by nice pools. One pool in particular lay at the bottom of a low cliff and held enough water to imply good-size trout. I approached it cautiously and found fish feeding on a hatch of midges. Beneath them several good ones were nymphing and flashing silver messages up through the clear water as they turned on their sides to feed. But the trout were difficult, feeding with extreme selectivity on the midges. I caught a couple of small ones before deciding the pool was spooked, then moved on vaguely acknowledging that I hadn't quite met the challenge of the midges. When flies get much smaller than size 20 and the leader lies on the water's surface like the footprints of water spiders, my confidence begins to dwindle.

Then, at the bottom of a small chute, I caught a nice brook trout. This is not the most common fish in Montana and, though it was introduced long ago, its accustomed venue is elsewhere. It is a wonderful thing to be reminded of the variety of beauties displayed in the quarry of trout fishermen. You want to cry, as a local auctioneer does at the sight of a matched set of fattened yearlings, "My, oh my!" The brook trout has a silky sleekness in the hand. Browns always feel like you expect fish to feel; rainbows often feel blocky and muscular; the brook trout exists within an envelope of perfect northerly sleekness. He is a great original, to be appreciated poetically, for he is not a demanding game fish. Some of the most appalling arias in angling literature are directed at this lovely creature, who was with us before the Ice Age.

I moved along the stream toward the end of my trip, thinking about my own part of the state. There the tawny hills had an almost glassy hardness from lack of water, and the handfuls of cattle grazing on them cast hard and distinct shadows, as if standing on tabletops or flooring. I intensely valued the stream-bred rainbows I'd caught, small-headed relative to their breadth and wonderfully marked with bands of stardust pink. This unpurposeful note of festivity is matched by their vital show when hooked, by their abandoned vaults for freedom. The great privilege is the moment one is released, when the small, strong fish moves from your hand to renew its hold upstream. Then it's time to go.

Midstream

I LOOKED OFF the wooden bridge and into the small river I had come to like so well. Nearly covered with yellow cottonwood leaves that diagramed its currents as they swept toward one another around the framework of the old boxcar out of which the bridge was made. A cold wind eddied down the river into my face, and I was ready to decide that to everything there is a season and that trout season was over. Fall gives us a vague feeling that the end of everything is near; here I felt that when the snow melted in the spring, my little river would be gone.

I don't know if it was literally the first time I saw that river, but it is the first time I remember seeing it. I came down the side of the basin riding a young mare. I could see, first, the treeline of the small river, then, here and there, flashes of its runs and pools as it made its way through the pastureland of its own small valley. There were a few bright and geometric lines where irrigation ditches cut diagonals from its more eloquent meanders, and a few small flooded areas where the water had stopped to reflect the clouds and the sky. It was a river with an indifferent fishing reputation.

Young anglers love new rivers the way they love the rest of their lives. Time doesn't seem to be of the essence and somewhere in the system is what they are looking for. Older anglers set foot on streams the location of whose pools is as yet unknown with a trace of inertia.

Like sentimental drunks, they are interested in what they already know. Yet soon enough, any river reminds us of others, and the logic of a new one is a revelation. The pools and runs we've already seen help us decode the holding water: the shallow riffle is a buildup for the cobbled channel where thick trout nymph with mirror flashes; the slack back channel with the leafy bottom is not just frog water but a faithful reservoir for the joyous brook beyond. An undisturbed river is as perfect a thing as we will ever know, every refractive slide of cold water a glimpse of eternity.

The first evening I fished the river, I walked through a meadow that lay at the bottom of a curved red cliff, a swerving curve with a close-grained mantle of sage and prairie grasses. It could be that the river cut that curve, then wandered a quarter-mile south, but there you have it: the narrow shining band, the red curve, and the prairie. As I sauntered along with my fly rod, hope began to build in the perceived glamour of my condition: a deep breath.

On the edge of meadow and next to the water, there was a stand of mature aspens with hard white trunks. The grass was knee deep. White summer clouds towered without motion. Once I'd crossed to that spot, I could make out the progress of small animals fanning away from my approach. I hurried forward in an attempt to see what they were, and a young raccoon shot up one of the slick aspens, then, losing traction, made a slow, baffled descent back into the grass. By shuffling around I managed to have four of them either going up or sliding down at once. They were about a foot tall, and something about their matching size and identical bandit masks, coupled with their misjudgment of aspens as an escape route, gave me a sense of real glee at the originality of things. The new river gurgled in the bank.

I walked in and felt its pull against my legs. Current is a mysterious thing. It is the motion of the river leaving us, and it is as curious and thrilling as a distant train at night. These waters, pouring from high in a Montana wilderness, are bound for the Gulf of Mexico. The idea that so much as a single molecule of the rushing chute before me was headed for Tampico was as eerie as the moon throwing a salty flood over the tidelands and then retrieving it. Things that pass us, go somewhere else, and don't come back seem to communicate directly with the soul. That the fisherman plies his craft on the surface of such an element possibly accounts for his contemplative nature.

I once thought this was somehow not true of aircraft, that they were too new and lacked mystery. But I lived for a time in the mountainous path of B-52 nighttime traffic. The faraway thunder that rose and fell to the west had the same quality of distance and departure one loves in trains and rivers. On a pale summer night, I made out the darkened shape of one of these death ships against the stars, casting its shadow against the prairie.

Today I stopped fishing to watch a little water dipper, one of those ouzel-like nervous wrecks that seem not to differentiate between air and water, and stroll through both with aplomb. I associate them with some half-serious elfin twilight, a creature that, like the raccoons, suggests a playful element in creation. I began to feel the focus that a river brings as you unravel the current in search of holding water.

The learning of this river corresponded with the waning of runoff. My casting arm was still cold from winter, and I waded like a spavined donkey. I am always careful to go as light as possible early on, knowing that mishaps are likely, and the matter of getting over round, slick rocks, judging the depth and speed of current don't come back immediately. You feel timid. Later in the year, you make long, downstream pirouettes in deep fast water that you'd never chance when you're rusty.

Getting rid of stuff is a matter of ceremony. The winter has usually made me yield to dubious gadgets, and I'm at war with these if the main idea of fishing is to be preserved. For example, the net can go; it snags in brush and catches fly line and if it's properly out of the way, you can't get at it when you need to. Landing fish without a net adds to the trick and makes the whole business better. Make it one box of flies. I tried to stick to this and ended up buying the king of Wheatlies, a double-sided brute that allows me to cheat on the single-box system. No monofilament clippers. Teeth work great. Trifles like leader sink, flyline cleaner, and geegaws that help you tie knots must go. You may bring the hemostat, because to pinch down barbs and make quick, clean releases of the fabled trout help everything else make sense. Bring a normal rod, with a five- or six-weight line, because in early sea-

son the handle you have on hatches is not yet sufficient and you must
be prepared to range through maybe eight fly sizes. Weird rod weights
reflect armchair fantasies and often produce chagrin on the water.

By now, I had begun to have a look at the river. Cutting deep
through hard ground, it was like a scribe line at the base of sine and
cosine curves of bank banded at the top with a thin layer of topsoil.
The river bottom was entirely rocks, small rounded ones, and on
either side were plateaus of similar stones, representing the water levels of thousands of previous years. A few mayflies drifted past in insig-
nificant numbers. I understand that mayflies bear a rather antique
genetic code themselves, expressed in size and color, and my hope is
that if things pick up, I have the right imitations in my box.

As I face new water, I always ask myself if I ought to fish with a
nymph or not. Presumably you don't walk directly into rising trout.
Camus said that the only serious question is whether or not to com-
mit suicide. This is rather like the nymph question. It takes weight,
a weighted fly, split shot. Casting becomes a matter of spitting this
mess out and being orderly about it. This requires a higher order of
streamcraft than any other kind of fishing, because it truly calls upon
the angler to see the river in all its dimensions. Gone are the joys of
casting, the steady meter and adjustment of loop that compare well to
walking or rowing. The joys of casting are gone because this ignoble
outfit has ruined the action of your fly rod.

Still, you must show purpose. American shame about leisure has
produced the latest no-nonsense stance in sport, the "streamside entomologist" and the "headhunter" being the most appalling instances
that come readily to mind. No longer content to contemplate the relationship of life to eternity, the glandular modern sport girds himself
against the waste of time. Small towns used to have a mock-notorious
character who didn't feel this way, the mythical individual who hung
the gone fishin' sign in the window of his establishment. We often
styled him a barber or someone equally remote from life-and-death
matters. Sometimes we let him be a country doctor, and it was very
rakish indeed to drift grubs in a farm pond against the possible background of breech birth or peritonitis.

In the shock and delight of new water, my thoughts were entirely ineffective. What is the relationship of the bottom to the surface, to the landscape through which it flows, to the life of the air around it all and the vegetation that alters the wind and interferes with the light? In other words, should one fish that deep outer bank—shaded by a hedge of wild junipers—with a nymph, or would it be better to imitate the few pale morning duns that are drifting around but not yet inspiring any surface feeding? In the latter case, that glassy run below the pool is the spot. For a moment, I avoid the conundrum by turning into another river object, a manlike thing with the unmoving fly rod. Because time has stopped, I really don't concern myself with an eager companion who has already put three on the beach.

Mortality being what it is, any new river could be your last. This charmless notion runs very deep in us and can produce, besides the tightening around the mouth, a sweet and consoling inventory of all the previous rivers in your life. Finally, the fit is so perfect that it creates the illusion that there is but one river, a Platonic gem. There are more variations within any one good river than there are between a number of good rivers. I have been fortunate in that my life-river has a few steelhead in the lower reaches, as well as Oregon harvest trout and the sea-run browns of Ireland; Michigan brook trout in the deep bends, braided channels in hundred-mile sections from the Missouri headwaters trout theme park; and, here and there, the see-through pools of New Zealand and the dark bends of Tierra del Fuego rivers where sea-run browns roll so profoundly. Fire and water unlock the mind to a kind of mental zero gravity in which resemblances drift toward one another. The trout fisherman finishes his life with but one river.

All this is getting fairly far-fetched. Still, like the trout, we must find a way of moving through water with the least amount of displacement. The more we fish, the more weightlessly and quietly we move through a river and among its fish, and the more we resemble our own minds in the bliss of angling.

I came to a pool where a tree had fallen. The leaves were long gone, and its numerous branches tugged lightly in the slight current that flowed through the pool. A remarkable thing was happening: a good-size brown was jumping among the lowest branches, clearly knocking insects loose to eat. Every three or four minutes, it vaulted into the brush over its window and fell back into the water. I knew if I could get any kind of a float, I would have a solid taker. I looked at all the angles, and the only idea I could come up with was that it was a good time to light a cigar. In a moment, the excellent smoke of Honduras rose through the cottonwoods. I waited for a solution to form, but it never happened. In the end, I reared back and fired a size 14 Henryville Caddis into the brush. It wound around a twig and hung in midair. The trout didn't jump at it suicidally, nor did I get the fly back.

Angling doesn't turn on stunts. The steady movements of the habitual gatherer produce the best harvest. This of course must be in the service of some real stream knowledge. But some fishing, especially for sea-run fish, rewards a robotic capacity for replicating casts, piling up the repetitions until the strike is induced. I once thought that the biggest things a steelheader or Atlantic salmon fisherman can have—not counting waders and a stipend—were a big arm and a room-temperature IQ. Now I know better, having found out the hard way.

The river made an angular move to the south into the faraway smoky hills. In the bend some workmanlike drywall riprap reflected the Scandinavian local heritage. The usual western approach would be to roll an old car into the river at the point of erosion. Instead I found neatly laid cobbles that gave the impression the river was slowly revealing an archaeological enigma or at least the foundations of a church. But for the next forty yards, the clear water trembled deep and steady over a mottled bottom, and I took three hearty browns that flung themselves upon the bright surface of the run. When I was young and in the thrall of religion, I used to imagine various bands of angels, differentiated principally by size. The smallest were under a foot in height, silvery and rapid, and able to move in any plane at will; these three trout fitted neatly among those imaginary beings.

The river lay down at the bottom of a pencil-thin valley, and though I could see the wind in the treetops, I could barely feel it where I fished. The casts stretched out and probed without unwarranted shepherd's crooks, blowbacks, or tippet puddles. I came to a favorite kind of stretch: twenty or thirty yards of very shallow riffle with a deep green slot on the outside curve. In this conformation you wade easily in thin, fast water and gain a bit of elevation on your quarry. The slot seemed to drain a large oxygenated area, and it was the only good holding water around. Where had I seen so much of this? The Trinity? The Little Deschutes? This, too, had slipped in the telescoping of rivers.

I couldn't float the entire slot without lining part of it. So I covered the bottom with my first casts, doping out the drift as I did, preparing for the long float through the heart of the spot where I was sure to raise a fish. The slot was on the left-hand side of the river and contoured the bank, but the riffle drained at an angle to it. A long, straight cast would drag the fly in a hurry. When the first casts to the lower end failed to produce, I tried a reach cast to the right, got a much better drift, then covered the whole slot with a longer throw.

The Henryville Caddis had floated about two yards when a good brown appeared below it like a beam of butter-colored light. It tipped back, and we were tight. The fish held in the current even though my rod was bent into the cork, then shot out into the shallows for a wild aerial fight. I got it close three times but it managed to churn off through the shallow water. Finally I had it and turned its cold form upside down in my hand, checked its length against my rod and removed the hook. These, I decided, were the yellowest, prettiest stream-bred browns I'd ever seen. Then I turned it over and lowered it into the current. I love the feeling I get when the fish realize they're free. There seems to be an amazed pause. Then they shoot out of your hand as though you could easily change your mind.

The afternoon wore on without specific event. The middle of a bright day can be as dull as it is timeless. Visibility is so perfect you forget it is seldom a confidence builder for trout. The little imperfections of the leader, the adamant crinkles standing up from the surface, are clear to both parties.

No sale.

But the shadows of afternoon seem to give meaning to the angler's day on about the same scale that fall gives meaning to his year. As always, I could feel in the first hints of darkness a mutual alertness between me and the trout. This vague shadow the trout and I cross progresses from equinox to equinox. Our mutuality grows.

A ring opened on the surface. The fish refused my all-purpose Adams, and I moved on to an even-depth, even-speed stretch of slick water that deepened along the right-hand bank for no reason: there was no curve to it. The deep side was in shadow, a great, profound, detail-filled shadow that stood along the thin edge of brightness, the starry surface of moving water in late sun. At the head of this run, a plunge pool made a vertical curtain of bubbles in the right-hand corner. At that point, the turbulence narrowed away to a thread of current that could be seen for maybe twenty yards along the smooth run. Trout were working.

I cast to the lowest fish from my angle below and to the left. The evenness of the current gave me an ideal float, free of drag. In a moment of hubris I threw the size 14 Adams, covered the fish with successive casts for about five minutes while it fed above and below. I worked my way to the head of the pool, covering six other fish. Quickly, I tied on a Royal Wulff, hoping to shock them into submission. Not a single grab. The fish I covered retired until I went on, then resumed feeding. I was losing my light and had been casting in the middle of rising fish for the better part of an hour: head and tail rises with slight slurps. There were no spinners in the air, and the thread of the current took whatever the food was down through the center of the deep water beyond my vision. This was the first time all day that the river had asked me to figure something out, and it was becoming clear I wouldn't catch a fish in this run unless I changed my ways. The selective trout is that uncompromising creature in whose spirit the angler attempts to read his own fortune.

I tucked my shirt deep inside the top of my waders and pulled the drawstring tight. I hooked my last unsuccessful fly in the keeper and reeled up the line. Wading into the cold, deep run, below the feeding fish, I felt my weight decreasing against the bottom as I inched toward the thread of current that carried whatever mysterious thing the fish were feeding on. I was suddenly very close to taking on the river and barely weighed enough to keep myself from joining the other flotsam in the Missouri headwaters. But—and, as my mother used to say, "it's a big but"—I could see coming toward me, some like tiny sloops, some like minute unfurling life rafts, baetis duns: olive-bodied, clear-winged, and a tidy size 18.

I have such a thing, I thought, in my fly box.

By the time I'd moon-walked back to a depth where my weight meant something, I had just enough time to test my failing eyes by connecting a little olive-emerger and a 6X tippet viewed straight over my head in the final light. At last, the thing was done and I was ready to cast. The fly seemed to float straight downward in the air and then down the sucking hole the trout made. It was another short, thick, buttery brown, and the fish that kept me from flunking my first day on that river. It's hard to know ahead of time which fish is giving the test.

Seasons Through the Net

T HE PUMP IN THE WELL kept shutting off. I messed around with the pressure switch to no avail, and when I restarted the pump by hitting the breakers, it belched rusty water into the sink and the pressure wasn't strong enough to sprinkle the garden. The pump is 180 feet down there with its own dark and secret life. I call the plumber.

An hour later the plumber's in the well pit. I look at him in that gloomy hole with his rusty wrench, the water up around his ankles, the pale tuberous roots of vegetation sticking out of the cold earthen sides of the well. He asks me how I've been doing; he means with fish.

I go out to the mailbox and run into a man taking in the sights with his wife. He wants to talk. They live in a trailer near Red Lodge, and he sells concrete animals for yard decorations. He keeps a good quarter horse and is a weekend jackpot roper. He's looking to catch him a large trout, he says. It must be in the air.

I stood with fly rod in hand on my first day of trout fishing for the year. We were a mile above the bridge that leads to White Sulphur Springs. They were retrieving a strange souvenir of winter. A Texaco wrecker was backed to the bank, hauling a dead horse out of the river, hauling him up by his hind legs, swinging him out through the willows on the end of the boom in black, wet-meat totality. A sandbank had gone out from under him, and he was lost to the river as surely as today's water and streamside pasture.

By the time the ice broke up, the flooded river had returned to its banks and the broad, dull woodlands had reshaped along the road in their loops and meandering symmetry. By June the spring storms were light-shot and prominent, quite unlike the homogeneous gloom of April: the first summer storms, perhaps. In the evening the Absaroka and Gallatin ranges overlapped like jagged sheets of palest slate under the pearly turbulence, and the river dropped from flood to a full canal gloss. Then, at last, the spangled river came out from under, braided in places like a glacial river or lying along sandy bars in a green, bending slot of oxygen and trout.

Sunup got earlier and earlier, until you woke under blue windows full of blowing cottonwood seeds, always with the feeling you had overslept. The pass above the ranch was already dropping its long lever of candied light into day. You could hear the creek from the bedroom window, racing down stony terraces among dry junipers.

It was clear that if you weren't careful, another summer would slip through the net, trailing wasted time, mortgage payments, and any number of things you might have saved.

The river stayed out of color well past the Fourth of July on our stretch. We hiked into the canyon of the Yellowstone to catch the last days of the salmonfly hatch, carrying rods and packs around geysers and poison springs with deer skeletons on their bottoms, and into pine copses through which sulfurous steam blew, and down long switchbacks of scree and crumbly rhyolite. The far side of the canyon rose trailless and miles away, seemed another world: absolute, remote, changing color with every hour's shift of light.

We were a true phalanx of trout bums, since dispersed as far away as New Zealand and as near as wives and families, that quicksand into which a troll's share is taken, generation after generation, spitting bamboo fragments and blue dun hackle, to join—with some decency—another of sport's secret mothball fleets.

Finally, at the bottom of this hot canyon, the river is a terrific surprise, the switchbacks jutting in to trail along its sides. The river seems quite literally a crack in the earth, here so exposed as to be principally rock. While our home stretch of the same river is still brown with spring runoff and irrigation, slough-connected and meandering among old ranches, here it is a lightning fissure in rock, empyrean blue and slightly unearthly.

In the canyon the trout's range of travel is bounded by falls, sudden declivities or change of altitude in the slab rock. The blue river turns green-white in a right-angle downward turn, a long ribbon of falling water, roaring and blowing away. The trout live above or below such a place; these are separate civilizations.

We cast our big, visible dries on the glossy rush, and quickly trout soar into focus and vanish with our offerings. Rods bow and lines shear through the water. Handsome cutthroat trout are beached and released in the gravel, wriggling back into deep water and flickering invisibly into the pale water curtain.

A mile below the trail's end, we found a feeder creek that dropped almost vertically from pool to minute pool. And each pool held handsome cutthroats that took flies readily and leapt down the plateaus until they were in the river itself. To hook fish at eye level, watch their descent, then finish the fight under your feet seemed unfathomable. Many of these fish were in their spawning colors and shimmered in the current as brilliant as macaws.

We ended the afternoon's fishing in time to save an increment of energy for the climb out. A great blue lid of shadow had started down one wall, and the boulders and escarpments bore eccentrically long panels of shade. Above us, a few impressive birds of prey sorted the last thermals. In two hours they were below us, turning grave circles in polite single file.

At Tower Falls we stumbled out of the woods. It was getting dark and someone fumbled for the car keys.

MIRAGE ON THE ROAD CROWNS as I spring along under sage-covered ledges, pools of water on macadam hills. Blackbirds scatter before my truck.

All the grass that seemed to indicate something about possibility, that turned up in mountain edges full of yellow-blossomed clover, was sun-dried like hard wire, annealed and napped in one direction or in whorls like cowlicks and distinctly dun-colored on the hard hills.

When the sheep yarded up in the orchard, their fetor hung slowly downwind with an edge that was less organic than chemical. In the heat of broad day I saw a coyote on a yellow grassy bench digging along the length of a pocket gopher's workings, throwing up a stream of dirt behind himself as industrious as a beagle.

In midsummer big streams like the Missouri headwaters can come to seem slumberous and unproductive. The great sweeps of river are warm and exposed, and the fishing can be perfectly lousy.

Then there's evening fishing on the spring creeks, streams that jump full-grown, quite mythically, from under ledges or out of swamp ground and flow for miles before joining a river, often at some secretive or wooded confluence. The stub ends of such streams are seen by passing fishermen, who seldom suspect the trout network lying beyond.

The angler parcels out the midsummer months with pocket situations, good for a few amusing visits. I always make two or three trips to my nearby beaver ponds, wallowing through swamp and chest-high grass to the beaver houses, beyond which stands water full of small brook trout. In the still ponds are the gnawed stumps of trees, big enough in diameter to suggest the recently solid ground which the advanced rodents have conquered.

If we fish here in the fall, we bring back wild crab apples for baking along with the easily gathered creel of brook trout. The fish in these ponds live on freshwater shrimp and their flesh is salmon pink on either side of their pearly backbones. The trout themselves are as surpassingly vivid as fine enamels, and the few meals we make of them are sacraments.

The stream that flows through our place is lost in irrigation head gates by August, so it has no trout. Obliviously, my young son fishes the pretty pool next to our cattle guard, increasing his conviction that trout are a difficult fish. Morbid friends say he is a sportsman of the future. I will explain to him as an acceptable realpolitik: if the trout are lost, smash the state. More than any other fish, trout are dependent upon the ambience in which they are caught. Whether it is the trout or the angler who is more sensitized to the degeneration of habitat would be hard to say, but probably it is the trout. At the first signs of deterioration, this otherwise vigorous fish just politely quits, as if

to say, "If that's how you want it . . ." Meanwhile, the angler quali-
tatively lapses in citizenship. Other kinds of fishermen may toss their
baits into the factory shadows. The trout fisherman who doesn't turn
dangerously unpatriotic. He just politely quits, like the trout.

IT'S OCTOBER, a bluebird Indian-summer day. Opening day for ducks,
it will be over eighty degrees. You're going to need your Coppertone.

Standing on the iron bridge at Pine Creek, I look upstream. I suppose it is a classic autumn day in the Rockies; by some standards, it is
outrageous. The China blue river breaks up into channels that jet back
together from chutes and gravel tongues to form a deep emerald pool
that flows toward me on the bridge with a hidden turbulence, a concealed shock wave. Where the river lifts upstream on its gravel runs, it
glitters.

The division of the river makes a multiplicity of banks, but the
main ones are shrouded with the great, almost heartbreaking cottonwoods that are now gone to a tremulous, sun-shot gold, reaching
over the river's blue rush. Where the pools level out, the bizarre, free-
traveling clouds with their futuristic shapes are reflected.

I can see my friend and neighbor, a painter, walking along the high
cutbank above the river. This would be a man who has ruined his life
with sport. He skulks from his home at all hours with gun or rod.
Today he has both.

"What are you doing?" I ask.

"Trout fishing and duck hunting."

Only fishing, I feel like a man who has been laid off.

"As you see," says the painter, gesticulating strangely, "I'm ready
for anything. I spoiled half the day with work and errands. I have to
pull things out of the fire before they go from bad to worse." Across
the river, the Absaroka Range towers up out of the warm valley with
snowcapped peaks and gold stripes of aspen intermittently dividing
the high pasture and the evergreen forest. My friend heads off, promising a report later on.

The last chance you get at overall strategy in trout fishing, before
you lose yourself in the game itself, is during the period called "rig-

ging up." I stand next to my truck, looking upstream and down, and remove the knurled brass cap from the aluminum tube. I am deep into the voodoo of rigging up. I draw the smoky-colored bamboo shafts from their poplin sack and join the rod. I fasten the old pewtery Hardy St. George reel my father gave me to the cork seat and knot the monofilament leader in place. Then I irritate myself over the matter of which fly to use, finally darting my hand blindly into the fly box. I come up with one I tied myself that imitates the effect of a riot gun on a love seat. I swiftly return it and take out a professionally tied spruce fly and attach it to my leader. I get into my waders, slipping the blue police suspenders onto my shoulders. Rigging up is over and now there is angling to be done.

Once my friend is out of sight, I scramble down the bank to the river, which here is in three channels around long willow-covered islands. By cautiously wading the heads of pools in these channels, one can cross the mighty river on foot, a cheap thrill I could not deprive myself of. Regardless of such illusions, I am an ordinary wader and usually have to pick my way carefully over the slippery rocks, my heart in my mouth. I have friends who are superior waders. One of them, a former paratrooper, glides downstream whenever he loses his footing until he touches down again, erect as a penguin all the while. At any and all mishaps when wading big rivers I tend to feel that I am too young to die, then fob off this cowardice as "reverence for nature."

This late in the year, the first channel crossing is child's play. I practically stroll over to the long willow island that is decorated on this shore by a vintage automobile, a breakaway bit of Montana rip-rap, high and dry, with river sand up to the steering wheel.

The brush willows form an interior jungle, all the details of which contrive to slap you in the face over and over again as you bushwhack through them. I come to a small clearing where a shallow sandy-bottomed slough has penetrated. A school of fry, a couple of feet wide and maybe ten feet long, dominates the end of the slough. With my approach these thousands of fish scatter toward the river; this is as fertile a nursery area as it is possible to imagine, dense and dark with infant fish.

I continue across the island, sweating in my waders, and end up at a broad, bright channel. The tenderloin of the spot is a 150-foot bevel of current, along the edge of which trout persistently hang. I wade into position, false-casting the necessary amount of line to get under way. Then I make my first cast, up sun, and coronas of mist hang around the traveling direction of the line. I mend the line, throwing a belly into it to make the streamer continually present itself broadside to trout holding upstream in the current. I have a short strike early on but miss it.

Then nothing except the steady surge of the river against my legs until I can feel it bending with enormous purpose toward North Dakota and its meeting with the Missouri. In the green of the river, ghostly orbs of white boulders are buried in running channels. The river is a fluid envelope for trout, occasionally marred by the fish themselves rising to take an insect and punctuating the glassy run with a whorl that opens and spirals downstream like a smoke ring. The boulders are constant, but the river soars away to the east.

After a period of methodical fishing, I finally come up tight on a trout. He holds throbbing for a long moment, then without any run at all is suddenly aerial. Four crisp dashes later and the trout is vividly alive and cold in my hand. As I return him to the river, I bend over and watch him hold briefly in the graveled current between my feet. Then quick as light he's gone.

I stand up and can feel that mild, aching joy of the first fish as I look to the long river moss in the crystal gravel channels, streaming and wavering like radio signals.

My trout memories precede any actual sighting of a trout. They go way back to a time when, inflamed to angling by rock bass and perch, I read hunting and fishing magazines and settled upon the trout as the only fish worthy of my ability, along with the broadbill swordfish. I had examined the Rockwell Kent illustrations in my father's copy of *Moby-Dick*. I didn't for the moment see what I could do about the white whale. Among my friends a rumor persisted of giant squid in the Humboldt Current that assaulted cabin cruisers and doused anglers with black ink before sinking a parrotlike beak into their brain pans.

Not even this enormity could compete with the trout for my attention, though putting the gaff to a wilderness of tentacles had its appeal for a bloodthirsty child.

The sun roosts deep in the aspens and spruce. Chickweed and wild roses flow down out of the forest carpet, around the garden, and up the sides of the compost heap. A sleeping bag floats on a clump of laurel, sunning out. You can walk in any direction of the compass from here and sooner or later you'll run into a trout. And you see, at some point, that you will keep making that walk.

The Indian-summer day ends with an edge, and during that night the temperature falls forty degrees. In the morning you squint out the kitchen door into a snowfield. The orchard looks like a corsage, and the poles in the corral are snowcapped in stillness. Trout season is over.

Southern Salt

I THINK THE IMPULSE to wander between northern and southern fisheries for as long as decency would permit came as a result of my boyhood reading of what I still consider a masterpiece of world literature, the catalog of the Paul Young fly rod company, *More Fishing and Less Fussing*. This delicious, slim volume of prose treasures, besides describing the virtuous Paul Young rods, hinted at styles of living I could only dream about. But one rod in particular was prescribed for the angler who, at the end of trout season, "went south with the birds." Even when I was explaining to the good monsignor who oversaw my little grade school, and who took a special interest in my graduating class of eight, that my dream was to be a Jesuit missionary—a ploy to defuse his annoyance at my disruptive behavior and drain a pint or two of blood from his weirdly livid face—my real dream was not the saving of souls but to go south with the birds, rod in hand, once winter had driven the trout into their winter holes. In the great Young book, luminaries such as Ted Williams found themselves "tickled pink" with rods that had "all the boys singing" down in the Keys. And in fact, getting away from baseball to fish, all he could say was, "Gee!" I had what Young described as "the finest all around daytime trout rod" and I thought the two of us just needed our walking papers for my life to be perfect. I would supplement my double-tapered fly line with the new "torpedo" line. From my remote angling venues, I would write testimonial letters to the Paul Young Company as to the quality of their products and sign them, as the others did, "Satisfied."

In time I did get there, and the first magic—so many years ago now—of walking across the palm fronds to the sea, lizards rattling in the brush, fishable water to the horizon, birds on the bait, is with me still. In the small west-coast Florida town where my family moved in the fifties, there were empty or under-construction CBS houses on saltwater canals whose roofs we climbed to sight basking snook in the shade of mangroves. One day, my brother and I spotted an alligator shaded up there. I got him to take a Lazy Ike plug and fought him, thrashing and spinning in the muck, and then landed him, whereupon he rose up on his legs and chased me into the brush. Half a day passed before I had the nerve to go back for my bicycle.

We went every day to the pier where the public fished. This was one of the many rubble-rock jetties that jut from the coast of Florida, and they are great and successful places for producing happiness. In some ways, there is nothing like the society of a good jetty. The retirees, the down-and-out, the economizing housewife, the driven boys, the exposure to the whimsy of all weathers, the fickle divination of angling destiny falling where it would up and down the length of the jetty, all contributed to a soap opera wherein each hooked fish produced a mob of hopefuls casting across one another's lines.

KEY WEST IN THE SIXTIES and seventies. Good heavens, a great and corrupt gardenia of an island in a wilderness of shoals and mangroves where we sometimes went from old wooden bars, shuddering with dance music and the heaving of like-minded characters. In the backyard of the Anchor Inn, an old Jaguar sedan that didn't run was used to store guns confiscated from the dancing fools. Closing time left four hours for the sleepy quiet of backyards and old streets before the sun came up, and once the engine of the skiff went down and several waves of sickness were fought back, we again were up and running—lust and booze banked down—off looking for fish in the glare. Nice to be young, though it was awfully hard work. Even today, when I am sure to go to bed early the night before a long day of fishing, I remember the special horror of fighting wild tarpon with a bar-life muzziness on my face and my clothes revealing beer stains, cigarette burns, and head shop perfumes. Looking back upon those days when nothing was expected of us and you could wait all day for a tide, live like dogs, and look for fish with an unreasonable zealotry, I wonder at the wisdom of making fishing "part" of my life.

Each year, Jim Harrison came down for a long stay and lowered already abysmal standards of decency wherein the awful polarity of our nightlife and daytime striving on the sea placed us all within easy reach of professional custodians. Guy de la Valdene was almost always there to help us remember that the idea was fishing, though when finally struck with the general sleaze he, too, became part of the problem, in the end challenging the limits of our sporting motto, "Nothing is too disgusting." This fishery lasted for many years, brought low only by a vague fear of being nabbed, though by whom and for what we were quite uncertain. Among the early signs was the presence of fellow anglers in regional prisons or in states of permanent exile under assumed names. It was a long way from Izaak Walton. Offshore lizards headquartered in the Chart Room Bar or the Full Moon Saloon, rootless and occasionally dangerous tourists and escapees, a complete collapse of the city's management of public services in a spontaneous crime wave, had begun to give our waters a sinister tone. We pined for cold water, the colder the better now that the real ghouls of Key West were coming out of the bag. The day-trippers on the Conch Train, we began to fear, might turn on the citizens in general butchery. We sold our skiffs and cleared out.

When I went back to Key West ten years later, I was astonished. The disreputable and rundown Duval Street had become a glut of T-shirt shops and tourist traps. The end of the street was frequently blocked to the height of several stories by cruise ships, while the city itself smelled of spring break barf twenty-four hours a day. Half the writers of the East Coast had moved here to immerse themselves in the sort of cannibalism they'd learned up north. Among the towering hotels and condominiums, the marina where I used to keep my skiff was encrusted with petrochemical grime and operated by the sort of surly rednecks with catfish mustaches who seem to have proliferated in the charter-boat trade around the world. The man on the forklift sported a gaping tip jar on the front of his machine and if you didn't take it seriously you were going to be a long time getting your boat. When I stopped in the bait shop to pick up a chart, uncertain if I could still find my way around these waters, waiting to be served by one of the several above-described idlers around the counter, a huge, drunken black man suddenly loomed in the doorway, gazed around the place and asked, "Which of y'all's the Grand Wizard around here?"

I once had the only flats skiff in town. Now, if you didn't have a skiff, you were viewed as some pathetic rebel without a cause. Idling out of Garrison Bight at No Wake speed, I found myself in a string of hostile skiffs that resembled a low rider parade on the border. I detected some wisdom in those skiff owners who used them exclusively for trailer rides on a1a. Once on the ocean or the Gulf back-country, the problem was finding a place away from the competition. On the oceanfront keys south of Key West, the tranquillity I remembered was disrupted by joyriding biplanes at low altitude, Jet Skis and confused new boat operators. On weekends, a trawler yacht anchored inside Ballast Key and sold drugs to the kids in the "Save the Bales" and "Key Wasted" T-shirts who roared up in personal watercraft for what amounted to curb service.

Half the people I knew had taken a Coast Guard exam and become "captains." Couples became captains together. I'd look in the phone book for old acquaintances and there they'd be: Smith, Captain Bill and Captain Sherri. I began to imagine a community where all were captains. Of course, many of these were realtors, though it was not out of the question for cosmetic surgeons or optometrists to be captains, too. It was very democratic, a homogenous world of captains.

Otherwise, my general impression was that Cayo Hueso had become part of New York, and not my favorite part. That would be the departure lounge at the airport. The same in-your-face style in the stores, the same goofy restaurant posturing so annoying to anyone who's merely hungry. Furthermore, Key West was having a waste-management crisis with grimly amusing results, like the notorious Mount Trashmore, towering over the Key West Memorial Hospital and often cited in speculative considerations of the remarkably high rates of multiple sclerosis among its employees.

But Key West has always been changing. Patrick Hemingway, who grew up there before my time, told me that when he went back after a long absence he was stunned by the impact of the overseas water aqueduct. He remembered Key West as "a goony bird island," a tropical, weather-blasted rock with humanity clinging to it in suitable humility. He marveled, too, that the black community in which he had so many childhood friends had missed the boom and was either disbursed or living in degraded vassalage to the tourism industry.

I certainly had seen enough. But it remains an odd pleasure to revisit these snapshots of the good times. There is nothing to compare to my years in the Keys as a reminder that Janis Joplin had it right: get it while you can. After that, it's too late.

The Longest Silence

Wで　HAT IS MOST emphatic in angling is made so by the long
silences — the unproductive periods. For the ardent fisherman, progress is toward the kinds of fishing that are never productive
in the sense of the blood riots of the hunting-and-fishing periodicals.
Their illusions of continuous action evoke for him, finally, a condition of utter, mortuary boredom. Such anglers will always be inclined
to find the gunnysack artists of the heavy kill rather cretinoid, their
stringerloads of gaping fish appalling.

No form of fishing offers such elaborate silences as fly-fishing for
permit. The most successful permit fly fisherman has very few catches
to describe to you. Yet there is considerable agreement that taking a
permit on a fly is the extreme experience of the sport. Even the guides
allow enthusiasm to shine through. I once asked one who specialized
in permit if he liked fishing for them. "Yes, I do," he said reservedly,
"but about the third time the customer asks, 'Is they good to eat?' I
begin losing interest."

The recognition factor is low when you catch a permit. If you wake
up your neighbor in the middle of the night to tell him of your success, shaking him by the lapels of his Dr. Dentons and shouting to be
heard over his million-BTU air conditioner, he may well ask you what
a permit is, and you will tell him it is like a pompano; rolling over, he
will tell you he cherishes pompano the way he had it at Joe's Stone
Crab in Miami Beach, with key lime pie afterward. If you have one

mounted, you'll always be explaining what it is to people who thought you were talking about your fishing license in the first place. In the end you take the fish off the conspicuous wall and put it upstairs, where you can see it when Mom sends you to your room. It's private.

I came to it through bonefishing. The two fish share the same marine habitat, the negotiation of which in a skiff can be somewhat hazardous. Running wide open at thirty knots over a close bottom, with sponges, sea fans, crawfish traps, conchs, and starfish racing under the hull with awful clarity, this takes some getting used to. The backcountry of the Florida Keys is full of hummocks: narrow, winding waterways and channels that open suddenly upon basins, and, on every side, the flats that preoccupy the fisherman. The process of learning to fish this region is one of learning the particularities of each of these flats. The narrow channel flats with crunchy staghorn-coral bottoms, the bare sand flats, and the turtlegrass flats are all of varying utility to the fisherman, and depending upon tide, these values are in a constant condition of change. The principal boat wreckers are the yellow cap-rock flats and the more mysterious coral heads. I was personally plagued by a picture of one of these enormities coming through the hull of my skiff and catching me on the point of the jaw. I had the usual Coast Guard safety equipment, not excluding floating cushions emblazoned Frost-Free Key West and a futile plastic whistle. I added a navy flare gun. As I learned the country, guides would run by me in their big skiffs and hundred-horse engines. I knew they never hit coral heads and had, besides, CB radios with which they might call for help. I dwelled on that and sent for radio catalogs.

One day when I was running to Content Pass on the edge of the Gulf of Mexico, I ran aground wide open in the backcountry. Unable to examine the lower unit of my engine, I got out of the boat, waiting for the tide to float it, and strolled around in four inches of water. The day was absolutely windless and the mangrove islands stood elliptically in their perfect reflections. The birds were everywhere—terns, gulls, wintering ducks, skimmers, all the wading birds, and, crying down from their tall shafts of air, more ospreys than I had ever seen. The gloomy bonanza of the Overseas Highway seemed far away.

On the western edge of that flat I saw my first permit, tailing in two feet of water. I had heard all about permit but had been convinced I'd never see one. So, looking at what was plainly a permit, I didn't know what it was. That evening, talking to my friend Woody Sexton, a permit expert, I reconstructed the fish and had it identified for me. Woody is very scientific and cautious. With his silver crew cut, tan clothing, and perfect fitness, he seems the model of reason. I believed him. I grew retroactively excited, and Woody apprised me of some of the difficulties associated with catching one on a fly. He made it clear that if I wanted to catch a permit, I would have to dedicate myself to it so completely that there really would be no time for anything else.

After that, over a long period of time, I saw a good number of them. Always, full of hope, I would cast. To permit, the fly was anathema; one look and they were gone. I cast to a few hundred. It seemed futile, all wrong, like trying to bait a tiger with watermelons. The fish would see the fly, light out or ignore it, sometimes flare at it, but never, ever touch it. I went to my tying vise and made flies that looked like whatever you could name, flies that were praiseworthy from anything but a practical point of view. The permit weren't interested, and I no longer even caught bonefish. I went back to my old fly, a rather ordinary bucktail, and was relieved to be catching bonefish again. I thought I had lost what there was of my touch.

One Sunday morning I decided to conduct services in the skiff, taking the usual battery of rods for the pursuit of permit. More and more the fish had become a simple abstraction, even though they had made one ghostly midwater appearance, poised silver as moons near my skiff, and had departed without movement, like lights going out. But I wondered if I had actually seen them. I must have. The outline and movement remained in my head: the dark fins, the pale gold of the ventral surface, and the steep, oversize scimitar tails. I dreamed about them.

This fell during the first set of April's spring tides—exaggerated tides associated with the full moon. I had haunted a long, elbow-shaped flat on the Atlantic side of the keys, and by Sunday there was a large movement of tide and reciprocal tide. A twenty-knot wind complicated my still unsophisticated poling, and I went down the upper end of the flat yawing from one edge to the other and at times raging as the boat tried to swap ends against my will. I looked around, furtively concerned whether I could be seen by any of the professionals. At the corner of the flat I turned downwind and proceeded less than forty yards when I spotted, on the southern perimeter, a large stingray making a strenuous mud. When I looked closely it seemed there was something else swimming in the disturbance. I poled toward it for a better look. The other fish was a very large permit. The ray had evidently stirred up a crab and was trying to cover it, so as to prevent the permit from getting it. The permit, meanwhile, was whirling around the ray, nipping its fins to make it move off the crab.

My problem was to set up the skiff above the fish, get rid of the push pole, drift down, and make a cast. I quietly poled upwind, wondering why I hadn't been spotted. I was losing my breath with excitement, the little expanse of skin beneath my sternum throbbing like a frog's throat, and I acquired a fantastic lack of coordination. Turning in the wind, I beat the boat with the push pole as if it were a gong and conducted what a friend has described as a Chinese fire drill. After five minutes of the most dire possible clownage I got into position and could still see the permit's fins breaking the surface of the ray's mud. I laid the push pole down, picked up my fly rod, and to my intense irritation, saw that the ray had given up and was swimming, not seeing me, straight at the skiff. The closing rate was ruinous. I couldn't get a cast off in time to do anything. About twenty feet from the boat the ray sensed my presence and veered fifteen feet off my starboard gunwale, with the permit swimming close to the ray but on my side. As soon as I could see the permit clearly, it started to flush, then slowed down and crossed to the opposite side of the ray. Taking the only chance offered me, I cast over the ray, hoping my line would not spook it and, in turn, the permit. The fly fell with lucky, agonizing perfection, three feet in front of the permit on its exact line of travel. Without hestiation the fish darted forward and took: the one-in-a-thousand shot. I lifted the rod, feeling the rigid bulk of the still unalarmed fish, and set the hook. He shimmered away, my loose line jumping off the deck. And then the rod suddenly doubled and my leader broke. A loop of line had tightened itself around the handle of the reel.

I was ready for the rubber room. Having been encouraged to feel it might be five years before I hooked another, I tried to see all that was good in other kinds of fishing. I thought of various life-enhancing things a fellow could do at home. I could turn to the ennobling volumes of world literature on my shelves. I might do some oils, slap out a gouache or two. But I could not distract myself from the mental image of my lovingly assembled fly rushing from my hands on the lip of a big permit.

I had to work out a routine that would not depend on such exceptional events for success. One technique, finally, almost guaranteed me shots at permit, and that was to stake out my skiff on the narrow channel flats that are covered with a crunchy layer of blue-green staghorn coral. Permit visit these in succession, according to tide and a hierarchy of flat values known mainly to them but intuited by certain smart fishermen. I liked to be on these flats at the early incoming tide—the young flood, as it is called—and fish to the middle incoming or, often, to the slack high. The key was to be able to stand for six hours and watch an acre of bottom for any sign of life at all. The body would give out in the following sequence: arches, back, hips. Various dehydration problems developed. I carried ice and drank quinine water until my ears rang. Push-ups and deep knee bends on the casting deck helped. And, like anyone else who uses this method, I became an active fantasizer. The time was punctuated by the appearances of oceanic wildlife, fish and turtles that frequented the area as well as many that did not. With any luck at all the permit came, sometimes in a squadron and in a hurry, sometimes alone with their tails in the air, rooting along the hard edge of the flat. The cast would be made, the line and leader would straighten and the fly fall. On a normal day the fly only made the permit uncomfortable, and it would turn and gravely depart. On another day the fly so horrified the fish that it turned tail and bolted. On very few days the permit would sprint at the fly, stop a few inches short, run in a circle when the fly was gently worked, return and flare at it, flash at it, see the boat, and flush.

On particularly hot days when the cumulus clouds stacked in a circle around the horizon, a silky sheen of light lay so fiercely on the water that my vision had to be forced through until my head ached. Patience was strained from the first, and water seemed to stream from my skin. At such times I was counting on an early sighting of fish to keep my attention. And when this did not happen I succumbed to an inviting delusion. The best place to fish was somewhere very far away, and it would be necessary to run the country. I reeled up my line and put the rod in its holder. I took the push pole out of the bottom and secured it in its chocks on the gunwale. Then I let the wind carry me off the flat. I started the engine and put it in forward, suffering exquisitely a moment more, then ran the throttle as far as it would go. The bow lifted and lowered on plane, the stern came up and the engine whined satisfactorily. Already the perspiration was drying, and I felt cool and slaked by the spray. Once on top, standing and steering, running wide open, I projected on my mind what was remembered of a suitable chart to get to this imaginary place where the fish were thick enough to walk on. I looked up and was reproved by the vapor trail of a navy Phantom interceptor. I ran up the channels, under the bridge, using all the cheap tricks I thought I could get away with, shortcutting flats when I thought I had enough water, looking back to see if I'd left a mud trail, running the banks to get around basins because the coral heads wouldn't grow along a bank, running tight to the keys in a foot-and-a-half of water when I was trying to beat the wind, finally shutting down on some bank or flat or along some tidal pass not unlike the one I'd just run from. It was as hot as it could be, and I couldn't see. The sweat was running onto my sunglasses, and I was hungry and thinking I'd call it a day. When I got home I rather abashedly noted that I'd burned a lot of fuel without making a cast.

The engine hadn't been running right for a week, and I was afraid of getting stranded or having to sleep out on some buggy flat or, worse, being swept to Galveston on an offshore wind. I tore the engine down and found the main-bearing seal shot and in need of replacement. I drove to Big Pine to get parts and arrived about the time the guides, who center there, were coming in for the day. At the dock, where the big skiffs with their excessive engines were nosed to the breakwater, guides mopped decks and needled each other. Customers, happy and not, disembarked with armloads of tackle, sun hats, oil, thermoses and picnic baskets. A few of these sporty dogs were plastered. One fragile lady, owl-eyed with sunburn, tottered from the casting deck of a guide's skiff and drew herself up on the dock. "Do you know what the whole trouble was?" she inquired of her companion, perhaps her husband, a man much younger than herself.

"No, what?" he said.

She smiled and pitied him. "Well, think about it."

The two put their belongings into the trunk of some kind of minicar and drove off too fast down the Overseas Highway. Four hours would put them in Palm Beach.

It seemed to have been a good day. A number of men went up the dock with fish to be mounted. One went by with a bonefish that might have weighed ten pounds. Spotting Woody Sexton, I wanted to ask how he'd done but knew that ground rules forbade this question around the boats; on the one hand, it embarrasses guides who have had bad days, and on the other, it risks passing good fishing information promiscuously. Meanwhile, as we talked, the mopping and needling continued along the dock. The larger hostilities are reserved for the fishing grounds themselves, where various complex snubbings may be performed from the semianonymity of powerful skiffs. The air can be electric with accounts of who cut off whom, who ran the bank on whom, and so on. The antagonism among the skiff guides, the offshore guides, the pompano fishermen, the crawfishermen, and the shrimpers produces tales of shootings, of disputes settled with gaffs, of barbed wire strung in guts and channels to wreck props and drive shafts. Some of the tales are true. Woody and I made a plan to fish when he got a day off. I gathered my engine parts and went home, where I had torn the engine to pieces on an old Ping-Pong table.

I worked out two or three bonefish patterns for the inside bank of Loggerhead Key. The best of these was a turnoff point where bonefish who were contouring the bank hit a small ridge and turned up onto the flat itself. By positioning myself at this, I would be able to get casts off to passing fish and to see a good piece of the bank, downlight, until noon.

One day I went out and staked the boat during the middle-incoming water of another set of new-moon tides. I caught one bonefish early in the tide, a lively fish that went a hundred yards on his first run and doggedly resisted me for a length of time that was all out of proportion to his weight. I released him after giving him a short revival session and then just sat and looked at the water. I could see Woody fishing with a customer, working the outside of the bank for tarpon.

It was a queer day to begin with. Vital light flashed on and off around the scudding clouds, and there were slight foam lines on the water from the wind. The basin that shelved off from my bank was active with diving birds, particularly great brown pelicans, whose wings sounded like luffing sails and who ate with submerged heads while blackheaded gulls tried to rob them. The birds were drawn here by a school of mullet that was making an immense mud hundreds of yards across. The slick glowed in the sun a quarter of a mile to the south. I didn't pay much attention until it began by collective will or chemical sensors to move onto my bank. Inexorably, the huge disturbance progressed and flowed toward me. In the thinner water the mullet school was compressed, and the individual fish became easier targets for predators. Big oceanic barracuda were among them, slashing and streaking through the school like bolts of lightning. Simultaneously, silver sheets of mullet, sometimes an acre in extent, burst out of the water and rained down again. In time my skiff was in the middle of it, the opaque water was inch-by-inch alive.

Some moments later, perhaps seventy feet astern of me, a large blacktip shark swam up onto the bank and began traveling with grave sweeps of its tail through the fish, not as yet making a move for them. Mullet and smaller fish nevertheless showered out in front of the shark as it coursed past. Behind the shark I could see another fish faintly flashing. I supposed it was a jack crevalle, a pelagic fish, strong for its size, that often follows sharks. I decided to cast anyway at a distance that was all I could manage. I got off one of my better shots, which nevertheless fell slightly behind target. I was surprised to see the fish drop back to the fly, turn and elevate high in the water, then take. A permit.

I set the hook sharply and the fish started down the flat. Remembering my last episode, I kept the loose, racing line well away from the reel handle for the instant the fish took to consume it. Then the fish was on the reel. When I lowered the rod tip and cinched the hook, the fish began to accelerate, staying on top of the flat, where I could witness its wildly extending wake. Everything was holding together: the hookup was good, the knots were good. At 150 yards the fish stopped, and I got back line. I kept at it until the fish was within 80 yards of the boat. Then it suddenly made a wild, undirected run, not permitlike at all, and I could see the shark chasing it. The blacktip struck and missed three or four times, making explosions in the water that sickened me. I released the drag, untied the boat, and started the engine. Woody started poling toward me at the sound of my engine, his mystified client dragging a line astern.

There was hardly enough water to move in. The prop was half buried, and even at full throttle I couldn't get up on plane. As the explosions continued, I could only guess whether or not I was still connected to the permit. I ran toward it trailing a vast loop of line, saw the shark and immediately ran over him. I threw the engine into neutral and waited to see what had happened and tried to regain line. I was again tight to the permit. Then the shark reappeared. He hit the permit once, killed it, and ate it, worrying it like a dog and bloodying the water. Then, an instant later, I had the shark on my line and running. I fought him with irrational care: I now planned to gaff the blacktip and retrieve my permit piece by piece. When the inevitable cutoff came I dropped the rod in the boat and, empty-handed, wondered what I had done to deserve this.

I heard Woody's skiff and looked up. He swung about and coasted alongside. I told him it was a permit, just as he had guessed from my starting up on the flat. Woody began to say something when, at that not unceremonial moment, his client broke in to remark that hooking them was the main thing. We stared at him until he added, "Or is it?"

Often afterward, we went over the affair and talked about what might have been done differently, as we had with the first permit. One friend clips a carbine on clips under the gunwale to resolve any shark problems. But I felt that with a gun in the skiff during the excitement of a running fish, I would either plug myself or deep-six the boat.

Also, I like sharks. Woody knew better than to assure me there would be other chances. Knowing that there might very well not be was one of our conversational assumptions.

One morning we went looking for tarpon. Woody had had a bad night of it. He'd awakened in the darkness of his room about three in the morning and watched the shadowy figure of a huge land crab walk across his chest. Endlessly it crept to the wall and then up the plaster. Carefully silhouetting the monster, Woody blasted it with a karate chop and now, at breakfast, he was nursing a bruise on the side of his hand. At 6:00 a.m., we were having grits and eggs at the Chat and Chew restaurant. A trucker who claimed to have driven from Loxahatchee in three hours flat was yelling for "oss tie." And when the girl asked if he really wanted iced tea this early in the morning he replied, "Dash rat. Oss tie." I couldn't wake up in the heat. Listless, half dreaming, I imagined the land crab performing some morbid cadenza on my pile of grits.

We laid out the rods in the skiff. The wind was coming out of the east—that is, over one's casting hand from the point we planned to fish—and blowing fairly stiff. But the light was good, and that was more important. We headed out of Big Pine into the calm water along Ramrod Key. We ran in behind Pye Key, through the hole behind Little Money and out to Southeast Point. The sun was already huge, out of hand, like Shakespeare's "glistering Phaethon." I had whitened my nose and mouth with zinc oxide ointment, and felt, handling the mysterious rods and flies, like a shaman. As Woody jockeyed the skiff with the pole, I put my leader together. I had retained enough of my trout-fishing sensibilities to continue to be intrigued by tarpon leaders with their array of arcane knots. The butt of the leader is nail-knotted to the line, blood-knotted to monofilament of lighter test; the shock tippet that protects the leader from the rough jaws of tarpon is tied to the leader with a combination Albright Special and Bimini Bend; the shock tippet is attached to the fly either by a perfection loop, a clinch or a Homer Rhodes Loop; and to choose one is to make a moral choice. You are made to understand that it would not be impossible to fight about it or, at the very least, quibble darkly.

We set up on a tarpon pass point. We had sand spots around us that would help us pick out the dark shapes of traveling tarpon. And we expected tarpon on the falling water, from left to right. Up on the bow with fifty feet of line coiled on the deck, I was barefoot, so I could feel if I stepped on a loop. I made a couple of practice casts—harsh, indecorous, tarpon-style—and scanned for fish.

The first were, from my point of view, spotted from too great a distance. That is, a long period of time would pass before they actually broke the circle of my casting range, during which I could go, secretly but quite completely, to pieces. The sensation for me, in the face of these advancing forms, was as of a gradual ossification of the joints. Moviegoers will recall the early appearances of Frankenstein's monster, his ambulatory motions accompanied by great rigidity of the limbs, almost as though he could stand a good oiling. I was hard put to see how I could manage anything beyond a perfunctory flapping of the rod. I had once laughed at Woody's stories of customers who sat down and held their feet slightly aloft, treading the air or wobbling their hands from the wrists. I giggled at the story of a Boston chiropractor who fell over on his back and barked like a seal.

"Let them come in now," Woody said.

"I want to nail one, Woody."

"You will. Let them come."

The fish, six of them, were surging toward us in a wedge. They ran from 80 to 110 pounds, slow, dark torpedoes. "All right, the lead fish, get on him," Woody said. I managed the throw, the fly falling in front of the fish. I let them overtake it before starting my retrieve. The big lead fish pulled up behind the fly, trailed, and then made the shoveling, open-jawed uplift of a strike that is not soon forgotten. When he turned down I set the hook and he started his run. The critical issue of getting rid of that loose line piled around one's feet now ensued. You imagine that if you are standing on a coil, you will go to the moon when that coil must follow its predecessors out of the rod. This trial went off without a hitch, and it was only my certainty that someone had done it before that kept me from deciding that we'd made a huge mistake.

The sudden pressure of the line and the direction of its resistance apparently confused the tarpon, so it raced in close-coupled arcs around the boat. Then, once it had seen the boat, felt the line and isolated a single point of resistance, it cleared out at a perfectly insane rate of acceleration that made water run three feet up my line as it sliced through the ocean. The jumps—wild, greyhounding, end-over-end, rattling—were all crazily blurred as they happened, while I pictured my reel exploding like a racing clutch and filling me with shrapnel. This fish, the first of six that day, broke off. So did the others, destroying various aspects of my tackle.

As the sun moved through the day the blind side continually changed, forcing us to adjust position until, by afternoon, we were watching to the north. Somehow, looking uplight, Woody saw four permit coming right toward us, head-on. I cast my tarpon fly at them, out of my accustomed long-shot routine, and was surprised when one fish moved forward from the pack and followed up the fly rather aggressively. About then they all sensed the skiff and swerved to cross the bow around thirty feet out. They were down close to the bottom now, slightly spooked. I picked up, changed direction, and cast a fairly long interception. When the fly lit, well out ahead, two permit elevated from the group, sprinted forward, and the inside fish took the fly in plain view.

The positive certainty of the take, in the face of an ungodly number of refusals and countless unrewarded hours, induced immediate pessimism. I waited for everything to go haywire.

I hooked the fish quickly. It was only slightly startled and returned to the pack, which by this time had veered away from the shallow flat edge and swung back toward deep water. The critical time of loose line passed slowly. Woody unstaked the skiff and was poised to see which way the fish would take us. When the permit was tight to the reel I cinched him once and he began running. The deep water kept the fish from making the long, sustained sprints permit make on the flats. This fight was a series of assured jabs at various clean angles from the skiff. We followed, alternately gaining and losing line. Then, in some way, at the end of this blurred episode, the permit was flashing beside the boat, looking nearly circular, and the only visual contradiction to his perfect poise was the intersecting line of leader seemingly inscribed from the tip of my arcing rod to the precise corner of his jaw.

Then we discovered that there was no net in the boat. The fish would have to be tailed. I forgave Woody in advance for the permit's escape. Woody was kneeling in the skiff, my line disappearing over his shoulder, the permit no longer in my sight, Woody leaning deep from the gunwale. Then, unbelievably, his arm was up, the black symmetry of tail above his fist, the permit perpendicular to the earth, then horizontal on the floorboards, where a pile of loose line was strewn in curves that wandered around the bottom of the boat toward the gray-and-orange fly secured in the permit's mouth. I sat down numb and soaring.

I don't know what this sort of occurrence indicates beyond the necessary, ecstatic resignation to the moment. With the beginning over and, possibly, nothing learned, I was persuaded that once was not enough. And indeed it wasn't. Thirty years have passed and none of the magic of permit fishing, not a trace of it, has gone.

Close to the Bone

ONE IS TEMPTED to think of bonefish as among the wildest of creatures, if a sensory apparatus calculated to separate them continually from man's presence qualifies them as "wild." Yet, when the serious angler insinuates himself into the luminous, subaqueous universe of the bonefish and catches one without benefit of accident, he has, in effect, visited another world, one whose precise cycles and conditions appear so serene that the addled twentieth-century angler begins to be consoled for all he has done to afford the trip in the first place. In his imagination he is emphatic about emptiness, space, and silence. He is searching less for recreation than for a kind of stillness.

Only the utterly initiated consider the bonefish handsome. Those new to or stupid about the sport think the fish is silly-looking, but those who know him well grant the bonefish a radiant, nearly celestial beauty. To me, he seems so perfectly made for both his terrain and my needs as a fisherman that he has the specificity of design seen in experimental aircraft. The nose, it is true, has a curious slant, and there is an undershot mouth that we, with our anthropocentrism, associate with lack of character, yet after a while you see that the entire head is rather hydrodynamic and handsomely vulpine.

The body is sturdy, often a radiant gray-green above and pure silver on the sides. The tail, like the fins, is frequently a gunmetal gray and is oversize and powerful, as exaggeratedly proportioned to its size as are the fish's speed and power.

A bonefish doesn't jump. From the fish's point of view, the jump is a wasteful and often ruinous enterprise. Tarpon customarily wreck themselves jumping, which is the only thing that enables us to take the large ones on light tackle at all. So people who like to be photographed with all the spectacle associated with themselves, their fishing paraphernalia and their aerobatic catch ought to forget bonefish and concentrate on tarpon. Hang a tarpon up at the dock and it will suck gawkers off the highway like a vacuum cleaner. A dead bonefish at dockside barely draws flies.

It took me a month to catch my first bonefish, and I regret to say that I killed it and put it in the freezer. I had no boat and haunted the roadside flats, especially at Ohio-Missouri Key, finally catching one at Big Torch after pushing my way through the mangroves and stumbling onto a mud flat where some gullible fish were feeding. For a long time, at the drop of a hat, I would take it out, rigid as a fungo bat, to show to my friends. One said it was small. Another noted that the freezer had given it sunken eyes and a morbid demeanor. I asked how you could speak of demeanor in something which had departed this world. It was the last bonefish I kept.

Hard as it may be to believe, the bonefish leads his life in his extensive multiocean range quite without reference to the angler. For example, off the coast of Hawaii he has taken himself to great depths, where he is of no earthly use to the light-tackle fisherman. His poor manners extend to the African coast, where he reveals himself occasionally to cut-bait anglers of the high surf who smother his fight with pyramid sinkers that a Wyoming wrangler might use to keep the horses handy.

For these transgressions of fair play the human race can best revenge itself upon the bonefish in the shallows of Central America, Christmas Island, the Bahamas, and the Florida Keys. From a topographical perspective, this immensely distributed fish seems to be all over the place, but the angler will resort to low tricks and importuning the deity for just one. In the back of his mind, he recalls that marine biologists describe the bonefish as "widely distributed." It doesn't help.

The marine shallows where the bonefish spends much of its existence, from the transparent larval stage to maturity, are accessible only to the fisherman or scientist who either wades or transports himself in a light skiff over the sand and turtlegrass. As much delicacy of approach is required of these observers as there is of the ornithologist. This essential condition of bonefishing makes it almost generically different from offshore angling.

Unlike almost any other game fish, the bonefish are not sought where they live. They live in deep water and only do some of their feeding on the flats. A trout fisherman, for example, seeking a particular fish, would attempt to ascertain where that fish lived, in which pool or under which log. The bonefisherman never has any idea where any given fish lives; he attempts to find combinations of tide and place that are attractive to feeding bonefish. Occasionally, a single fish will appear with certain regularity, but this is exceptional.

Flats used by feeding bonefish are flooded by tide. They are flooded at unequal rates, depending on the location of the individual flats relative to the direction of tidal bore and current, and the presence of keys and basins, which draw and deflect the moving water. One flat, for instance, might have rising water while another, located a mile away, may not get its first incoming water until an hour later. Even this is not constant, since wind can alter the precise times of rising and falling water.

The beginning bonefisherman often feels humiliated to learn that flats he found empty could produce bonanzas for anglers with a better sense of timing. A tide book and a good memory are the first tools of the bonefisherman. With experience, a pattern begins to emerge—the shape of the life habits of a wild species.

The novice starts with a simple combination—early incoming water in the morning or evening—and gradually, by observation, begins to include the mosaic of tidal information that finally becomes the fabric of his fishing knowledge. Tide in the Tropics, where only a foot of water moves on the average, seems rather ethereal to the new bonefisherman. To him it hardly seems reasonable that three- or four-tenths of a foot of tidal variation can mean the difference between a great and a worthless fishing tide.

Tide can work in another way: you are poling across a flat in less than a foot of water. A fish tails high on the flat. You begin your approach, closing in deliberately. There is the small sound of staghorn crunching against the skiff's bottom, then the more solid sound of sand. You can't go any farther. The bonefish is still tailing, still out of reach. You get out of the skiff and wade toward him to make your cast. His tail disappears as he tilts out of his feeding posture, follows your lure or bait, takes, is hooked and running. For ten minutes you live as never before. Then the bonefish, a fine eight-pounder, is released.

When you return to the skiff, it's high and dry; the tide has dropped out from under it. You've got a six-hour wait before you can budge the skiff, so you pace up and down the flat like an angry executive. If you're a smoker, you smoke more than you have ever smoked before. Can't someone get me out of this?

Now, if you have gone aground in the morning on a summer's day and have not brought water, you will be truly sorry. If you have gone aground in the afternoon and can't find your way home in the dark, you'll be sleeping in the skiff. Pick a breezy place where the mosquitoes have taxiing problems; a certain number will crash-land on your person anyway, but the breeze will discourage the rank and file. Curl up in your little flats boat, listen to the wave-slap, and, watching the deep tropical night, think upon the verities of your choice. Tantrums, it should be mentioned, only keep you from getting to sleep.

Tide, that great impersonal pulse of earth which brought you that eight-pounder on a platter, has cooked your goose.

Bonefish are hard to see. You train your eyes to find them by a number of subliminal signs which, after you have fished the flats extensively, give you the opportunity to amaze your friends with feats of vision. "Bonefish right in front of you!" you say as one ghosts past the skiff, visible only by the palest shadow it casts on the bottom.

"Where?" asks your good friend, whom you really shouldn't treat this way. "My God, where?"

"Right in front of you!" This starts your companion casting, even though he sees nothing.

"Flushed fish," you say, gazing at the horizon.

The difficulty in seeing fish gives the veteran a real opportunity to lord it over the neophyte, gives him a chance to cultivate those small nuances of power that finally reveal him to be the Captain of the Skiff. After that, the veteran can relax and radiate generosity.

Of the fish that concern the flats fisherman, bonefish are the smallest and probably the hardest to see. Water and light conditions dictate how they are to be sought with the eye, but again intuition eventually takes over. In the Florida Keys, where bonefish are characteristically seen swimming rather than tailing (and perhaps this is true everywhere), you must make a disciplined effort to look *through* the water surface. While it is certainly something very inviting to look at, the man who confuses angling with relaxation and lets his eye linger here will miss nine out of ten fish. In the beginning, especially, the task must be borne down on, for it is hard work. Eventually you will learn to sweep, or scan back and forth, over the area of possible sighting. At the first sweep, your mind records the features of the bottom; on subsequent scans, if anything is out of place or if the small, unobtrusive, and utterly shadowy presence of a bonefish has interrupted those features in your memory, you will notice it.

Polaroid glasses are an absolute necessity. There is some disagreement about which color is best. Green lenses are the most common, but things show up a little better with amber. Many people find the amber lenses hard on their eyes on brilliant days and so confine their use to overcast skies. I have used the amber glasses on brilliant July days and been plagued by headaches and strobelike afterimages.

In very shallow water, bonefish manifest themselves in two other ways: by waking and by tailing. Fish making waves are often seen on the early incoming tide, and I think these are more important to the angler than the tailing fish. Singles make a narrow V wake, not always distinct, and pods of fish make a trembling, advancing surface almost like a cat's-paw of wind, called "nervous water."

The most prized discovery, however, is the tailing fish. And wading for tailing fish is the absolute champagne of the sport, the equivalent of dry-fly fishing during the hatch. These fish can be harder to take than the swimmers—their heads are down and it is necessary to get the fly near them so they can see it, yet this close presentation tends to frighten them—but the reward is commensurately greater and the corollary that they are usually hooked in the shallowest kind of water makes their runs even more vivid. Since there is often more than one fish tailing at the same time, the alarm of a hooked fish is communicated immediately and its companions will explode away from the site like pieces of a star shell.

The sound that a hooked bonefish makes running across a flat cannot be phonetically imitated. In fact, most of the delicate, shearing sound comes from the line or leader as it slices through the water. The fish will fight itself to death if not hurried a little and if care is not taken in the release.

Anglers of experience speculate a good deal about the character of their quarry, doting on the baleful secrecy of brown trout, the countrified insouciance and general funkiness of largemouth bass, or the vaguely Ivy League patina of brook trout and Atlantic salmon. The smallmouth enthusiast who accedes to a certain aristocratic construction to his sport is cheerful and would identify himself with, for instance, Thomas Jefferson, whose good house (Monticello) and reasonable political beliefs about mankind (democracy) have been so attractive to the optimistic and self-made.

The dedicated trout fisherman is frequently an impossible human being capable of taking a priceless Payne dry-fly rod to an infant's fanny. One hardly need mention that more lynching has been done by largemouth bass anglers than by the fanciers of any other species, just as Atlantic salmon anglers are sure to go up against the wall way ahead of Indiana crappie wizards.

But the bonefisherman is as enigmatic as his quarry. The bonefish is as likely to scurry around a flat like a rat as he is to come sweeping in on the flood, tailing with noble deliberation. So, too, the bonefisherman is subject to great lapses of dignity. A bonefish flat is a complex field of signs, quite as difficult a text as an English chalk stream. The bonefisherman has a mildly scientific proclivity for natural phenomenology insofar as it applies to his quest, but unfortunately he is inclined to regard a flock of roseate spoonbills only in terms of flying objects liable to spook fish.

The bonefisherman is nearly as capable of getting lost between a Pink Shrimp and a Honey Blonde as the lone maniac waist-deep in the

Letort plowing through his fly box from Jassid to Pale Evening Dun, though, because a boat is usually required, he may be slightly more oppressed by equipment.

As the bonefisherman is sternly sophisticated by his quarry, his reverence for the creature increases. Undeterred by toxic winds, block meetings, bulletproof taxicab partitions, or adventures with the Internal Revenue Service, he can perceive with his mind alone bonefish moving on remote ocean flats in the tongue of the flood.

Weather

SITTING UP IN the pilot house, we could see with our own eyes that a serious storm was coming. The Weatherfax hadn't shown a good picture of it the day before, but you could see it on the radar, streaming through above Cuba, across Grand Bahama, and now it was on top of us. Chris went forward to the windlass while Phil laid down another hundred feet of chain between us and the anchor. The slight shifts in the boat's position were revealed in the apparent movement of the sandy bottom under deep, clear, pale-green tropical water. We were on good holding ground. There wasn't really much to worry about though it couldn't help the fishing. And there were the compensations of a tropical squall: the supercharged atmosphere of deep, humid wind, the unpredictable tide slipping through the roots of heaving mangroves. It was interesting weather.

We were in a remote part of the Bahamas, a long way from even the smallest village. There were so many small cays and deep green cuts that if things abated at all, we could get in a lee somewhere and go on looking for fish. Meanwhile, we hung on our anchor, transom directed at the low, broken coast, covered in spindly pines well spaced in their sandy footing by incessant sea winds.

At the last village we'd bought bread from the local bakery. The people were cheerful and smiled quickly. Most had little to do. Their modest gardens were ruled by stingy rainfall; commercial fishing seemed reduced to supplying a hotel or two. The people were scattered along the roads that left the village, strolling or carrying sacks. Coconut palms bowed over the roadway, and as one of my companions said to me, a coconut did not reach a great age here. These pedestrians weren't the first poor natives to roam the luxury home sites of the future.

The boat was owned by a friend of mine, and in his foresight and wisdom she was equipped with good electronics, shipboard refrigeration, and comfortable places to eat and sleep. And she carried two bonefish skiffs in davits. Phil, her captain, also acquitted himself as a cook, and the night we ate all the fresh mangrove snappers or the night we had all the crawfish and black beans illustrated the compensations of life on that part of the South Atlantic, which seems at once a global dropoff and shelf of copious marine life, a buzzing cross-section of the food chain with fishermen briefly at the very top. One could raise the poetry as a nonconsuming naturalist, but who besides the angler crawls to the brook at daybreak or pushes his fragile craft to the head of the tide to come out on the flood with the creatures that breathe the water?

The weather broke and we began to fish, poling the skiffs among the myriad small cays in the fragrance of mangrove blossoms, the ceremony of angling holding our minds on all the proper things. Bananaquits, the active little Bahamian honey creepers, flitted along the sandy shore. At one small cay we disturbed a frigate bird rookery, iridescent black birds, the males adorned with red inflated throats. They pushed off the branches of mature mangroves and soared with the amazing low-altitude slowness that their immense wingspans allowed, practically at a walk. For a moment the skiff seemed surrounded by magnified soot, then they climbed steeply and soared away.

We spotted two nice fish well back in the mangroves in inches of water, their backs out of the water as they scoured around the bases of the bushes for crustaceans. Their silvery brilliance was startling. We stopped the skiff and watched. They didn't seem to want to come out, so I decided to give it a try. I cast the fly into a narrow space between the mangroves and watched the two fish circle toward it. I moved the fly slightly and the first fish darted forward and took. I set the hook and the bonefish roared out of there so fast that for a brief moment the small mangroves swept low by the pressure of my fly line and the fish was off.

At the edge of a turtlegrass flat I hooked a bigger fish that forced a sheet of water up my leader with the speed of the line shearing the water. At about a hundred yards into his run, the hook broke. Now, that's very rare. I chatted less with my companion and more to myself and tried to stare through the water to the bottom or concentrate on the surface for the "nervous water" of approaching schools. We found one right at the edge of the mangroves. I hoped if I could hook one here, it would head for open water. I made a rather long cast that fell just the way it was supposed to. One strip and I was solid tight to a good fish. He ran straight at the boat and I had fly line everywhere as he passed us and stole line, causing it to jump up off the deck in wild coils that were suddenly draped around my head and shoulders. The fish was about to come to the end of this mess. When he did, I felt the strange sensation of my shorts rising rapidly toward my shoulder blades. At the point they came tight in my crotch, the leader broke with a sharp report: The line had hooked the button of my back pocket. My companion was hunched over the push pole in a paroxysm of laughter. I looked at him, I looked at the open sea, I tied on another fly.

I was in that state of mind perhaps not peculiar to angling when things seem to be in a steep curve of deterioration, and I had a fatal sense that I was not at the end of it. Bonefish are ready takers of a well-presented fly but once hooked, they are so explosive that getting rid of slack line and getting the fish on the reel can produce humiliating results. Their speed and power are so far out of proportion to their size that a bonefish, finally landed, seems to have gone through a magical reduction from the brute that burned line off against the shrieking drag to the demure little fellow one holds in one's hand while gently removing the fly. With his big round eyes and friendly face the bonefish scarcely looks guilty of the searing runs he just performed. And the fastest individuals are the ones that look fat, bright little pigs that root around the shallows. They're almost always moving, and if they rest, they prefer to get in among the mangrove shoots where barracuda can't get a straight run at them. Their reactions to anything overhead are instantaneous, so one good way of locating fish is to watch a low-flying cormorant cross the flats; every bonefish touched by the bird's shadow will explode to a new position, then resume feeding. You slip up to where you have seen them move and perhaps you make a connection, the slow-stripped fly line jumping rigid in a bright circle of spray.

After a wonderful meal of roasted razorback hog, garden vegetables, and big in-season Florida tomatoes, I sat up listening to my host's wonderful stories of life in the thirties: training fighting cocks in Bali while recovering from malaria, roading birds from his bicycle, tossing roosters from the balcony of his hotel to the bellhop down below to build up their stamina. Once, when he was waiting to catch the flying boat to the Orient, his plane was so late that he went to Idaho to learn to ski in the meantime. And I enjoyed his cultural views: "The Italians are my favorite! They adore their little pope! Then they put on their condoms and fuck everything in sight!"

Afterward, I went up on the foredeck and sat next to the windlass to watch the full moon rise. We were in a small tropical sea trapped between the Atlantic and the Caribbean. The Gulf Stream, that great violet river, poured northward just beyond my view, regulating the temperature of the world. Once the moon was up, it appeared as a fixed portion of the universe while the clouds and weather of planet Earth poured over its face. I thought of all the places and times in my amusing life I had looked to a full moon for even one suggestion I could do something with. I thought about John Cheever stating that man made a better traveler than a farmer and how the motion of clouds against the face of the moon always made me crave motion or pine for the sound of waves breaking on an empty shore. Or how Roger Taylor said a boat was meant to improve your position for watching the weather, or how Hemingway said, "Always put in the weather." Weather on the Gulf Stream included the northern gale when we were headed to Cuba on my sloop *Hawksbill:* winds that built the seas up so high that the spreader lights thirty feet above the deck lit the waves from the side, and the big graybeards with their tops blowing off chased us high over the stern until they caught us and knocked us down at three o'clock in the morning. Weather is one of the things that goes on without you, and after a certain amount of living it is bracing to contemplate the many items not dependent upon you for their existence. But tonight the moon shone broadly on the tropical sea. I could make out the radio faintly from the wheelhouse; Reba McIntyre, Roseanne Cash, Tammy Wynette, the big girls were out on world airways. I was supremely happy.

I had a good night's sleep. By the time we arose and went hunting fish, I had a healthier view of loose fly line, the messages from the moon, and my place in the universe. It was as if the bonefish were in one room and I was in another: it was just a matter of opening the door in between. And indeed, one nice, round fish, swimming along where a snapper-filled creek poured onto the flat, came to my fly at the end of the long cast. And I landed him.

A World-Record Dinner

"MUTTON SNAPPER" is hardly a prepossessing title. The sheep, from which the name derives, is not much of an animal. No civilized person deals with him except in chops and stews. To bleat is not to sing out in a commanding baritone; to be sheepish is scarcely to possess a virtue for which civilization rolls out its more impressive carpets.

And it is true that the fish is not at all handsome, with its large and vacant-looking head, its crazy red eye and the haphazard black spot just shy of its tail. Yet its brick-orange flanks and red tail are rather tropical and fine, and for a number of reasons it deserves consideration as major light-tackle game. After you've been incessantly outwitted by the mutton snapper, you cease to emphasize his vaguely doltish exterior.

To begin with, mutton snappers share with the most pursued shallow-water game fish a combination of hair-trigger perceptions. They are wild and spooky, difficult to deceive and very powerful. Taken under optimum conditions, they are as enthralling as any species that haunts the flats.

Like most flats fish, the mutton snapper is primarily a creature of deep water, another individual thread in the ocean system that, following its own particular necessity, crisscrosses the lives and functions of the animals that share its habitat. Which is to say that in looking for one fish you find another—and maybe, in the end, you find it all.

After a long winter's flats fishing, I had naturally acquired a ready facility for recognizing most anything that came along. A flat is a circumscribed habitat so far as larger fish are concerned. The first time I found mutton snappers was while poling for permit on flood tides close to the keys. They were wild fish, hustling around in their curious way and pushing abrupt knuckles of wake in the thin water. Their red tails made them unmistakable.

They seemed so conscious of the skiff that it was hard to see how they might be taken on a fly rod. Besides, they were somewhat harder to find than permit, for example, and they were every bit as alert and quick to flush.

One long-ago day in May, Guy de la Valdene and I began to fish for them in earnest, spurred on from time to time by the sight of brilliant red forks in the air. The fish often seemed hurried, and after we had poled to the spot where we had seen a tail, there would be nothing. Most of the first fish we found were in a grassy basin south of Key West, a shallow place usually good for a few shots at permit. The basin was little more than a declivity in the long-running ocean bank that reaches from just below Key West to the Boca Grande Channel across from the Marquesas.

A long convection buildup of clouds lay along the spine of the keys, like a mirror image of the islands themselves, all the way to Boca Grande, and then scattered in cottony streamers to the west. So we fished in a shadow most of the day, straining to find fish in the turtlegrass. With the leisurely, wan hope that comes of being on a flat at no particular tide, I was poling the skiff. We passed a small depression and suddenly spotted two mutton snappers floating close to the bottom with the antsy, fidgeting look they so often have. Guy made an excellent cast and a fish responded immediately. My hopes sank as it overtook and began to follow the fly with the kind of examining pursuit we had come to associate with one of the permit's more refined refusals. But, with considerable élan, Guy stopped the fly and let it sink to the bottom. The snapper paused behind it at a slight forward tilt and then, in what is to the flats fisherman a thrilling gesture, he tipped over onto his head and tailed, the great, actually wondrous, fork in the air, precisely marking the position of Guy's fly.

I looked toward the stern. Guy was poised, line still slack, rod tip down. He gave the fish three full seconds and I watched him lift the rod, feeling foredoomed that the line would glide back slack. But the rod bowed in a clean gesture toward the fly line, which was inscribed from rod tip to still-tailing fish. Abruptly, the fish was again level in the water, surging away in a globe of wake it pushed before itself. A thin sheet of water stood behind the leader as it sheared the surface.

The first long run ended with the fly pulling free. As Guy reeled in his line and backing, I let the boat drift on the tide toward the little community of stilt houses standing mysteriously in spiderlike shadows off Boca Grande Key. Nearby, an old sail-powered commercial boat rusted on the bank that had claimed it, a long row of black cormorants on its crumbling iron rail.

"Well," said Guy, "I guess they'll take the fly."

By late afternoon Guy was poling. I stood in the "gun seat," as we called the casting deck, trailing my loop of fly line. We zigzagged around in our grassy basin, fishing out the last of the incoming tide and getting shots from time to time at permit. From directly out of the light, a large stingray swam, and in front of it were two large fish, indistinguishably backlit. Because they were with the ray, these were necessarily feeding fish. I had time to roll my trailing loop into the air, make a quick false cast, then throw. The left-hand fish, facing me, veered off and struck. I had him briefly, yet long enough to feel an almost implacable power, enough to burn a finger freeing loose fly line. Since mutton snappers frequently accompanied rays into this basin from deep water, we presumed that is what had taken my fly.

Rays are a common sight on the flats. The game fish seldom follow the pretty spotted eagle rays, whose perfection of shape and movement is beyond quick description. They are dark and beautifully spotted like a fawn or leopard; as a wing is lifted to propel them, the exquisite and creamy ventral surfaces are exposed. Spotted eagle rays mud less than stingrays; their oval mouths seem made for more exact procedures. When the boat is upon them they flush with long perfect sweeps of their wings, and when they are lost to the eye the swirls and turbulence of their surprisingly powerful movements continue to disturb the surface.

The platitudinous stingray with his torpid, carpetlike movements, on the other hand, holds some special interest for game fish. Jacks, snappers, and permit will follow a feeding stingray throughout the tide, using the ray as a kind of stalking horse to scare up small fish and crabs. When a fish is found with a ray, it may be assumed that he is feeding rather than traveling. A suitable presentation must be made.

We knew where to find rays, having often seen them on the soft backsides of banks whose harder edges we fished for permit. Our grandly complex set of banks stretched from the Atlantic to the Gulf of Mexico; we had laboriously laid out its tortuous inner channels and developed some sense of the sequence in which permit used its individual flats and banks. But always we had fished the edges.

Today we wanted to go into the interior of the banks on incoming water and fish well up on the soft bottom. We made the long run from Key West in the early morning, the scattered keys looking deep, wet and green on the slate sea. We passed Mule, Archer, Big and Little Mullet, Cottrell, Barracuda, Man, Woman, Ballast, and Boca Grande, on out past the iron marker, west into the first gut.

The flat was dotted with mudding rays. Guy took the pole and we tracked them down one by one, seeing the fleeting red forks or discovering the nervous snappers too late.

Eventually we found a single large snapper working a stingray. The ray was making such an extensive mud that it seemed unlikely the snapper could even see a fly. In any case, the excitement of watching the tailing fish collaborate with the ray and the measuring in my mind's eye of the breadth of that fork went a long way toward totally eroding my composure.

The mutton snapper was tailing when I cast, and I threw well beyond the ray and retrieved the large fly through the edge of the slick. The tail dropped abruptly, and my first thought was that I had flushed the quarry. Then I saw the wake directly behind my fly and hoped for a take straightaway, but none came. I had to stop the fly and let it go to the bottom, an act that has always felt entirely unnatural to me. The fish tipped up, tail entirely out of the water. I lifted the rod tentatively, then came up tight, and the fish was running.

Water streamed up the leader and the snapper peeled off in a bulge of water tinted by his own brick-red hue. The flat was broad and the snapper failed to clear it to deep water on his first run, at the end of which he turned perpendicular to the line and held there for awhile, implacable as a fire hydrant. Then, with an air of having made the decision himself, he allowed me to retrieve him at his own sullen rate. I began to look around for the net but found Guy one step ahead of me, the big net at parade rest.

My glances for the net were premature. A number of runs remained to be endured. With a fish badly wanted, it is always simple to imagine the hook pulling free, the leader breaking, the dead feeling in the slack rod. Five minutes later the fish was at the boat, succinctly netted by Guy.

It seemed bigger than I expected. A short time after landing the fish we ran into a local guide who weighed our fish: a little over fifteen pounds, the world record on a fly.

That night this best-of-breed was dispatched as follows: deprived of head and innards, he was stuffed with shrimp, shallots, buttered crumbs, parsley, tarragon, and mushrooms, then rinsed down the gullets of hungry anglers with gouts of cold domestic Chablis. I would wish a similar fate upon all world records that are not released at the boat.

The next day Guy took another big fish, this one thirteen pounds, and we began to feel we were getting the hang of it. This fish was given to a Cuban friend at the yard who remembered mutton snappers in the Havana markets. He carried Guy's fish around in a formal march, under the stored hulls, through the dry shed, and out to the carpenter's shop, before giving it the place of honor on the front seat of his pickup.

When we looked for the snappers in the next few days we couldn't find them anywhere. The rays came in on the same tides, but now they were alone. A week or so later the commercial fishermen located the snappers on the 120 contour offshore, 118 feet out of our depth.

Tarpon Hunting

B Y MARCH IN the keys you're thinking of tarpon. The fish have been around in small numbers all winter—not quite fishable numbers, somehow—when bonefish and permit have seemed the more logical subjects of attention. Night trollers and drifters have been taking tarpon in the channels and killing them for advertising purposes; they make the only sign a tourist will believe when hung up at the dock. The shrimp basin in Key West and the harbor always have quantities of fish, but these are domesticated brutes, feeding themselves on the culls of the commercial fishermen and rolling and burbling with the reptilian presence that half-tamed alligators used to have on Florida golf courses. We just stare at them unable to account for their feral behavior.

But usually, sometime in March, while permit fishing or bonefishing on an edge adjacent to deeper water, we spot the first string of migrating tarpon, often juvenile fish up to fifty and sixty pounds. Below Key West they inevitably appear to be travelers, pushing wakes and rolling with their eyes coming out of the water. You are absolutely sure they see you in the skiff, transfixed and watching. The whole mystery of their cycle seems contained in the absolutely deliberate way they travel, deliberate as caribou or spring warblers.

"Mystery" is not an altogether misplaced word regarding tarpon. Much serious research on the fish was dropped when schemes for converting these unparalleled creatures to fertilizer and cat food were abandoned. There seem to be vertical migrations of fish from deep to shallow water, in addition to the fish that appear to be traveling from the south, very probably Central America. But facing a lack of hard information, the angler feels the invitation to elaborate his own sense of the fish's presence. An awareness arises of the distinction between a species like the tarpon and the offshore pelagic fishes with which, as a game fish, the tarpon is often favorably compared. But in the tarpon, the aerodynamic profiles and chameleonic coloring of blue-water fish are replaced by something venerable; they are inshore fish, heavily scaled; they gulp air; and as if to seal their affinity for the land masses of the earth, they require fresh or brackish water to complete their reproductive cycle. They migrate, as many fishes do, and when we touch or intercept these migrations, we sense, subliminally, the dynamism of the earth: tarpon migrate by season, season is a function of planetary movement, and so on. Which is no more than to say you can face bravely those accusations of loafing when you have ruined a month chasing tarpon, racking your brain to understand their secret, sidling lives.

It is quite early in the morning. Not first light, because a higher angle of sun is required to see fish on the dark bottom we are working today. But it is early enough that as we cross Key West the gas stations are being swept down by sleepy attendants with push brooms, and the Cuban men are over on their end of Duval Street drinking cups of their utterly black coffee and eating *bollos*. In the still air you can smell the smoke from City Electric on the other side of town. The groundswell of Latinate noise—that first of all the things that make Key West another country—has not yet started, and as we go up Caroline Street all the side streets running down to the shrimp basin, marked for us because of the great trawling booms sticking up among the old wooden houses, are quiet. The shrimpers always line up first under the awning of the Fisherman's Cafe. No one there yet, though someone is arranging ship-to-shore radios and fathometers in the window of Key West Electronics across the road.

It feels like a tarpon day. Spring tides will give us a good push of water. The wind has swung almost into the full south and it's already hot. Up the keys the yellow mosquito plane will be skimming in over the mangroves, its cloud of spray hanging and settling in the windless air.

There are sponges drying on the balconies of some of the old wooden houses, and as if you might forget that the town is at sea, gulls and frigate birds soar high overhead. Next to Key West Oxygen Service, in an ugly asphalt parking lot that rivals the La Brea tar pits in midsummer, a bonefish skiff sits high on its trailer, bridging the imagination from the immediate downtown of Key West—both an outrageous honky-tonk and a memento of another century—to its gauzy, impossibly complex backcountry surrounds. When you're at the drive-in movie in Key West, watching adult fare with all the other sweating neckers, the column of light from the projectionist's booth is feverish with tropical insects blurring the breasts and buttocks on their way to the screen. At low tide you smell the mangroves and exposed tidal flats nearby, and you're within a mile of sharks that could eat you like a jujube. Once the movie is over and you've hung the speaker back on its post and are driving home, palmetto bugs and land crabs pop under the tires.

This morning, when we get to Garrison Bight, we turn off before the causeway and pull into the dry shed where my boat is stored. Across the bight at the ramp, a skiff is being launched behind a station wagon. I take out the binoculars and look. It's a Hewes guide boat. I see the chairs, the enormous engine, the push pole, the Teleflex steering up in the forward corner, and over me and my companion, Guy de la Valdene, comes that specific competitive tension you feel when another skiff is working the same country. If Saint Francis showed up with a guide boat behind his car, we would rather he stayed home. Every shallow-water fisherman down here is cordial on land, monstrous at sea.

It's not Stu Apte; his skiff has a center console. It's not Bill Curtis; his is yellow, and furthermore he fishes Key West mainly on permit charters. Woody Sexton is in Loggerhead today. Jim Brewer fishes out of a Fibercraft and this is a Hewes. Bob Montgomery has an offshore charter. Cal Cochran? He's supposed to have plenty of fish in his backyard at Marathon. Same with Steve Huff. Page Brown fishes out of a Mako and he would have told us if he was fishing Key West. It would be nice to know who it is so we could avoid running the same pattern. Possibly one of the sports from an angling club, chasing points, mounts, and records.

Richard, the manager of the boatyard, comes out and says, "Morning, Mister Tom," with that special look of philosophical resignation that is the hallmark of the Key West Conch. He climbs up on the forklift and heads into the shed for the skiff. I had it built right here at the yard only last winter, and the first rip of boat fever has not passed off. I love to watch the skiff come out on the fork so I can see the long, precise chine running from stem to bait wells. When the boat emerges, Guy says, "Yes, I know it's beautiful, but please don't say it again."

"I know, but—"

"Don't say it."

Richard rolls the forklift forward onto the concrete dock and lowers the boat into the slick water. To the untutored eye, nothing about the skiff is exceptional: bare nonfouling utility has been taken as far as the mind could create demands for the boat-builder.

The glass hull, brought down bare from the mainland, is white, low, and spare. From the side it looks like a simple linear gesture, the blade of a scimitar or an arrow. It is seventeen-feet, two-inches long, not counting the integral bait wells. The boat was built up from this bare hull with three-quarter-inch marine plywood, the arm-and-a-leg variety. From above, the skiff appears as a succession of bare surfaces over which a fly line can blow without snagging; the forward casting deck is continuous with the broad, flat gunwales. The aft deck is set slightly below the gunwales and, like the casting deck, overhangs the bulkheads by half an inch. Set into the aft deck are the lids of two dry-storage boxes, a battery box, and an insulated icebox. All topside surfaces are blue-gray.

The steering is forward and starboard, with the wheel set horizontal to the deck. Donald Duck's picture is in the hub; a pacifier hangs from the ignition. The throttle and gearshift controls are in a single lever, and there is a tachometer with which I pretend to monitor my engine's performance. I monitored my previous engine's performance, noticing not a thing right up until the idiot light turned on, a plug blew out of a cylinder and the whole thing froze like a tractor in quicksand. There is a toggle on the dash for the power tilt, the 125 Evinrude on the transom being too heavy for hand-tilting as frequently as flats fishing requires.

Guy is at the gas dock, filling the stainless forty-gallon tank under the casting deck. I get a block of ice and put it in the cooler with our lunch and twelve soft drinks. The rods go under the port gunwale, rain gear under the seat. The tackle box goes aboard with a couple dozen of Guy's shock tippets rolled like surgeon's suturing materials. And now we're ready, suddenly feeling the anticipation that is the result of the watching weather, reading the Coast and Geodetic Survey tide book, and listening to all the baloney and general hearsay from guides and other anglers about just where it is the tarpon might be.

Along the starboard gunwale, flexed tight against it, is the big kill gaff with its seven-foot hardwood handle, never to be used on a fish less than a world record, though Guy and I agree that the goal is to train oneself to release that fish, too. But at this early stage of development the gaff still goes along. Someday, when we have grown enough in the fishing, the gaff will be nailed up over my desk, with the stainless-steel gaff head that I wrapped and epoxied myself, a rather handsome old souvenir of barbaric times. On top of the port gunwale, resting in two teak chocks and secured with aviation shock cord, is a seventeen-foot push pole.

Choked and started, the engine idles on the transom; the boat trembles and laps gently against the dock. Guy slips the lines and pushes us away from the dock and I put it in forward, easing us out past the crawfishing boats and two or three sponge boats with tongs laid across the seats, then out into the basin in the low angle of light. Idling along, the boat rides low in the water with radically little freeboard. This is a skiff that will run forty miles an hour in less than a foot of water; offshore, it would be as reassuring as a waterlogged mahogany plank. Its design, derived from numerous other boats but primarily those built by Eddie Geddiman, is a pure, indigenous product of the fishing conditions of the Florida Keys. A fast, shallow-water boat.

We pass under the Garrison Causeway as morning work traffic is beginning to rush overhead. We can smell its exhaust with the same emotions with which we perceive the hamburger stands over by the charter-boat docks. Once on the other side, there's that damned guide boat we saw being launched, up on a plane now and way out at the front edge of a fan of wake. I hear the honking overhead and then a siren as a policeman runs down some sorry gob in a GTO. The brilliantly painted Cuban fishing boats are off to our left, gaudy as Arab smacks; behind them is the institutional slab of the navy bachelor officer quarters, built with the military's usual flair for grace in design.

By now the guide boat has upped and gone. We don't know where he could be and are just hoping that our two skiffs don't go wandering over the ocean making the same stops, tripping over each other as in some mistimed, syncopated dance step.

I run it up to 4500 rpm. The bow lifts, then the stern comes up under the power and kicks the bow down. I slack off to 3600 and we bank and turn through the markers. Key West drops quickly behind and finally clusters at the end of our long arrow of wake. There is a sense of liberation as we run, civilization melting away while another country—mangrove keys, shallows, and open seas—forms around us.

When you pass them, the mangroves empty themselves of cormorants; the birds drop down slapping the water with their wing tips, then shudder as though it had been a close call. The backcountry is full of pelicans, frigate birds, ospreys, bitterns, egrets, and herons, not to speak of that mass of small shorebirds such as plovers, avocets, turnstones, surfbirds, and phalaropes or a number of glamorous "occasionals," as the bird books call them: ibises, eagles, and the utterly incredible roseate spoonbills, the color of a Miami streetwalker's lipstick, that wheel out behind a sandy little key.

We stake the skiff in a small basin near the Northwest Channel. The shrimpers are coming in sporadically from the Gulf of Mexico, trawling booms swaying and diesel engines sounding like farm tractors at this range. We are watching for tarpon moving in the big channel to graze off or shortcut toward the smaller channels shoreward of us. We are staked—that is, tied to the push pole, which is shoved into the bottom along a sandbank that separates the channel from the basin, knowing it will deflect tarpon up into shallow water, where it is hoped they will be moved to take the fly.

We are using the big rod. It carries a No. 12 saltwater taper line and is a very effective rod for fighting a fish, if not exactly a wand to handle. It is powerful, with a second grip just short of the stripping guide. We have rigged a grizzly-and-orange fly on a 3/0 hook, using an 80 pound shock tippet. Ten inches above that, the 12 pound starts and it is this breaking strength that brackets what pressure the angler can put on the fish.

We take turns with the rod, watching for incoming fish that can appear and blow by too quickly if one's alertness flags. Very early on, some tarpon roll in the big channel. They are clearly travelers, though, and will keep right on going—to Mexico, for all we know.

After a bit, a good-size shark glides under the boat. Touched with the rod tip, he moves off in a surge. A little later a hawksbill turtle peers up at us from green water, then, frightened, races off at a speed one doesn't associate with turtles; his front flippers are a blur of effort, while the back ones cross and trail.

Guy stands up on one bait well and looks intently through the binoculars. "The damned guide boat," he reports, "is sitting on our next stop." Sure enough, the skiff is at Mule Key, exactly the place where we would be getting the phase of tide we wanted in another half-hour. "And you know what else?" The answer was posed in the tone of his question.

"Yes," I said ruefully, "he's fighting a fish."

We start looking at our watches. We're not getting any shots on this spot, have been cut off on the next, and when the men in the guide boat are done with their present fish, they very well might make a move to our next stop. Guy looks through the glasses.

"What's he doing?"

"He broke the fish off," Guy said. "There are two of them. They're sitting in the boat to rerig."

"I feel sort of frustrated here," I said.

"I do, too."

"If we don't crank up—I know this is irrational—if we don't crank up I'm afraid we're going to be following him all day long."

"Let's slip the stake," said Guy, "and blow all the way to Big Mullet before he gets his nose out of that tackle box."

I slip the pole out of the bottom, coil the line on the bow, put the pole on its chocks and secure it with the shock cord, then start the engine. I idle into Northwest Channel, then run it up to 5400 rpm, all the way to the stop, so that we are truly flying, running through the banks with a mean tide chop beating our back teeth loose.

We get two-thirds of the way across Northwest Channel and the rival guide sees the push pole on our gunwale and realizes what is happening to him. He quick-hands the rod he's rigging to his companion and starts the engine. Our problem is to hit the run-through channel in the Mule Key bank directly on the nose or else we'll be sawed off by our opponent.

The guide boat wheels around and things are still at the educated-guess stage. From here the bank looks solid and we appear to be heading on a collision course: running aground. Now the other boat is flying full tilt as well, on an interception course. It is sufficiently neck and neck that we'll have to find another place to fish if I'm forced to shut down the engine on the shallow bank and feel my way along for a place to sneak through.

But then a piece of the bank seems to peel away before our eyes and suddenly we spot a solid green creek running through the hard stuff. We cross the bank at 5000 rpm and shut off. In our new silence we hear the drone of the guide boat taper to an idle a short distance behind us.

"You look back," says Guy with a smile. We are both of us pretending to survey the basin as though we hardly knew another boat was anywhere in the country. I turn around and see the two men hunched in the idling boat, staring at us without love.

Alas, it is a far cry from the genial gatherings of anglers on the Test or the Itchen. When flats fishermen run into each other on the water, smiles and jolly waves notwithstanding, it is more like war. When information is asked for, a bum steer quite naturally springs to the lips. I rather suspect, though, that the true scoop on the Test and the Itchen would indicate that those anglers, tweeds and all, have the needle into each other as thoroughly as we do.

Soon the guide boat is running again, the big engine offering what we interpret as a mild trumpet of resignation. While we fully expect to see them at another stop, at the moment, we have the place to ourselves. Meanwhile, it is as quiet as can be, the water lapping gently on the sides of the skiff and pearly summer clouds resting along the horizon.

We tilt the engine and Guy begins to pole. He was a collegiate rower and poles better than I do, with a steady, persistent beat that is perfect for surveying an area when you are not absolutely sure of finding fish. Immediately we begin seeing life; clusters of spotted eagle rays bustle around like nuns, barracudas appear near the boat without ever having been seen in the act of swimming over, small sharks come, stingrays and houndfish. But not, for the moment, any tarpon. We're not talking very much. I feel the successive pushes of the pole and hear its steady rise and fall in the water. Occasionally we glide to a stop and I hear Guy lighting a cigarette behind me, and in a moment the boat surges forward again. The bottom is dark with turtlegrass and we look hard to penetrate its surface. At the same time we try to survey a wide range for rollers and watch the surface for the faint wakes that look like a thumbnail pulled gently along under a sheet of silk. What you see more than anything is movement; the laid-up or sleeping fish are the toughest to spot.

There is a little breeze now and a few horsetail clouds high in the sky, brilliantly white and lacquered. A radiant drop curtain of fuchsia light stands on edge from the Gulf Stream south of us. East across the channels Key West can still be seen, like a white folding ruler, in sections on the blue expanse.

Guy says "tarpon" so quietly that I wonder if he means tarpon in general, but with a certain dread I realize he has spotted fish and a moment later I see a large single swimming with easy sweeps, quite black and bulky looking, moving on a course we will easily intercept. This means it will be entirely up to me. I'm trailing enough line for my false cast and have already begun that rather tense process of trying to figure our range as it is modified by the progress of the skiff in one direction and that of the tarpon in another. That the fish itself looks about as manageable as a Cape buffalo is little help in the finer calculations of the mind. I know from experience that this peaceful meandering fish can offer a scarifying performance, calling into question (if usually theoretically) whether or not the angler is actually safe.

Guy poles to an interception point and turns the skiff in such a way we're at rest by the time the fish is in range. The pole is down and away from where my backcast could foul it. I roll my trailing line into the air, false-cast, shoot, false-cast again, shoot, get my range, and cast. The fly falls acceptably and I strip sharply once to get the fish's attention, continuing with a quick, jerky retrieve. Then the tarpon turns almost imperceptibly: the enthralling, terrifying moment when, unbelievably, the great fish alters its course, however slightly, to take the fly.

Now the fish is tight behind the fly, so close as to seem cross-eyed as he watches and follows it, a dense reptilian presence in pursuit of the streamer. Then comes his slight elevation and gain of speed, the mouth opening, and one last forward surge as the fly vanishes.

I strike him too quickly and feel little more than a bump as the fly comes free. The tarpon muscles about in confusion, making a depth charge of disturbance when he sees the boat, and turns over on himself clearing out. We should be fighting that fish now, one reflects gloomily. Yes, one is inclined to admit, one has blown off a good fish.

To seize the rod with a pontifical sigh and hand me the push pole would be Guy's every right, but he remains in the bow, camera around his neck, ready to record each new faux pas.

I return to my post in the stern with that special determination that surely prepares the angler for more garish errors than those which produced the determination. This is the vicious circle of angling, the iron maiden of a supposedly reflective pursuit.

We pole for a good long time without sighting another fish. We are beginning to lose our tide here, and the time has come to think of another move. We sit down in the skiff, drifting under the dome of unsoiled marine sky. Guy hands me a sandwich and we have our lunch, chewing and ruminating like cattle. We are comfortable enough together that we can fall silent for long periods of time. A flats skiff is a confined place and one in which potentials for irritation are brought to bear as surely as in an arctic cabin, but this comfort of solitude enhanced by companionship is the rarest commodity of angling. Pure solitude, nearly its equal, is rather more available.

Lunchtime, between tides, with the boat drifting before the wind: our piddling inclinations toward philosophy begin to emerge. My recent failure with the fly rod exaggerates my proclivity for higher things. We talk about "the meat bucket." Originally, the term indicated a particular place in the water that held fish in quantity. Then, gradually, it came to mean whole rivers or bays or banks that were good and, finally, states and regions where someone could live who could not live where the country was all shot to hell. In the end, the meat bucket was a situation of mind where everything was going to be okay. When you had gone and messed up your intelligence with whiskey or worse, jacked yourself all out of shape, the meat bucket was the final pie in the sky, the universal trout or steelhead or permit or what-all run, the place where you always threw the perfect loop and never had to live with righthand winds, cold rain, broken homes, failed religion, or long-distance releases.

The meat bucket was Bill Schaadt pantomiming coming up tight on a fifty-pound chinook on the Smith River, saying, "I'm into one!" loudly and reverently. The meat bucket was Russ Chatham making a precise delivery at a hundred feet with a hangover. The meat bucket was Jim Harrison screaming that his knees were buckling and "He's got all my line!" on his first hundred-pound tarpon. The meat bucket was Bob Weddell laying his ear to your Hardy reel that a twelve-pound steelhead was making scream, and saying with rapture, "They're playing our song!" The meat bucket was Bob Tusken's lead-filled Bitch Creek nymphs hitting you in the head when you tried to cast them, Guy de la Valdene skinny-dipping between two guide boats full of glowering anglers at Cutoe Key, Chico Horvath miming a gang bang in his waders on the banks of the Firehole, Rudi Ferris sleeping on the garage floor waiting for "the bite," Woody Sexton looking with horror at the bad housekeeping in my skiff, seawater and Lucky Strike wrappers in the dunnage box. In the end it was all the unreckonable fragments of the sport that became the reference points of an obsession that you called the meat bucket, or, among the archdiocese of angling maniacs you had come to know, more simply, the M.B.

The push pole is secured once more in its chocks; the engine is down and again we are running. This time we head southwest toward Boca Grande Key. The light is so good we can see the stilt houses from where we ride. The spongers browse around in their little boats, standing in the bow and steering the outboard motors with clothesline tied to their waists, raking up sponges like oceanic gardeners.

We are heading for Ballast Key, where we expect to find tarpon and where I have every hope that I will not fall apart and bungle either the cast, the hookup, or the sometimes appalling fight that ensues.

The keys down here have a considerably less swampy character than those above us along the Gulf of Mexico. They are higher and, in some cases, have headlands, beaches, and woods. In the spring these are great meeting places for migrant warblers headed for cool northern forests.

We shut off next to an empty beach of wild palms amid clouds of wheeling white seabirds, and Guy begins poling down the face of Ballast. There is a wash here that raises and drops the skiff. The bottom is rock and packed sand, dotted with sea fans, a desperately difficult place to pole without falling out of the boat. When fish are spotted the poling is so noisy that the tarpon are often spooked, and the boat cannot be easily or quickly positioned for incoming fish. So you abandon yourself to the combinations and hope they come up in your favor.

Almost to Woman Key, we find tarpon: a string of fish, they are traveling on a bright sandy bottom, as distinct as fractured sections of pencil lead.

We are in good position and it is now only a question of waiting for them to come within range. At first we see them from afar, splashing and marking their progress purely in surface movement. At this remove, they are no more scary than a school of feeding jacks.

Then, as they approach, their above-the-surface presence of wakes and splashes is replaced perceptually by the actual sight of fish as specific marine entities, individual torpedoes coming at you. It is hideously unnerving, if you care about fishing.

I like my cast and at the first strip two fish turn out of the string to follow. Then one of them quite aggressively takes the fly and turns off to the side. I continue the strip I started with my left hand until I come up tight. Then, with the butt of the rod in my hip and the rod tip low and to the side, I hit two or three times hard.

The fish is in the air, upside down, making a noise that reminds you of horses, thunderous and final; your eye remembers the long white rip in the ocean. Then a short accelerated run is followed by an end-swapping jump by a game animal that has pulled all the stops. At the third jump the run begins. The fourth jump would be better observed through binoculars; the line no longer even points at the fish.

The tarpon has burned off a hundred fifty yards in such a way that the centrifugal surge is felt in the reel, shuddering my arm. Now he must be followed in the boat. The backing goes onto the reel at the expense of a painful swelling of the forearm and the shirt clinging wetly. After some time the fish is close enough that we can reasonably exert some pressure. Guy keeps the boat parallel to him, silver and brilliant in the deep green water, and the fight goes on, interrupted by inexorable fifty-yard runs from which we patiently recover. Now the fish makes a number of sloshing, head-rattling jumps, after which, in his new weakness, I can turn him slightly on his side.

In a moment he is beside the boat, bright and powerful-looking. I take the pliers and seize the shank of the hook, and with a twist the tarpon is free, though he is slow to realize it. I reach down and hold him for a moment, and I sense in this touch his ocean-traveling might. An instant later he has vanished.

Guy tells me firmly that it's my turn to pole.

Silver King: A Glimpse

W E WERE LOADING LUNCHES, rods, and tackle into my skiff
by the glare of the car's headlights. The weather was deteriorating. I turned to marine weather on the skiff's radio and learned that
we were in a tropical disturbance and that a hurricane plane had been
sent out to view the center of it. George Anderson and Jimbo Meador
were my companions, men who never confuse angling with male bonding: fine dining and gentlemanly hours were out the window. We had
fueled up at the dock instead of siphoning gas from the rental car with
a borrowed garden hose as George and I had done in the past. We were
going to look for tarpon in a new place, a stretch of beach, a deep pass
and broad, sandy banks that looked ready to receive spring migrants.
We had a watermelon in the icebox, sandwiches, a couple of gallons of
water. With George aboard, this would be all there was to eat until
the last drop of gas had been burned looking for fish.

He had tied up a supply of leaders, cautioning us to lubricate our
knots with Chapstick instead of spit. "Use spit and you overheat these
copolymers. You break off a lot of fish." George had been chasing tarpon so long this spring in the keys that he had tendinitis from pulling
up leader knots. Jimbo had never caught a tarpon before and right now
it was the only thing in the world he cared about. I had made a blind
guess that this area would hold fish, but I couldn't be sure.

I eased the skiff up onto a plane. The quartering chop was coming at us from the southeast and the boat pounded up sheets of spray

that stung our faces. I strained into the darkness ahead of the semi-airborne skiff, trying to remember any obstructions that might lie in front of us. "I remember this old boy from Baldhead Island," came Jimbo's Alabama drawl above the wind, "going from Southport across the Cape Fear River headed for Frying Pan Shoals, I guess . . ."

"What about him?" I hollered.

"Well, he hit something in the dark. Found him dead in his skiff." I looked even harder into the blackness ahead, picking out a few lighted markers, a few house lights along the shore, those of a barge and then a tug. We didn't realize what a lee we'd enjoyed until we got around the island. The wind was gusting up to twenty-five knots and prospects for fly-fishing were bleak.

By the time dawn began to break under scudding clouds and gray skies, we were searching for tarpon. George scanned the water intently. I stripped out line and false cast the twelve-weight line when a gust of wind flattened the backcast and sank a size 3/0 tarpon fly into the back of my head, the barb buried well below the skin. "We've got fish!" George shouted, then suggested I kneel on the deck so he could examine the fly. I doubt that he ever took his eye off the fish as he seized the fly with his pliers and yanked it out of my scalp. Next he removed a long file from the pocket of his shorts and retouched the hook point. Stepping back to the casting deck I felt a trickle of blood going down the back of my neck. Later, when I told a friend at the dock how George had helped me, the friend asked, "Does he do children's parties?"

The fish were, in fact, traveling slowly toward us, rolling with open mouths and looking like a nest of enormous baby birds awaiting a worm. I cast to the edge of the school and was able to turn one fish, who then gathered himself under my fly and sucked it down. I hooked him and he burned off for about fifty yards. Out of nowhere, a hammerhead shot through the school looking for my tarpon. I tightened the drag and broke the fish off, leaving the shark sluicing through a piece of empty ocean. Re-rig, start over.

Hours later, we found the most beautiful big school of tarpon under a sky burnished pearl by the tropical wind. They were barely moving, their thick green backs just under the surface and their steeply angled, gunmetal-gray fins piercing the surface in such numbers that, from a distance, they looked like a small island. We eased up on the school and Jimbo cast into them, stripped, and hooked a fish. Stepping backward off the casting deck, he nearly went over the side. There was a circle of white around his eyes as the fish headed for the sky in the first of a series of ocean-bursting jumps. George stood next to Jimbo and coached him to keep a deep bow in the rod and put maximum pressure on the fish. After several hundred-yard runs, the vaulting leaps were reduced to surface lunges and the fish was soon alongside the boat. Jimbo sat down, pouring with sweat. George and I could reimagine our own first tarpon as we looked at the silvery bulk of this great game fish. We knew the euphoria our friend was feeling, and the odd, pure relief at the moment of release; the tarpon eased itself back into the darkness under the skiff and resumed its migration.

While I ran home against the falling tide, a happy Jimbo indulged a reverie about his grandparents, Osceola and Naomi, who fished for gars with whole croakers. "Benny Jones worked for us then and he cut those gar into steaks with an axe and took them to Gertie Pearl to sell in her nightclub." Jimbo smiled, either at the memory or at the Gulf of Mexico; it was hard to say.

But that was a whole other story. George was still looking for a fish.

The Hard Way

I'VE BEEN FISHING for permit for thirty years and I will simply not state how many I've caught. I once lived next to the permit flats and I have caught *some*. Fishing alone, with friends and with guides I have had the meager success that generally must suffice. But each one of those fish has meant so much and the struggle has been so enduring in memory that I know I'll go on trying, however feebly, to catch another for as long as I can cast. Anyone who has ever caught a permit feels the same way. New flies have proven effective and new fisheries have developed in Central and South America. The definitive permit though is still a fish from the keys, where for so long anglers have attempted to make some sense of its habits.

This year I again borrowed a spare room from my brother-in-law in Key West, scattered my clothes and tackle about, established the code for the CNN news loop, bought the *Key West Citizen* and a book of tide tables—in general, raising all the antennae for local orientation and preparing myself for four days of fishing with my friend and guide Gil Drake, who has dedicated forty years of his life to understanding permit. I doubt any other fish could have held his attention for so long. I caught my first one in 1969 and have felt the same unwavering passion ever since.

We left Key West and headed southwest along the Gulf of Mexico flats in a glaring stillness. I stripped off enough line to present the fly and stood in the bow as Gil poled us across what seemed to be a large, vague area of shallows. Until you acquire enough knowledge of flats fishing to convert this lack of definition into the intricate and highly patterned habitat that it actually is, the sport is little more than a series of accidents, and maybe not even that. There are times when it is an impenetrable tedium from which you emerge desperate for home waters.

Because of the stillness of the day, the low mangroves stood mirrored in a chromium glare. Small flocks of migrating gannets passed by, the blinding white of their bodies shining against the green shallows. These excellent birds winter at sea but their advent among the islands in search of nesting sites accompanies spring permit fishing and the first runs of tarpon. Warblers have begun to appear, mangroves to put on new foliage; the storm-clouded waters are clearing and the flats are astir as global heat starts north.

A squadron of permit appeared on the flat, feeding steadily, tips of dorsals and tails making incisions in the slick water, their deep bodies taking on their surroundings as they moved. At a range of about a hundred feet, Gil began to position the skiff. I checked and rechecked the loose fly line on the deck, made my best effort at estimating our closing speed, and raised my rod to begin casting. The fish exploded in the general direction of Mexico.

With this slick, transparent water, we were hoping for intent, feeding fish. Any fish that looked up at all was bound to see us. We hoped, too, for an afternoon breeze that never came. Instead we found through this long day numerous permit, some of very substantial size, but all well out of reach; some simply dematerialized in the glare. They induced futile casting, among other defiant gestures; so when the water jug was empty and the last Cuban sandwich swallowed, we felt as far from catching a permit as we had when we began.

To pass the time, Gil and I talked about how we've changed the way we fish for permit. The flies are heavier and more realistic. We cast much more directly to the fish, as close as possible, instead of the long leads we used to throw out for fear of spooking them. Knowledge of tides and seasons, as well as the extremely specific "trails" used by permit, has improved. Catching a permit on a fly has gone from nearly impossible to extremely difficult. The fish are around in good numbers, thanks to a persistent practice of releasing them. Key West remains at the center of stateside permit fishing, and if the attempt to ban Jet Skis from the White Heron National Wildlife Refuge is successful, we may look to a long future for this exalted fishery.

The breeze picked up the next day and our ability to reach the fish rose accordingly. Of course the wind makes accurate casting harder. And there were fewer fish around. One fish after another refused the fly; several lifted in the chop as I cast, and saw the boat; another tried to tail on the fly but lost it in the grass. And then the sun went down. Afterward, I drove into town to buy sandwiches for the next day at Uncle Garland's. We went from Cuban Mix, to roast pork, to a belly-buster called the "Midnight Special." So far, lunch was providing the only punctuation in the search for fish.

The third day enlarged our sense of struggle. The nice cobia I caught off the back of a stingray early on did little to mitigate our frustration. I had several opportunities through the long hot day and none of them came to anything. You find yourself looking at jet contrails, wondering when they're going to open up Cuba, trying to remember the names of the bartenders at the Anchor Inn on Duval Street in 1971. The light was at a low angle and the cormorants were homeward bound. We crossed a shallow flat at the middle of which was a kind of trough. A nice permit was swimming up the trough with the lazy movements of a feeder; I could just make out the edge of fins around the deep, shadowy body. I made a cast and the fish responded. From his vantage point on the platform, Gil called out suggestions for working the fly. My hope was still low when I felt the slight tightening in my line. I struck and the fish streaked off so fast that I had loose fly line ten feet in the air. Once he was on the reel, a satisfying *whirr* from the drag indicated his progress throughout a long, fast first run. Fighting a permit is pure worry. I worried about my knots and about the line to backing splice I'd done the night before. I worried about the hinging effect, after hours of casting, on the knot at the fly. I worried that fishing with a barbless hook had been taking sportsmanship too far. I desperately wanted to land this fish.

I began to believe the permit was coming to the boat but at the range of sixty feet, he went on another wild run, this one ending in a dogged halt a long way off. Gil kept up our pursuit with the push pole and after a while the fish was a rod's length from the starboard side of the skiff. But when Gil started for the net, the fish shot straight under the boat. I plunged the rod tip underwater to keep the line clear of the hull and waited for the fish to continue his run out the other side. He didn't reappear. My hopes began to vanish. I reeled until the leader was inside the rod and felt the dread certainty that my leader had fouled on one of the trim tabs under the hull. I lay the rod down and hung over the transom. Below the hull, the tail of the permit projected, finning evenly, the leader fouled on the bottom of the boat. I had one chance left. I reached down and tailed the fish and lifted him into the boat with one motion. Caught! I felt the cool solidity and strength of the fish between my hands. After Gil removed the hook and eased the fish back into the water, I watched him surge off into the evening glare.

Tomorrow, we were going permit fishing.

The Sea-Run Fish

I AM PASSIONATELY interested in Atlantic salmon, steelhead, and sea trout, all kin. More than any other fish, they have carried on their backs centuries of hare-brained theories and demented off-season reflection. Yet each of them have created different sport fisheries. Some are quite difficult, others are set up so that the well-heeled may be successful. Atlantic salmon fishers have fallen into several groups, of which the following is an incomplete list.

The Rich, Old and New

Awaiting a bush plane or gut-festooned aluminum outboard boat in flannels, cordovans, a signifying necktie or bowtie and the oddly imprisoning drapery of a J. Press blazer, these men often own the rivers they mean to fish. However, given the tedium of riparian owners' meetings and unpredictable encounters with native peoples who are increasingly armed, if not with Kalishnikovs then with counsel, they sometimes have transferred ownership to the credulous and more recently well off, demonstrating once again how they have hung on to money for so long.

The newly rich aren't discernible from the old by visual references. If they now often own the river, they seem left holding the bag by their predecessors who continue to exercise a sort of *droit du seigneur* through frequent visitation, on the theory that they add tone and continuity to the old camp. With experience at their backs, they can jubilantly outfish the new owners. Only loose tongues as to the odious rise of the Irish or the poor job done by land grant colleges can get their rod privileges pulled. So many of the children of the old rich have given up their club memberships and are now in rehab that this group of anglers is discovering a hard-won humility and is getting along with the new rich better.

Corporate Groups

These are growing more common. Say you're on the edge of the tundra hoping to spot the great skua in his hunt of the arctic seas, when a Gulfstream jet, with the logo of a world-renowned widgetworks on its fuselage, lands in a cloud of jet exhaust, scattering caribou, penguins, and reindeer. The door opens, the stairway descends, and here they come! All hard-driving executives with new gear, they fly well below the radar of annual reports which do not reflect this use of the multimillion dollar aircraft. Shareholders know a G-3's "out there" but they think it's going to merger meetings or is being used as a kind of attack aircraft in hostile takeovers. Retirement-minded investors would be hard-pressed to imagine their benefactors at forty thousand feet, stretching nine-weight flylines in the aisle while *Debbie Does Dallas* plays in the little lounge area where the steward brings peanuts and cocktails, or relaxing in the always-open cockpit where you can sit with the pilots and study the gray seas below while pondering the mystery of salmon.

Time Sharers

Yes, people, they are condominiumizing rivers. With a group of angling writers, I was once invited to a Scottish river as a guest of the syndicate which was preparing to sell shares. I declined to attend, but the very able fishermen who did go fished hard and got one fish in a week between them. I don't think these guests helped the owners' cause, releasing as they did many sardonic reports that poorly concealed their hysterical boredom. Nevertheless, I am told the river "sold out." The new owners, I'm confident, will be made to know that the Atlantic salmon, in addition to being the king of fishes, is a difficult fellow; and that while awaiting the bite it is advisable to reflect upon the advantages of services, cuisine, and clean towels.

Spongers

To this group, which is comprised of guests and writers, I belong. My wife, less flatteringly, says that I am a salmon-steelhead whore. When I have phone calls to return and she prefaces her listing of them with the suggestion that I get into my net stockings and high heels, I know that anadromous fish are at issue. I try to be a good guest. I save up jokes. Sometimes I have to bunk with a nincompoop and am thus made aware of the nature of the hole I have filled. I suppose I don't care, not when I'm on the river. Yet at dinner, there are times when I am keenly aware of a great gulf. Here is where the early bedtime comes in. Still, it's possible to feel the shame that makes the modern hooker call herself a "sex worker" and attempt to start a respectable union like the AFL-CIO. But when streetwalkers go on strike or writers refuse to salmon-fish unless every condition is met, that's entirely less impactful than when airline pilots or teachers go on strike.

The Poacher

I find the rod-and-line fellow rather attractive as an amiable sort of buccaneer, not necessarily with a family to feed but more likely with a lack of sporting opportunity to redress. I used to fish the Blackwater River in Ireland with a local poacher. When we caught a fish we took it straight to the landowner's door, generally an Anglo-Irishman, whom Brendan Behan defined as a Protestant with a horse. We would sell him the fish at a pretty penny, as it was so fresh as to be hard to hang on to, lurching about in our hands. The few shillings thus attained looked remarkably at home on the counter of the local pub, where the miracle of economics transformed them into foamy-headed black stout. In the words of the immortal Flann O'Brien, "A pint of plain is your only man."

And so there you have it. To ascend this ladder in the salmon hierarchy is possible if you have the pluck and aplomb of Becky Sharp or Willie "the Actor" Sutton. Otherwise it is hard to maintain your salmon privileges and you most certainly must study the societal underpinnings of this arcanum or else will be banished to a high-volume bonefish camp in the Tropics, where guides, management, and local idlers alike will abuse you, steal from you, and say unspeakably nasty things about your mother, whom they haven't even met.

Steelheaders fall into a very different set of troupes. The first group, distinctly, are the original California steelheaders emanating from the Bay Area. In fact, wherever you go in steelhead country, there will be a remarkably high number of San Franciscans, because their home fishery has all but disappeared. The situation from which these anglers emerged was unique and will never be seen on earth again. Mostly city dwellers, they had a casting club in Golden Gate Park that for many years was the cutting edge of fly casters' technology and produced almost all of the world's great casters from Jon Tarantino to Steve Rajeff. What can never be replaced is the steelhead run on the Russian River, a short distance outside the city, a run of over thirty-thousand wild, big, beautiful steelhead in public water. And not very far beyond were other great rivers, including the Gualala, Eel, Klamath, Trinity, all of them now pitiful remnants of their original selves. To put yourself in fishing anywhere near this quality would take a very substantial outlay and probably it can no longer be done, even with jets and dollars.

I first arrived on that scene in the middle sixties, and by then it was on the way out. Many of the prominent anglers, exemplified by the peerless Bill Schaadt, had moved on to other things, from king salmon in the Smith and Chetco to stripers in the bay. What remained of the steelhead fishery was in the form of lineups, a string of anglers, shoulder to shoulder, moving at a prescribed pace down the pool. I must admit that I was unprepared for the competitive nature of California steelheading, the heaping of scorn upon one another, the invidious comparisons: it was very much an urban scene transported to the river. But they had certainly brought the craft of fishing fast-sinking shooting heads to its apogee. A more recent wave of Californians have introduced the dead-drifted nymph and Glo Bug techniques, and it is even more deadly than the shooting heads. In my view, both of these methods are inappropriate to today's hammered fisheries. Happily, there are signs of repentance, and more and more steelheaders are returning to the floating line, accepting its limitations just as we accept the net in tennis.

Another group of steelheaders are the "locals." Some of these are anglers of high refinement and exquisitely tuned sensibilities, people like Bill McMillan and the monks of the Skagit who pioneered for North Americans the rediscovery of the double-handed rod. "Locals" are now scattered more or less between Portland, Oregon, and Prince Rupert, British Columbia, and while they have an understandable level of turf consciousness, they are no match for the animals who oversaw the last days of California steelheading. If you are sufficiently self-effacing to soak up a certain amount of social abuse, and willing to accept that locals have utter contempt for any other kind of fishing you might have done, you might eventually be able to spend some time around them. Your next job is to outfish them, which they don't think is possible; and after that, socially speaking, they're fucked. Now you can lay all the bad stuff on them, early rising, persistence, and the rest of it. Locals often fail to see this coming or to realize that nothing is more abhorrent than an out-of-towner with a plan.

The lodge denizens form another group. I am sometimes one of them and I think this is often a good deal. The lodge has the unenviable job of maintaining living facilities, waterborne transport, and guides, as well as some level of communications and emergency medical capability in remote places. The logistics underlying this can resemble what in military parlance is called a task force, but it enables one to arrive with clothes and tackle only, and depart with no responsibilities for maintenance and other ordeals of the off-season, a real luxury. The downside is that it's not cheap and you never know who you'll be bunking with. By and large, you are housed with collegial spirits, some of whom will end up as friends. Still, there is always an element of risk and if you travel long enough to so-called destination angling, you will meet some unparalleled Twinkies and monsters. A Frenchman of our acquaintance had his trip to an Alaskan steelhead camp ruined by some bearded slimeball of a Denver lawyer who didn't like the French and threw rocks into the river ahead of him while he tried to fish. My son and I had the depressed manager of an aluminum plant cast a glum shadow over a promising week of bonefishing. The CEO of a worldwide construction company dominated the services of one steelhead camp and treated the staff with painful rudeness. And of course, a certain amount of regimentation is necessary in the operation of a lodge, and so the usual eccentricities of the dedicated angler are not necessarily appreciated. Real fishing camps don't like to be turned into love nests by philanderers and their dates. Vegans may starve to death, and while the companionship of men is a common thing in such places, drumming and hand-holding are thought to take the mind off the real work at hand.

Mostly, however, it works quite well. Besides, if you are not a "local," some sacrifices must be made. You are free to camp near the fishery or work out little innovations with cheap motels or indulgent friends. If you take this latter course, plan to have plenty of time at your disposal; after arranging all the food, shelter, and transportation, you'll have little time left for fishing. It is easily possible to get in sixty hours of angling in a week of fishing from a lodge or fishing hotel. It takes twice as long to get in the same amount of fishing if you are looking after yourself. Yet both options have their charms and place, and I'd never give up either one. It must be said, though, that it is nearly impossible for the out-of-towner to make much of a hand at Atlantic salmon fishing without lodgelike arrangements. While that is still possible in steelheading, it remains to be seen if the fish themselves can survive these democratic times. Certainly one sees little on steelhead rivers of the patrician ways noted on Atlantic salmon fisheries. In fact, only with the recent advent of double-handed rods have tony sport trappings heretofore unknown among steelheaders become apparent: single malt Scotch, good cigars, tweed caps, and the somewhat random use of the word "heritage." And it is a great relief when these high-falutin' new steelheaders continue to fracture the English language in their customary way, referring to MacAllan whiskey, for example, as "some good shit." And when the Number Six Ring Gauge Upmanns are unavailable, the Lucky Strikes will do quite nicely, thank you.

The final type, a derivative of one already described under Atlantic salmon, and the classification to which I ardently aspire, is the roaming sponge. This angler, grinning, obsequious, excessively convivial, seems too stupid to have a plan. Sleeping in or next to the vehicle in which he arrived, he cuts such an unarresting figure that he has bored in past the ejection level before the locals are on to his game. Too late, they realize he has increased the pressure on their favorite water. I feel it's the duty of the roaming sponge to make up for this to his hosts, especially in good works of river conservation. Consider it a form of life insurance. The sponge must acknowledge his indebtedness and work hard to pay it off. Only when he himself becomes the target of continuous sponging can he be said to have arrived.

However you accomplish it, every salmon, steelhead, or sea trout river you manage to get under your belt is something to be treasured. Obviously, it may be neccessary to put self-esteem to one side or to give remarkably inaccurate impressions of your character to people whom you like. A private agony may ensue—indeed may haunt your old age—but it gets you on the water.

Wesley's River

RECENTLY, and among people we didn't know that well, my eleven-year-old daughter said something that made jaws drop. Having heard the phrase "the F-word," possibly from a potty-mouthed sibling, and assuming in our house that it must mean fishing, she told a group of guests, "All my dad cares about is the F-word." In the astonished silence that followed this showstopper, she added, "When he's not doing it, he's reading about it."

Well, it's true, but I don't like every kind of it, and some of the latest forms of trout fishing as applied in my home state of Montana make me loath to bump into any of its practitioners for fear I will again see the tall man on the banks of Poindexter Slough who was tint-ing his neutral-colored flies with Magic Markers to match the may-flies rising around him. There's always some little rivulet no one else wants: a brushy bend, a pond back from the road under wild apple trees. Go there.

This summer I jumped at the chance to escape the latest teched-out fly-fishing with its whirring splitshot, 7X leaders, and transitional subaqueous lifeforms imitated in experimental carpet fibers. I spent a week in a portageur canoe with Wesley Harrison who was guiding for his fifty-third year on the Grand Cascapedia River of Quebec. A portageur canoe, which is what Wesley called it, "Not a Bonaventure and not a Gaspé," is a broad-bottomed and commodious rivercraft big enough to carry nets and rain gear, light enough to be driven by a small outboard, and lithe enough to slip along quietly in the river from drop to drop, as the precise settings of the killick or anchor are called. This task calls for a bowman, in this case a cheerful young Canadian named Jeff, who deferentially helped Wesley move the boat through its daylong ballet on the rapids and meanders of the great river.

I was warned that if I did not fish seriously the entire time that we were on the river, if I repeatedly misstruck fish or failed to turn over my leader in the wind, Wesley would return to shore and put me off the boat. He has taken more than one sport in early with the recommendation that he go elsewhere to learn to fish before coming back. I was tuned up by such admonitions forty years ago on the Pere Marquette River by my father and my "uncle" Ben Ruhl, and there was a certain solace in having the majesty of a great river presumed as a place of seriousness, if not solemnity. These men grew up before the advent of Jet Skis and other entertainment doodads of this dubious age. The river was your great wife and the very hem of her skirt must be honored.

I rose from bed in the wonderful music of birds in the forest surrounding the camp. To my western ears, the sliding notes of the redstart made a summery mystery. I thought of the warm haze in the skies, the nearness of the sea, the plain thrill of fishing for strong North Atlantic ocean fish whose legend required their seasonal presence in what otherwise was a woodland trout stream. The mind of an angler is stretched to account for this.

I had breakfast with my hosts, who took very good care of me with homemade pastries and jams, tawny local bacon and farm eggs. I gathered my rod and sweater, a book of low-water salmon flies on Patridge Wilson-style hooks, some hard candy to suck on at tense moments, then walked across fields of wild strawberries swept by a warm, balsamic breeze. My only fears were that I would be struck by lightning or that news of a world war would come over the little radio in the kitchen or that Wesley would kick me out of the canoe.

Whereupon, I met the man himself and his bowman, Jeff. Wesley Harrison was a tall, strongly made, and cheerful man in his seventies, flannel sleeves rolled over arms that had poled his canoe thousands of miles. Jeff was that rare, quick-witted youngster without a phony bone in his body. He kept one eye on Wesley to be sure of the right syncopation of effort.

The river was a little dark and I mentioned this to Wesley. He shook his head faintly. "Not good," he said. "The old Indian calls this poison water." We pushed off and started the motor. Sitting in the middle of the canoe, I rested my fingertips on the fly rod I'd laid across the thwarts. I kept one eye on the unscrolling river behind and one on Wesley, whose billed cap shifted left and right as he sized up our course.

We passed another canoe with two Mic Mac men guiding a well-dressed sport who failed to acknowledge our passing. "Oh, that old Indian feller there now," said Wesley, "he's quite comical. I asked him yesterday if they were catching anything and he called out, 'Nothing! Fisherman no good!' He's a comical one, that one."

Wesley shut the engine off and tilted it on the narrow transom. Then he grasped the paddle and, finning it skillfully alongside the ribbed hull, eased us silently downstream to the head of a long pool. "Let 'er go, Jeff," and our bowman dropped the iron.

The canoe settled into a stop as the Grand Cascapedia whispered past the hull. "No shipwrecks with a lad like Jeff," said Wesley. He thought for a moment. "If we drowned, poor old Jeff's girlfriend would be running up and down the riverbank crying her heart out." Jeff was gazing at the sky and I got the feeling this had been going on for a while. Then, to me: "We'll fish this one to the right."

I thought of my host's father sitting one previous evening deep in a chair on the screened porch above the river, reciting Izaak Walton: "When the sun is bright and the moon is right, the fish will bite. Maybe." And the great proverb of my Celtic forebears: "It's better to be lucky than to rise early." All sorts of things run through your mind when you look at new water, especially great new water with all its manifold concealments and prospects. This really was a fine pool, cut out of stone and the roots of old trees, with a long, deep run trembling down its center. The water was tea-dark from alder stain but clearing rapidly.

I cast my fly, a Green Highlander, in widening arcs, extending one arm's length of line per cast until I'd reached my longest distance, all under Wesley's hawklike gaze. I reeled up, thus signaling Wesley to resume his crouch at the gunwale with his paddle and Jeff to lift the killick, as we moved to the next drop. The current here was different and Wesley kept his paddle in the water to control the yaw of the canoe.

We resumed conversation. I had, for example, noticed a small valley that stood at an angle to the river. "Oh, a tough life there," said Wesley, "more mealtimes than meals." I murmured—I thought compassionately—but did catch a glint in Wesley's eye. "There's an old feller up there so poor he has to take his dog down to the gate in a wheelbarrow to bark at strangers."

While I burned a hole in the river looking for a moving shape under my fly, Wesley told me about a Frenchman who lived nearby, a high-spirited man whose wife had twins. When Wesley inquired after the babies, the Frenchman replied in a heavy accent as imitated by Wesley, "Oh, they're cute little things but they're an awful bother."

I fished this drop very slowly, thinking we were in the heart of the matter. Every so often, a seagull flew overhead reminding me of the ocean not so far away but somehow unimaginable in this beautiful sweetwater stream. At the bottom of the pool, the river went through a cleft in the rock and I thought that must be the end of it. Wesley stared at the pool as my line moved on top of the current. "What's the matter, Mr. Salmon? A hot day like this, we'll put you in the cooler and save you the trouble of swimming all the way upstream."

We discussed life in Cascapedia, a small place which, like all places, had most of the world's problems, even drugs. "Fine young fellers," said Wesley, "good fellers get on these drugs. Couple of months they look like they crawled through a knothole." And, of course, nature: "The Old Indian says the hummingbird goes south by getting into the feathers of the wild goose." He looked at me and shrugged: maybe, maybe not. Then he apologized in case the bowman seemed a bit sleepy. Late night with the girlfriend.

At that moment, an astonishing thick shape sucked a section of water down around my fly and I hooked a salmon. My reel screeched at the first run and then with wonderful power as the fish vaulted high over the surface of the pool. I got my fingers inside the arbor of my reel to slow things down, though it was clear the fish wasn't going to be entirely under control for some time. Another jump, this one sideways in a real rip. Without my noticing, the killick had been weighed and now Wesley was slipping us over to the gravel bar opposite the pool. I got out to fight the fish while Wesley readied the net and Jeff slid the canoe ashore. Then the fish jumped again and broke the leader. Wesley walked over to me, looked at my straight rod. For a moment all was silent. Then he asked, quite coolly I thought, "What happened?"

Now he wanted to examine my tackle. The leader, a finely tapered thing, he actively disliked. I buried my own views of leaders and took one of his, tied on another fly, and began fishing the drop below the one where the salmon, a big salmon, had taken my fly. I knew how it was. The next take could be a week away. There was a cavernous silence in the canoe. I resumed my methodical fishing of the drop, cast, lengthen, cast, lengthen. The waterspeed was picking up lower in the pool and required more careful mending of the line. I kept seeing the fish in the air, hearing the erratic screech of the reel, feeling that slump as the dead rod straightened.

But then I hooked another fish, a hard-running ocean-bright fish, and this one, after several wonderful leaps, ended up in Wesley's net, a big deep-hanging silver arc. With a wide smile that confirmed my absolution, Wesley said, "A fresh one, right from the garden!"

We bounced along the river toward camp, tall ferns thrust through the gunwales to announce our fish. When we landed, Wesley shook my hand and said he'd see me in the morning. "You can't leave us now," he told me. "We're well acquainted from fighting the salmon together!"

I headed back up through the banks of wild strawberries considering a nap, the river poems of Michael Drayton, considering the notion that no one owed me anything.

Sur

ABOUT THE TIME the Administration decided that the problem with our economy was all these welfare recipients, I decided it was a sovereign time to go trout fishing in Argentina. The long flight south was half empty, and in order to avoid the in-flight movie, I tried to read the pile of magazines I'd bought at the airport which, whatever their subject, had a movie star on the cover and inside culture, politics, and sports, in pellet form. Reaching into my "hospitality kit" past the little elastic stockings and mouthwash, I produced the eyeshade which, pulled over my head, must have made me look, like the other passengers, as though I was facing a firing squad. Contemplating the rivers that drain the Andes—the Andes!—I quickly slipped off into a pleasant sleep while my feet swelled and my body dehydrated without me, the elastic of the eyeshade embedded in my hair and the soundless film, a stylish getaway item with perky bankables, played on. On a night flight, much is left in the form of the long vapor trails that follow the aircraft in the darkness: imperfect dreams, vanished childhoods, the residue of souls. The envoy, the coke whore, and the basketball player in the Japanese league alike fly from country to country on this basis alone, sharing an armrest, taking only that portion of the overhead bins to which they are really entitled.

Some time later I tottered into the Plaza Hotel in Buenos Aires and in a kind of twilight zone turned on the television set and watched a documentary about a black rock 'n' roll band from Oakland, I think. I tuned in too late to get the name of the band but dully marveled at their apocalyptic music and hyper-athletic antics. Halfway through this thing, the band did an extended "It's Only Rock 'n' Roll" with my contemporaries, the Rolling Stones. I looked on in startled gloom as a rickety and wooden Keith Richards tried to stay out of the way of these rocketing black men. Jagger showed less mother wit in attempting to hold his own with the lead singer, who filled the air around him with chaotic energy. After singing his part of the chorus, Jagger tried to steal away in his patented "Little Red Rooster" strut, yet managed only a melancholy impression of a formaldehyde-injected yard chicken on its very last legs. I watched with subdued dread as Mick and the gang tried to find someplace on the stage to be safe from these exploding rhythm meatballs from California. I knew I was jet-lagged, but it seemed I was witnessing Whitey eat dust as the Third World thundered past. I wondered if this was behind the Administration's fear of welfare recipients, the sense that by hoarding all the items on the Keynesian wish list, we had let Others make off with the things that actually mattered.

By the time I got to the Plaza San Martin, I had my feet under me but was in something of a cloud. Assailed by fishing memories, I sat on a park bench near the memorial to the fallen of the Falklands War, listening to a local fundamentalist harangue the crowd as he walked back and forth with his Bible open in one hand, pulling the collar of his boiled shirt away from his sweating neck with the other. I hadn't known they had guys like him down here. Squads of vivid, provocative females were pouring into the park for a sort of evening paseo. Buenos Aires is known for this, but still it was a shock. I'd flown all night long, napped at the plaza, made a late-afternoon visit to the Basilica de Santissimo Sacramento to think about several people who are gone, and now I dazedly occupied a park bench while this bone-rattling parade of Argentine women passed before me and briefly displaced my preoccupation with sea-run brown trout at the foot of the southernmost Andes where I would be tomorrow. What sort of man would these beauties of the Southern Cross consort with? Well, though I'd been enveloped by their colognes as I made my way down the side-walk, smirking at their Versace knockoffs, the men were more than presentable, and no middle-aged trouter from the States was going to change the balance of power by merely showing up in the plaza. I had a better chance of snagging my waders than a comely dinner compan-ion, and so I returned to my room and slept quietly with my fly rods until it was time to head back to the airport for the trip to Tierra del Fuego.

The Argentines have a refreshing lack of reverence for the won-ders of modern transportation and wandered the aisle of the 727 with rowdy enthusiasm. We stopped at Río Gallegos, the scene of Butch Cassidy and the Sundance Kid's last bank robbery, then at my desti-nation, Ciudad Río Grande. Each time the plane touched down, the Argentines leapt to their feet and, braced in the lurching aisle, flung open the overhead bins in a cascade of sweaters, wine bottles, bird-cages, groceries, diapers, and Styrofoam coolers. When I got off the plane and looked around, I thought I was home in Montana as flakes of sparse snow blew across the sere landscape.

I went out to fish that night, bounding along the roads of Estancia José Menendez in a Russian Lada. At the very point I meant to remark on the similarity of this landscape to my backyard to Mike Leach, my Anglo-Argentine guide, a flight of flamingos lifted up from the pasture, an anomaly like Mike Tyson's voice, and wheeled off to the south. I had never seen such bird life and none of it familiar: Magellan geese, ashy-headed geese, strong-flying creamy-breasted ibises, Southern fulmars and other antipodean seabirds, silver teal, the carnivorous caracaras, numerous falcons, including the aplomados I saw so rarely, big night herons. Patagonian foxes the size of cats looked on modestly from the weeds; and, stratospherically high overhead, Andean con-dors with their twelve-foot wingspreads trained their mystical telem-etry on the ancient plain. Looking across these superb distances to the Andes beyond—a series of almost whimsically odd peaks—it was hard to avoid feeling that the greatest thing man can do for land is to stay off it.

As a sop to the visiting Yanqui, my guide gave me the latest synonyms for "vagina," always handy in the outback. I began to fish. What, ho! I caught a nice big sea trout and went back to the estancia for a midnight supper. Even the wild wind of Tierra del Fuego had ceased to blow. My companions were companionable and Maria José, my cheerful hostess, told me I was a fine fellow to catch a sea-run fish on my first evening. As I lit into roasts and puddings, I was too absorbed to imagine that my luck might already have run out. I was happy to be dining in the middle of the night, contemplating my siesta after the next morning's fishing. We were out of phone and radio contact and I lolled in this vacuum of accountability.

The next morning I was fishing another stretch of the Río Grande, which has a unique quality: it is a prairie river that runs to the sea. The sloughing banks and undercut meanders would be familiar to any western angler, but the seagulls walking its banks and the mighty sea-run trout in its shadowy corners give it a thrilling strangeness. We fished it with shooting heads and the demanding T-300 lines. As yet, the wind was eerily quiet, not a hint of the forty-knot gales that make you rip your underwear trying to cast into it. I cast for four or five hours without a sign of anything and rode back for lunch and an afternoon nap. I wondered if I had appreciated that fish the night before as I should have. The water temperature had dropped into the thirties and fishing had slowed down, though a few fish had been caught elsewhere.

As I retired, several of my Argentine companions, out of the earshot of the peerless Maria José, made sly references to "La Manuela," the local equivalent of Miss Palm. I told them of a friend so in love with La Manuela that he bought her a ring, which he showed everyone and which looked suspiciously like his high school class ring, on his own hand of course. They held up magazine photographs of Argentine bathing beauties at Punta del Este. No, no, I protested, slipping off to my room with a slim volume of Belgian love sonnets. There I stewed about the fishing for a minute before falling asleep.

A few hours later, it was again time to fish. We went to a remote stretch of the river this time, and though the wind stayed down and fish rolled along the grassy bank with heavy surges, none approached my fly. I cast inches from the bank, limiting myself to a single false-cast and covering the water with the care of man laying the last roll of linoleum on earth. A cold, full moon rose above the Andes. "Perhaps, with this moon," said my guide and companion Federico, "they are doing their eating in the middle of the night." I had been casting a four-hundred-grain leadcore for five hours and should have been looking forward to my midnight supper; but I felt rather sunk.

All the jokes at the dinner table, particularly those told by a fellow who caught two fish, were stupid. The next windless day, after eight or nine hours of casting on either side of the siesta and no fish, Maria José remarked that soon my luck must change. I looked at my meal and wondered how people could eat at such a time. The others didn't think the fishing was so bad. Actually, one did. He was having a spell and had asked God to get him out of it. More to the point, he sat down on the bank and told himself to grow up. I thought of the opening of *The Old Man and the Sea*, where the old man is "definitely salao." I remembered a long bad spell on the Dean River in British Columbia. You just keep casting day after day until your hand swells up. That's the only way out. If you're a fisherman, you can't just leave. The other hard luck case told me he just said to himself, "Look, this is crazy. It's not the end of the world."

By that midnight meal I was a vampire pariah of failure, flinging my tackle and waders into my room. Into the vast allure of Maria José I ventured the sentiment, *"Soy un perro infermo!"* I am a sick dog! In years past I might've sucked down the cordials for the pain but now had to content myself with the Belgian couplets and the rising wind to rattle my shutters.

By morning the wind had become a gale, with birds hurtling overhead and grass flattened on the wild pastures. A gaucho went past with his horse and a little dog, all three leaning into the wind. A guanaco appeared beyond a tempting bend of river, a sort of primitive creature that resembles a small camel. With his melodious whinny he seemed a veritable modern novelist. As I watched his splay-footed retreat over the land of the forgotten monster Patagon, a maledroit wobble of his neck in retreat, I thought, "There but for the grace of God go I." The morning ended without a fish.

My siesta was a torment. I actually felt sick. I thought I was throwing strikes but it wasn't working. I was now thinking only of escape, perhaps to the seafood cafes in Buenos Aires. No Belgian couplets for me. I stared at the ceiling of my room and tried to imagine what I had in mind in four decades of throwing a fly line, and counted up how I'd lied to myself about it not really mattering if you actually caught a fish. But these were such great fish, the biggest brown trout in the world. It was a tormenting paradox.

That night I fished the Polo pool with Kevin. He was a guide but first he was a fisherman. He said, "It happens when it happens." As the eventless evening wore on he showed me the lies, the green bank, the fallen bank, the beaver lodge, the gravel bar. It was a readable run. I couldn't daydream, couldn't cast automatically. Each one had to be placed, and the water covered had to be continuous and steady. I released myself into my bad luck and felt a kind of liberating indifference. The moon started to come up and I watched the line straighten on the water. Mend, drift, retrieve, cast again. The full moon rose again. The line flowed across the pool, angle to angle, an easy slide.

And then it stopped. The curve in the line straightened and I hooked a fish, a big fish. The long rod bowed deeply and then the fish soared into the air, wild and rattling in the silver light of the moon, then fell back into the water. I backed up onto my bank and fought the fish downstream. Kevin got in the river with the net but couldn't see the fish. I was trying to tell him where it was when another fish jumped out in the darkness, and Kevin started toward it until I persuaded him that my fish was coming down the bar. Kevin put a flashlight in his mouth and illuminated a circle of black water in front of him. Suddenly the fish was there, its spotted back breaking the surface, then up showering streamers of silver from the mesh of the net. I leapt like a guanaco off the riverbank and danced Kevin around the shallows. "I'm a human!" I shouted. When I held the fish in the water, the hook simply fell from its mouth. He was a big male, over eighteen pounds, the biggest trout I had ever caught, to put it mildly. I stood in the river for a long while, holding him into the current and feeling the increasing strength in a kicking tail I could barely encompass with my grip. To the north, the Aurora Austral raised a curtain of fire in the cold sky. My trout kicked free and continued his journey to the Andes.

THE CONTEXT FOR ANOTHER TRIP to South America was building outside my window: four feet of Montana snow, thirty-five degrees below zero and the very special familial tensions produced by constant confinement and small things gone wrong, a condition of late winter known locally as "the shack nasties." The dogs wanted to go out and then come in and then go back out in some sadistic drill they decided to impose on us. Furthermore, the decorating scheme of my house seemed like the set of *The Little Shop of Horrors:* piled books, windrows of family photographs, unanswered mail, too many chairs, too many rugs, an always-lost cell phone, a channel changer especially lost during football playoffs, every doorknob a coat hanger, every bedpost a clothes peg, the ominous rings of ice around the windows, the mud boots, the snow boots, the coveralls, the mismatched gloves, the face mask in case we'd like to go for a little walk that usually began with one spouse dropping the other off in the car, well upwind so that the elements could shove you a couple of miles back to the house for health purposes. But it was a remark of my wife's that sent me halfway around the world in search of sea-trout "None of my friends has a home so underfurnished as ours," she said.

Hasta la vista, baby.

Flying into Ciudad Río Grande is an arresting experience. The winds are generally gale-force and rather alarming as the plane bucks and surges toward the long tongue of concrete runway. Aircraft already on the field, though tied down and unoccupied, surge against their restraints. Even our big Buenos Aires jet continues to lurch about as the passengers unload. Experienced locals grab tight to everything that is loose—from packages to their hair to the bottoms of their dresses—as they emerge onto the runway, barely able to free up a limb to wave to their friends and relatives waiting inside. One thinks immediately of the uncertain destiny of the fly line liberated in these latitudes. In Tierra del Fuego, anything disturbed is soon airborne. I have fished while the wind carried the gravel off the bars and streamed it into the air. If you smile too often, your lips will hang up on your teeth in the dusty grimace that distinguishes a new angler. The old hands have a sort of pout that's not so much an indicator of mood as an attempt to keep dirt out of the intake.

Sea trout are enigmatic fish to be polite. They are brown trout and therefore subject to that species' notorious moodiness. Sea trout have inflicted compulsive fly changing, night fishing, pool stoning, and further extreme belly crawling measures upon their devotees. That they bring an oceanic rapacity to the smaller world of the river makes them no easier to understand.

We had favorable full moon tides which we thought would send us new waves of fresh fish. Winds which had been gale force for weeks began to abate. There were several generations of fish in the river at the same time, ranging upward from superhot little jacks that would be the crown jewels of a sea-trout fishery anywhere else and ranged on up to sizes we could only dream about. Our host, Estevan, was by now an old friend. "Stevie" loved to fish, knew his river well and kept us amused with his detached sense of humor wherein anglers and all their passions were regarded with the objectivity of a top researcher closeted with a houseful of laboratory mice. If one party returned with six fish while another returned with four, Steve would note, "Six beats four." Later, this took on a life of its own and Stevie was heard to note, "Eighty-one beats eighty" without any explanation as to what this referred, though it had to be something other than fish. For mishaps, he had an elegant South American shrug which meant, "What can you do?" and contained no hint of condescension. The strongest negative emotion he ever revealed was occasioned by an angler who made every mistake possible in order to lose a fish that would have been a world's record. Stevie spent the rest of the day staring through the windshield. When I asked him about his rage, I learned that it wasn't the loss of the great fish that disturbed him, but the fact that the angler had resumed casting after the fish got away. "That," said Stevie, "was too much. I went to my car." This particular vehicle is a low mountain of caked Tierra del Fuegian mud, rod racks on top, rap tapes on the front seat, and a United Colors of Benetton sticker in the rear window. In it we rumble across the grasslands, sheep fleeing before us in flocks, condor shadows racing from the Andes and, to a deep, throbbing beat, the Fugees ordering Chinese food in a New York restaurant. Stevie looks around, takes it all in. "Thirty-seven beats twenty-nine."

My friend Yvon Chouinard believes in going deep. I go deep only when utterly discouraged. When Yvon notices me reacting to the sight of his four-hundred-grain shooting head landing on the surface of the river like a lead cobra in its death throes, he states, "To save the river, first I must destroy it." This Pol Pot–style remark fired my determination. On the Río Grande, he got into a pod of bright sea trout and caught one after another with devasting efficiency. Some yards above him, I held a cold stick and consoled myself with the cries of my success-gorged partner, "*I feel like a shrimper!*" Fish must have been running as their silvery rolls and huge boils were increasing and at last I began hooking up. These fish were beyond big. They were heavy and violent, taking the fly with a brutish malevolence. By the standards of two lifelong fishermen—and we had a hundred years between us—we were so far into the zone that not even approaching night could drive us out.

I put on a small bomber and began working the far grassy bank, enjoying the provocative wake the fly pulled behind it, enjoying the evening as the Darwin Chain receded into the stars. A kind of hypnosis resulted from the long hours of staring into this grasslands river. Suddenly, a fish ran my fly down, making an eight-foot rip in the silky flow of the river. I could feel this one well down into the cork of my double-hander. The fight took us up and down the pool, and the weight I perceived at the end of my line kept my anxiety high. Several times I thought I had the fish landed when it powered out of the shallows. In the end, netting the fish, Stevie said, "Look at those shoulders!" We weighed her in the net and Yvon came up for a look at this twenty-five pound female. To judge by her brilliant silver color and sharp black spots, she was just out of the ocean. I never imagined such a trout belly would ever hang between my two hands. As she swam off the shelf, she pulled a three-foot bow wake. In the sea yesterday, she was now heading to the mountains. We were glad to watch her go.

Yvon noted that with twenty-one sea-run brown trout, nineteen of them over fifteen pounds, we had had the best fishing day we would ever have. We were tired and vaguely stunned. There was also a sense that wherever we'd been going as trout fishermen, we had just gotten there today.

Stevie contemplated all this, let his eye follow a flight of ashy-headed geese passing overhead, and said, "Twenty-one beats twenty."

Fly-Fishing the Evil Empire

I WAS IN HELSINKI, waiting for a plane to Russia, and had walked downtown via the agreeable strand along the Baltic. The coal-fired city electric plant and the old mercantile buildings on the shore looked out on the sparkling water of the northern sea. Numerous watercraft lay along the quay, along with small vendors doing an active trade. Farmers from coastal villages, moored stern-to, set up scales on the transoms of their vessels and sold vegetables. No bellowing, no casbah, no plucking at your sleeve, just quiet northern transactions between women of the city and big-handed, modest farmers. I was fortunate enough to see one of the heroic Finnish icebreakers, languishing now in summertime. I then went into a lovely old enclosed market, over which soared glistening seagulls and big gray and black Finnish crows, to look at the fish—salmon fresh from the sea and trout from Finnish lakes. The red-cheeked fishmonger beamed over his offerings and seemed to understand that I only wished to admire them. Outside, a businessman leaned against a fish stall reading *Firma* by John Grisham. A young man rowed past in a graceful wooden craft, carrying his girlfriend and a pair of gloriously matched boxer dogs whose elevated chins and half-closed eyes suggested a patrician abandonment to the moment.

I crossed through a residential area thronged by many of the young people who had adopted the ubiquitous Brit rocker look, learned from newsclips of soccer riots. Others wore T-shirts dedicated to the Hard

Rock Cafe, the Chicago Bulls, and the darling of northern Europe, Bruce Springsteen. A French youth sported a sweatshirt that read "Soft Ball Coach. Fifth Avenue." Along either side of the street large signs advised the use of condoms, which were depicted as rocket ships heading into the stars. "What a voyage!" you could picture Little Willy saying. "I'd better be aboard!"

Beneath a poster advertising a bungee-jumping meet the following Saturday was an energetic Bolivian band, five young men in black hats and serapes, playing their native music and dancing as a Baltic cloudburst descended over them. Among the dark old buildings, an amalgamated architecture offering the occasional Eastern-looking onion dome, the little band seemed impossibly fresh (I didn't yet know that Jerry Jeff Walker was playing down the street from my hotel that night). And so I subjected them to my bad Spanish. That we should fall upon one another as lost junketeers of the other hemisphere is beyond analysis. The Americas shrank to a neighborhood as we wrote down addresses under the falling rain. Once again their feet began to shuffle, the guitars to throb. The piercing Bolivian flutes seemed to annoy the Europeans. Across the street, a youth with long blond hair looked on, apparently eager to suck in whatever our little concert contained. His T-shirt depicted the skyline of a desert city, palm trees thrusting up through the searchlights. This pictorial matter was surmounted by a desolating, one-word message:

SCREENPLAY

I wanted to see the Helsinki railroad station, designed by Eliel Saarinen, a leading example of the National Romantic style, and one of the most appealing public buildings in the world. I looked at it from the front of the Atheneum. The scale was wonderful; it seemed to belong to a city in the past, to a time whose scale was more human. It was cool and eccentric and appeared to serve the right number of people. I went inside and browsed among the flower sellers and newsstands, and watched the well-behaved people in ticket queues. Directly beyond the main hall with its easygoing throng, doors opened to the platforms. Outside, beautifully cared for trains sat on parallel sets of tracks that shrank away into a distance that implied the half-lit solitudes of the North. Heroic white clouds towered in the blue sky. I sat on an iron-and-wood bench to watch the arrivals and departures, Finns in town to shop, Finns going to their lake cottages. There were seagulls in the railroad station, and from a waste basket next to my bench an amiable crow polished off a package of biscuits.

I wandered around, noting buildings by Alvar Aalto, and among the quirky neighborhoods, the art nouveau apartments and the quickly changing marine skyscape, I attempted to detect the spirit of Sibelius. A Finnish gentleman of a certain age took me aside and made it clear that Suomenlinna, Lorkeasaari, Seurasaari, and the great beach at Phlajasaari should not be missed. I assured him I would follow his advice. When I travel, there is usually one rhapsodic instance of telling myself, "I must learn the language!" It is an innocent impulse, resulting in no action, that I felt not once in Finland where even a sprinkling of words sound monstrously impenetrable. But pictures were another thing. I looked at rooms full of them in the Atheneum. Some of the sculpture was so conservative I thought it was Roman, but the painting was another matter, the best possessing a sequestered domesticity, a pleasing lack of European references.

There are beautiful public gardens behind one of the inlets, slightly unkempt, but every bit as handsome as English gardens sometimes are and as most French gardens are not. These were dominated by vast winter greenhouses that faced modest ponds and beds of replacement plantings. A very old woman, surely more than ninety, had been wheeled up to one of the ponds by her nurse. The nurse, you could see, hoped the old woman would take an interest in a family of mallards feeding on the pond. I noticed one of the woman's legs had been amputated and it was clear she didn't see the ducks. She seemed beyond indifference. Despite the nurse's good intentions, this business with the ducks was insufferable. To grin at such a sight would spell defeat. I admired her refusal and watched this little drama by standing next to a wall of viburnum, pretending to be interested in the ducks myself, and stealing glances at the old woman.

She caught me. I averted my eyes. When I looked again in her direction, she was smiling at me in a sly way. The length of shore along the pond dividing us seemed a tremendous distance. When she gestured for me to come over, I affected a saunter but my guilt betrayed me. Once I reached her side, I saw that her silver hair was in thick, complicated braids. She reached out her hand and I took it. She was from another century and her hand was cool and full of strength. The nurse shrank to the size of a pinhead and the wheelchair seemed poised for flight. We watched the ducks. Our eyes shone. We were flying.

Back to my hotel for a snack of perch soup, reindeer, and cloudberries in the dining room, then dreams of Atlantic salmon in Russia.

THE TARMAC AT MURMANSK was under repair and so our small group of Americans and Brits were diverted into a military airport. We stood near a plywood shanty, awaiting transport to the Soviet helicopter, its red star painted over. It would carry us to sixty-seven degrees north latitude, above the Arctic Circle, to our camp on the Ponoi River, three hundred fifty miles of wild Atlantic salmon water springing from a tundra swamp and flowing to the Barents Sea.

We took the time to inspect the pale blue fighter planes parked in front of bulldozed gravel ledges. They looked like state-of-the-art military equipment, but canvas had been thrown over the canopies, there was at least one flat tire, and they now belonged to a discarded chapter of world politics and other cerebral fevers. The hearty, cheerful Russian woman who was our translator for the moment gestured to the airplanes and said, "You like some military secrets?"

We boarded the enormous helicopter and put in our earplugs, sitting on benches amid duffel bags and rod cases. The Russian crew nodded in that enthusiastic, mute way that says, We don't know your language. The helicopter lifted off to an altitude of about two feet. I looked out the window at the hurricanes of dust stirred by the rotors and then the helicopter roared down the runway like a fixed-wing aircraft and we were on our way.

In very short order, the view from the window was of natural desolation, rolling tundra, wisps of fog, and alarming low-level whiteouts. Even through my earplugs came a vast drumming of power from the helicopter's engine. As I often do when confronted with a barrage of new impressions, I fell asleep, chin on chest, arms dangling between my knees, looking like a chimp defeated by shoelaces.

After an hour and a half, we stopped at a rural airfield and got out to stretch while the crew refueled, a task they performed with cigarettes hanging from their lips. Parked on this airfield were enormous Antonov biplanes built in the 1940s. A Russian mechanic told us that some of them had American engines. These were great cargo-hauling workhorses in Siberia, and from time to time we would see them flying over the tundra at a snail's pace.

We reboarded, joined by a very pretty Russian girl carrying an armload of flowers. She smiled at everyone with the by now familiar mute enthusiasm while the helicopter once again roared into flight. We all mused on this radiant flower of the Russian north, working up theories about her life and dreams. Everything was so wonderfully foreign that later we were slow to acknowledge that she and her husband were our talented cooks from Minnesota.

Landing on a bluff above the Ponoi River, we could see both the camp and the river. The camp was a perfectly organized congeries of white tents of varying sizes, and once I was installed in mine, I briefly stretched out on my bunk to take in that bright sense of nomadic domesticity that a well-appointed tent radiates. In this far north latitude, I knew that the sun would be beaming through my canvas day and night. In one corner was a small Finnish woodstove that in our sustained spell of warmth would never be used.

We were instructed about the angling at the first dinner. An amusing and slightly imperious Englishman named Nicholas Hood picked the first pause between syllables during the official briefing to forgo dessert and descend to the river with his sixteen-foot Spey rod. I was impressed by his deftness in effecting a warp-speed fisherman's exit without getting caught at it. I had just given an old household toast of ours, "Over the lips, over the gums, look out stomach, here it comes." To which Hood responded, "Cerebral lot, your family," and was out of there. One of my companions, Doug Larsen, a superb outdoorsman, remarked that Hood slept with one leg in his waders. I do like to hit the ground running in these situations, but by the time I could disentangle myself Hood was stationed midway down the Home Pool cracking out long casts and covering water like one who'd bent to this work before. "Any sense of the protocol on fishing through here?" I asked.

"Go anywhere you like," he said, far too busy to get into this with me. So I went, I thought, a polite distance below him and began measuring several long casts onto the tea-colored water. English salmon anglers think that our single-handed rods are either ridiculous or inadequate or simply bespeak, especially when combined with baseball hats, the hyperkinetic nature of the people who use them. One Englishman fishing here earlier in the season had stated plainly that he didn't think Americans should be allowed to fish for salmon at all.

At the end of one quiet drift, a salmon took, ran off with the fly line and, well into the backing, cartwheeled into the air. He put up a strong, fast fight and I had to follow him down the beach to a small cover, where I tailed him. I looked down at the salmon, at eight pounds not large, but a wonderful, speckled creature, a pure and ancient product of the Russian arctic. I slipped the barbless hook from the corner of his mouth and this brilliantly precise fish, briefly in my hand, faded like an image on film, into the traveling depths of the Ponoi.

When I returned to my spot on the pool, there was Nicholas Hood, beaming and fishing at once. "Well done!" said Hood, showing surprising pleasure at my catch. As we would see, Hood was much too able a fisherman to be insecure about anyone else's success.

So was the talented Doug Larsen, who fascinated me with his expansion of the carp family: the specklebelly geese so popular among Texas gunners were "sky carp," the grayling with their tall dorsal fins that darted out after our flies were "sail carp." I know he wanted to place the enormous salmonid of the Danube and other waters, the taimen, into some remote branch of the carp family. But it wouldn't go. The Russians who fished for them, he explained with ill-concealed disgust, waited until the taimen made his first jump, then let him have it with a twelve gauge. The only way to land them, really, and one that put aesthetically pleasing or even polite tackle out of the question. You would be at one with the shark assassins of Montauk and other brutes.

Larsen had brought with him our third companion, a Mr. Duff, who listed among his shadowy achievements giving investment tips to

Mookie Blaylock. During the course of our week's angling it became clear to me that the suave, well-dressed, and neatly coiffed Mr. Duff, introduced to me as having warmed up for Atlantic salmon by float-tubing for bluegills on their spawning beds, was a werewolf. His attempts at angling innocence, like asking whether a Near Nuff Frog would be a good fly to tie on, didn't fool me even in the beginning. Something about the space between his eyes put me on the qui vive. He was into fish all week and stood on the banks of the tundra river at evening and howled like a Russian wolf to commemorate each catch. Not quite physically powerful enough to pinch down the barb on his hook, he had other strengths. Setting off on my middle-of-the-night excursions, I realized that when I reached the river, the wolf would be there. In the end, we accepted Mr. Duff as he was, a wild dog, saliva glistening in the corners of his mouth, chastely marcelled waves of blond over his forehead, and a gymnast's ability to fish up to, around, and past you, nipping continuously at your water, as well as an unswerving, otherworldly need to catch the most fish. In other words, a werewolf.

Larsen and I were no longer comfortable with our considerable experience in angling for sea-run fish. We were being hunted down by this bluegill jock and had to exhaust our reserves of strength and knowledge to stay ahead of him. And the Ponoi rewarded him frequently as he gazed reflectively through his cigarette smoke. Incidentally, while he always had a cigarette smoldering between his lips, I never saw him light one. This primeval or eternal cigarette ought to be a final clue for any reader who needs one.

After a few days, you imagine you will be on the river forever. This is one of the few places I have ever fished where salmon seemed truly eminent. One fished with ongoing concentration, trying to throw strikes with every cast, mending as exactly as possible and looking into one's fly book like a fortune teller. The world of the river became more enclosing, the hurtling power of the fish ever more emblematic of the force of wild things and the plenitude of undisturbed nature.

One afternoon I fished in the trance state of repeated casting. The river was so comfortable, I did without my waders. The clouds were long, thin streamers on the northern summer sky. On the cliff face above me was a nest of arctic gyrfalcons; the parents wheeled around the nest bringing food while the pale, fierce youngsters' screams echoed across the canyon.

We had passed a place where villagers had come out and built a fire. The ground was trampled and there were empty vodka bottles and pieces of roasted reindeer tongue. These people had been here for thousands of years and had some old habits, not readily discernible to our eyes.

A fish came with a slow rolling motion and started back to his lie with my Green Highlander in the corner of his mouth. I let him tighten against the reel and raised my rod. And now we were off to the races, me running over the round rocks in wading shoes while the fish cartwheeled in midriver, the thread of Dacron backing streaming after it and the reel making its sublime music. We had earlier noted Nick Hood bounding like Nijinsky behind a fish, springing from stone to stone, and I felt more than the usual pressure to stay on my feet. But this fish was landed in a slick behind boulders. I released him without ever taking him out of the water and he flickered away into the depths of his ancestral river.

While Larsen continued to catch fish steadily, Mr. Duff started showing some of the deficits of his otherworldly auspices. He would catch fish at a good clip, then become possessed by a "hoodoo." By this time we'd become well enough acquainted that he could share some of the special problems he experienced. A hoodoo evidently is some sort of bird, or possibly a bat. When it settles, imperceptibly, between the shoulder blades of the unsuspecting angler, it becomes impossible to catch a fish. One can hook them, but they always get off. So, for a while, the wolf's echoing howls were less frequent. Sport that he was, though, he finally shook it. From time to time the hoodoo settled on Larsen and me. We also began to acquire some of his other problems; by midweek, for example, Larsen had begun taking great pains to precisely part his hair.

That night, when I left the dining tent with its many pleasures of good food, pleasant companionship, and a fly-tying table where the silliest notions may be brought to life, I knew I had to keep fishing. However, it had been a long day and a small nap was in order. Larsen and

Mr. Duff, now transmuted into a bon vivant, refilling drinks, telling golfing stories, and smoking the very cigarette I had watched glow all week long, were in the dining tent for the foreseeable future, actively being corrupted by an English farmer, James Keith, who promoted late-night card games and a general shore-leave atmosphere.

I awakened at three, gulped the cup of cold coffee I'd left beside my bunk, and soon was walking through the sleeping camp with my rod over my shoulder. Snores issued from several tents and the sun was shining merrily. Wagtails had seized this time to hop among the tents looking for food. I noted Hood's sixteen-foot Spey rod leaned up in front of his tent. Hood was in for the evening and there was every chance I would have the magnificent Home Pool—one of the great salmon pools in the world—to myself. I climbed down the path along a small stream, waving away the mosquitoes, and was soon casting out onto the great river and discovering how tired my muscles really were.

I caught a small grilse right away, a silver-bright fish only a day or so from the ocean. Then it got still and not a fish was rolling. Though sleep kept rising through my mind, I was in the river and the casts were still rolling out. About halfway down the pool I felt a jolting strike. After ripping forty yards into my backing, a terrific salmon made one crashing jump after another well out in midriver. Then it started back toward the ocean. I put as deep a bow in the rod as I dared and began following the fish downstream. I beached this big male on a small point, beyond which I might not have been able to follow. His lower jaw was so hooked it had worn a groove in the upper, and I was delighted to make certain this individual could make his contribution to the gene pool. I've always thought that it would be nice after landing an exceptional fish to go straight to bed. And so I did, drifting off in my glowing tent to a dream of sea-run fish.

We stopped in Murmansk for a couple of hours on the way out. I went to a small museum and looked at some wonderful paintings of submarines—some in the open sea, some in remote ocean coves with snow on their decks—and the portraits of their captains. This glimpse of military glory was at sharp odds with the beleaguered municipality all around us. As I looked at the cheerlessly monolithic public housing towering over raw, bulldozed ground, I remembered that the leading cause of domestic fires in Russia is exploding television sets. But no one in the world has wild, open country like the Russians, a possible ace-in-the-hole on a strangling planet. Poets and naturalists could have understood this so much more comprehensively than I did, dragging my fly rod, but without it I probably would never have gotten there or stood for a week in a river coursing through the tundra to the Barents Sea.

Mr. Duff gazed at me with the faintest of smiles as I dragged my duffel to the boarding area. A thin plume of motionless smoke extended vertically from his cigarette. Then he looked away, resuming his scrutiny of a back issue of *Golf Digest*. I was conscious that the weight of my duffel had come to seem tremendously heavy as I dragged it from boarding area to boarding area that day and night, in Murmansk, in Helsinki, in New York, in Salt Lake City. By the time I got to Bozeman, I apparently had become so weak that I could barely lift it. Finally home, I dragged it out of my car like a corpse. I hated it so much that I slept a full day before unpacking it. When I did, beneath the soggy wading shoes and dirty laundry, I found the most beautiful round river rocks and heard a distant howl from the shadows along the far shore of the Ponoi.

Of the Dean

THERE IS A MOMENT when you are waiting to meet a fishing companion, or you may even be by yourself, in the big lobby of a city hotel, the bellhop looking askance at your peculiar luggage, when you question whether this journey will really end in fishing. This is a frequent perception of today's destination angler, whose often conventional background in angling hasn't entirely prepared him for this approach. I like to compare it to the angling hotels that used to exist, especially in the British Isles. The best places, or those I like best, provide food and lodging in places where logistics are tricky and transportation specialized and indispensable. No one should ride a jet boat or bush plane if hiking would get it done. The serious angler, while no Luddite, likes to use the least machinery possible.

Yvon Chouinard, a real adventurer and great alpinist, has built his case on coolheaded coping; being unflappable has seeped into everything he does. Whereas I drag waders and rod tubes and carry-on bags into a corner like a sweating squirrel, Yvon, equally far from home in this Vancouver hotel lobby, merely appears ready to fish. My thought is, the airport shuttle may not go to the bush planes at Vancouver's South Terminal at all. His thought is, we'll get there. The first year we fished the Dean together his tackle and luggage never made it. He expected useful things to turn up and they did. I'd have broken my rosary over this one, spraying beads all over the Wilderness Air Terminal.

This year, we get to the airport, we get to Bella Coola, we get to our little cabin on the Upper Dean, we have all our stuff. I lie on my back the first night pinching a black Egg-Sucking Leech just behind the yellow lead eyes, making it do a little dance on my chest. "If the river comes up," I say, "I'm putting this baby to work."

"Don't be a pawn of the gods." Yvon yawns from his bunk.

The year before, I'd admitted to him my guilt about fishing constantly and going home mostly to do my laundry. I had decided that I had reached the time of life for less hesitancy in diving into the things I had always loved. Of my four fly rods, only one was left. The rest got siwashed on various rivers.

"Your wife has worked hard," Yvon said. "You deserve a vacation."

Our English friend, Bo, working on his duffel bag, suddenly sounds exasperated. "There goes the sodding zipper." Through the haze of jet lag, he contemplates the ruptured duffel. "I bought this from the Iranian next to the office. It was marked down from fourteen quid to eleven. He said I could have it for nine. I said, 'I didn't ask for a discount.' He said, 'Six then.' Good God, the same price as a prawn cocktail!"

On the Dean again. What would I do without this river? I design my year around this week, these pools, these beautiful fish. Dean fish are always appearing in articles about steelhead fishing. These dream slabs are just better-looking than other steelhead. Fishing the Dean puts us in an extreme state of mind that encourages the refashioning of our sport every single day. Last year, after the river blew out, we went to the bottom with evil sea snakes made of marabou feathers and kept catching fish. They couldn't see well enough to run and chugged around like big brown trout, afraid of ramming into something. Each night, one of us would rise to urinate under the stars, only to come back inside having reinvented the wheel of fly-fishing. Twice during the same day, Yvon waded out deep, only to be turned back to the beach by the need to take a leak. He surmised his prostate was gone, a condition associated with shooting heads weighing more than three hundred grains. For diversion, we discussed evil luck in steelheading, when your companion once again has a deep bow in his rod, and you are on cast 62,509 without an eat. You get a terrible feeling: you're not a man anymore. And whenever we can't hook up, we become concerned with our diet, which in this case was high-octane North Canadian all-day power food. "Maybe we've reached the point in life where we ought to travel with our own cook," said Yvon. "On the other hand," he said before I could disagree, "we're still pissing off the porch." He unceasingly takes the balanced view except when noting the fact that the world will soon end.

Across the river, Bo is plying the run with regular strokes of his double-handed rod, single-Spey casting off his right shoulder and then, cigarette at his right hip between thumb and forefinger, watching the drift. One mend and the line comes up tight. Bo sets the hook, takes a last drag off the cigarette, drops it in the water, and witnesses a bright silver steelhead aerialize about sixty yards away while every drop of this mountain water hurries to the Pacific.

This has been a wonderful trip, each of us catching fish at the same rate. Steelhead can be quite unfair. A couple of years ago, one of my friends, a fine fisherman, shared a camp on the Dean with a drunk and disorderly orthopedic surgeon, a blowhard who never cast a straight line or tied any knot but a granny, but he outfished everyone nevertheless. He had been sure these steelhead bums were ninnies before he lit into the joy juice and headed for the river, and now he knew it; he went home to Texas without ever seeing his bubble burst, and every fish a photo opportunity. A twanging Texan in English tweeds is a hard pill to swallow, but my friend chose to consider it a kind of acid test.

My latest view of fishing, one I believe to be the evolutionary product of forty-five years of fly-fishing, is that everything has to do with smoothness, and that constant changing of one's mind results only in not catching fish. Lee Wulff once said, along these lines, that the last thing to change is the fly. I have especially tried to practice this in steelheading, despite the fact that the available methods are all, at any given time, extremely tempting. Still, there is no better way to fish across and down than with a double-handed rod and a floating line;

that's how I fish steelhead. My exception to this is that, for summer fish, I usually switch to a sinking line when the sun is on the water; otherwise it's the floater. Bo fishes the floater, stroke after elegant stroke. Yvon reaches deep into his toolbox and, unless forcibly convinced he's on the wrong track, eases that fast sinking head right on down to the pebbles, further enlarging his prostate by trying to put the fly in a place where not much of a decision is required of the fish. At winter fishing, Yvon is far more realistic than I about how deep one must go, always fishing while I am sometimes merely casting. Sometimes I forget that a loop is an empty thing as compared with a tight line jumping off the surface and showering water drops.

Bo fishes the way he wants to, floating line, sheer, good-natured steadiness. When he fished Tierra del Fuego, he fished the same way, even though some of the dredgers in his camp were having more activity. Though it didn't get to him, it would have gotten to me. I'd have dredged. Bo calls Tierra del Fuego the land of the T-300 and the black Bunny Leech, a place to be fished "no more than once in ten years." He has a tolerant but persistent approach to his fishing. I spent a week with him a year ago on the Sustut River in British Columbia and in all our conversations he neglected to mention that just before we met he had caught an Atlantic salmon of more than fifty pounds. I had to read it in *The Atlantic Salmon Journal*, where it was given the same emphasis ordinarily accorded land speed records.

Therefore, when Yvon and I came upriver to pick up Bo, waiting with Spey rod furled at his side, we responded to his beaming statement, "I just caught a huge fish," as if to a joke. I said, "Are you sure it was a steelhead?" Mildly exasperated, Bo told me that of course it was a steelhead, with a big red stripe down its side. From his description, it was indeed a large fish, well over twenty pounds, a big male that never jumped but crossed the river at will more than once, which made me wonder if I'd inadvertently deprecated his moment of triumph. All steelheaders are cruelly incredulous about fish caught "around the bend," even if the catch was witnessed by Mother Teresa.

There were anglers on the other side of the river. On a steelhead river, fishermen one doesn't know are more or less the enemy; these made a great point of not observing the fight. Later, when Bo bumped into them, they wanted to know if it was a dying chinook he'd snagged. I was beginning to see why he hadn't mentioned the fifty-pounder. On the great rivers, salutes can be rare.

THE FIRST TIME I fished the Dean was more than ten years ago, when El Niño conspired with the gillnetters to reduce the run to a smidgeon. A friend had invited me to join a group of what at first sounded like angling conceived on an imperial scale. It was and that was the problem. The first issue was finding a way to load his cases of wine and foodstuffs, his PVC sewer pipe filled with rods, onto the plane to Bella Coola.

We stayed on a sort of ministeamer in the Dean channel with a helicopter on deck. We had three-wheelers on the shore. We would ride in the helicopter up the river to the pools. Below us, the Totem anglers and other groups of real fishermen jumped up and down and gave us the finger. I cringed in the chopper and was afraid to get out when it landed. Anyway, never mind, there were no fish. So we persuaded the young pilot to take us about the countryside. We descended upon a grizzly bear who jumped up as though to catch a giant moth. Every living thing hated our alien technology. Finally, we went fishing for the lowly pink salmon, caught hundreds, and the pain began to lift. Back at the ship, our leader, a manic-depressive director of angling tours, tied hundreds of Green Butt Skunks, awaiting the run; he could no longer speak. We set crab traps from the side of the ship and pretended that a seafood dinner was all we were after, up the Dean channel with all this gear. The leader tied flies; the helicopter pilot suggested crazy side trips to run up some billable hours; the real fishermen were poised on the beach to kill us; the steelhead waited around the Queen Charlottes without any immediate plans. Finally, a friend and I talked the helicopter pilot into flying us back to Vancouver. No one had the heart to go upriver again, soaring over the countless fists and fingers.

The coast swam by under our plastic bubble windshield. As the sun shone in, the tension began to leave me and I fell asleep. The other anglers joined us at the hotel later that night. When I looked in on them, they were all in their underwear surrounded by Chinese prostitutes; it didn't seem the right time for fish chat.

All winter long I received upward-revised bills from the manic depressive. But that wasn't the true debt. For years, I ran into visitors to this beautiful river. "You were on that goddamn ship?" they'd inquire. "In that helicopter?" Ever since then I've been trying to treat the great river right, trying to get out of its debt. I was the guy who'd farted in church. It would be a year before I was restored to grace.

THE SHOOTING woke us up. A grizzly sow and her three large cubs had come into a camp and they were fighting over something in the yard, cuffing each other into the sides of the cabins. During the rest of the night, the guides tried without luck to send them on their way. Only sunrise sufficed, by which time the four seemed consumed by guilt from their all-night party. They slipped into the brush on the west side of camp and moments later were racing over the round stones of the river bar on their way out of Dodge.

Bears are exhilarating. They'd been around before, and in a previous year had even chewed up the proprietor's airplane. This year, more than a few were dining on spawned-out salmon: an easy life on the verge of winter, but grizzlies did not require ease. If necessary, they would ascend the high, exposed scree slopes and snatch a mountain goat who thought he could safely watch the passing seasons in the valley below. Their rare excursions into camp certainly gave new piquancy to late-night trips to the outhouse. But this was the British Columbian wilderness, and anything that starkly contrasted with our everyday world, like the grizzly bear, the raven, the wolf or the eagle, was welcome. To the robust cubs backing around the cabins with garbage sacks and low growls, I wished to say, Have at it.

I was back on the Dean. As always with anadromous species, the question was whether or not the fish were in. These days, any delay in a run fills the angler with the fear they may not come at all. River fish that are subjected during part of their life cycle to the rapacity and lawlessness of high seas commercial fishing face a serious question of survival.

The steelhead of each river system are separate races, their characteristics derived from deep time in a particular place. Dean River fish are known for their speed and wild strength and they will come to a dry-fly better than other strains, though the depth and clarity and prevailing temperatures of the river itself have much to do with this.

I caught a small fish on the first day, then fell into a long dry spell. Casting from daybreak to sundown, wading deep in clear green water as it sweeps past the gravel bars and wooded foothills, is stirring exercise. And with a floating line, the pleasures of casting are alone fulfilling. But when the second day rolled around and I had not moved a fish, I could feel the slight clench start—the clench that suggests you might never hook another steelhead if you cast for a thousand years. Suspecting I'd sinned against the river with ship and helicopter, I sat down on the rocky abutment of an old logging bridge where tame winter wrens explored for insects in the sunny cracked stones. Half of the second blank day was over and I knew I was pressing. For some reason that's hard to pin down, pressing won't work on steelhead. Covering the water is all-important, but so is fishing out each cast, mending and controlling fly speed. Elements such as fly speed and the look of the fly making its small V-wake on the surface require a delicacy born of composure. An effective steelheader must control his temperament and master his touch through long hours of disappointment and the wild conditions of Northwest coastal rivers.

The boat dropped me off at the top of the most beautiful steelhead run I had ever seen. I had a quiet moment to look the water over and tie on my favorite steelhead fly, the October Caddis. There was a sparkling chute of white, boulder-strewn water at the head that quickly dissipated in the deep, flowing pool. Across from me was a high rock wall covered with lichen. A ribbon falls descended its face and made a circle of bubbles in the water below. The tailout was a shoal of small stones where the entire Dean River rushed toward the sea, accompanied by impossibly rare music.

I began casting, swept away by the radiance of this place and by the high sense of possibility this handsome water suggested to the angler. Very early on, a steelhead rose, took my fly lightly, released it and disappeared. I felt a bit sunk but went on casting in case the fish had not been touched and might move to my fly once more. Four casts later and the fish rose under the sparkling wake of the October Caddis, backed down a yard with it and vanished.

This was too much, and now almost technically hopeless, but since steelhead will come several times before they really line up on the fly, I kept casting. I tried to make the turnovers of the cast such that the fly always landed with a dead straight leader, and this turned out to be the right play because on what must have been close to my last cast, the fish instantly rose and sucked down the fly. I set the hook against a surge of power as the fish fought its way across the pool. It felt so strong that I recognized my chances of landing it weren't particularly good. About halfway down the pool, the fish made a greyhounding jump and scared me with its size. I remember thinking it was like a picture of a jumping steelhead in some old-fashioned fishing book: parallel to the water, amazingly high against the dripping rock wall at the far side of the stream. By the time we reached the tailout, I had to make a stand. If the fish got into the rapids, it was gone. I raised the pressure until the rod was bent into the cork handle. The steelhead held in the pool for several long moments, then yielded. I felt it turn and then miraculously come my way. In a short while, I slid the fish into a small cove and tailed her, for it was a great big hen of about eighteen pounds, a beautiful slab of silver with a cloud of rose down her side. I removed the barbless hook and sent her on her way, daring to believe that I had received absolution.

Snapshots from the Whale

I HAD AS MY GUIDE that day a young man who was perhaps simple, and whom we shall call "Alfred." He lived on the North Shore of the St. Lawrence River where he crabbed, lobstered, fished for cod, and assisted in the building of pretty lapped strake inshore skiffs of about twenty feet. Each December, Alfred told me, he set out for a week or two in the black spruce forest with a sled, a twelve-gauge pump shotgun and several hundred rounds of shells. He traveled in the snowy forest until the ammunition ran out and the sled was piled high with grouse, which he trailed home for his mother to cook and can for the winter. His companion was a small Indian dog of a kind that fascinated me, as they were distributed mostly among the Montaignais who bred them carefully and held on to them against all odds, including the offer of significant monies. These dogs were small and mean, particolored, and loyal only to their owners. Anyone else who came near them, they bit. The First Nations people believed if they weren't mean, they weren't any good. They were too small to do much harm: in fact, as will be seen, they did much good.

The North Shore grouse woods are so densely forested that to blunder around in them hunting grouse is futile. So the hunter who has surmounted the terrific difficulty required in obtaining an Indian dog walks the old loggers' traces while the dog, well out of sight in the forest, hunts. Upon finding a grouse, the little dog flushes him up a tree, then sits at its base barking until the hunter finds him and shoots the bird. On they go, for long days. They are subsistence hunters. The fates of dog and hunter are intertwined, and there is something terrific about the way they work together in order to survive. The little dog never lets the man out of his sight and the man, though impoverished, will not sell the dog to anyone.

My reason for remembering Alfred is more succinct. Every time I hooked a fish—not so often by the way—he would tilt his head back and shout in that North Shore accent which sounds like and might well be Cockney, "Fuck, what sport!" Or as pronounced by him, "Fook, wot spawt!" I don't know who taught him to talk like this, but he put a lot of lung to it while conveying extraordinary merriment and victory. More disconcerting was when I managed to put a fish in the boat and he thundered around in his drooping hip boots, baying *"Blood!"* I picture myself with a genial smile, rod crossed on my lap, waiting for Alfred's fervor to pass, as it soon did, restoring my gifted boatman. I had never seen anyone quite so bonded to his environment, alert to the movement of birds and game, the movements of water, to the possible arrival and positioning of new fish in the river. I imagined I could see his entire life at a glance, steadily weathering in the sometimes terrible seasons of this rind of the North Atlantic to one day disappear into the very minerals of its decaying rock. I could imagine him at the very end, staring into the abyss: "Fook, wot spawt!"

One of our group, who later would try to burn our camp down, stood on the float wearing a blue blazer and a polka dot bow tie, waiting to board the great, battered seaplane. The rest of the group displayed the usual plumage of a fishing party, excepting only the Aussie Akubra hat sometimes seen on spring creeks these days and the cracker camo-jumpsuit of the angler-predator.

On the dock was an old friend of my companions. We reviewed the quality of fishing he'd just had, a usual mood-setting pretrip information plunge. He told us equitably about his catch, about good flies, water levels, the usual. Then he added that this trip, after a couple decades of regular visitation, would be his last. He was dying, he said, and would be gone by the New Year. "Tight lines," he said, without a trace of irony, and boarded his outbound floatplane.

ON MY SEVERAL VISITS to the Whale, I took pictures in my usual haphazard way. My photography has a way of converting the beautiful expanse of wildflowers to a "before" shot from an acne-aid commercial, ocean liners to houseflies, and my daughters' boyfriends to corpse-feeding zombies of some nonstop nightmare. But with the Whale my failures were different. The point-and-shoot camera seemed to choke on the light, leaving my fish-holding companions suspended in the shining fog of Nowhere, having apparently found their quarry in some astral spare parts depot.

This is a riverscape as from an Ingmar Bergman film, a lowering arctic sky, a braided riverbed, small old trees, and high rocky shores streamlined by the centuries of ice, feeder creeks that trotted noisily out of infinite backcountry to fall into the mighty stream. A head-swinging caribou cow appeared among our tents one morning, out of her mind with wolf bites. Close enough to touch, she never seemed to see us, then threw herself into the river and just kept going. The sun fell soon after and we imagined hearing the wolves move through our camp in the dark, still on her trail.

The Whale has been fished sufficiently to have had some of its pools named, although the process is recent enough that you know the people for whom the pools are namesakes. One time I had an indifferent guide, whose preference was to sit on the bank chain-smoking. I was unhappy with him for carelessly knocking a big male salmon off my line with the end of his net. When I caught another fish, a small grilse, standing on a small stone at the edge of the run, he came out, netted it and, in conciliatory fashion, pointed under my feet and said, "Tom's Rock." It looked like every other rock in sight.

MY TENTMATE, Dan, was the most spectacular snorer I've ever encountered. Given that there was no pattern or rythmn to his snoring, it was difficult to get used to it and drift off. One minute he sounded like he was sawing wood, the next like he was drowning in molasses. Each night he said, "Tom, I know I snore. When it gets unbearable, please just wake me up and tell me to roll over." Each night it became unbearable, and each night I said, "*Dan*, wake up and roll over!"

"Why?"

"Because you're snoring very loud."

Each night he took in my claim sleepily and replied, "Oh no, I'm afraid you're mistaken about that." And went back to snoring.

AT PRICE'S POOL you climb down a rocky embankment to where the river drops off immediately, then you must wade out among enormous, deeply submerged boulders to get a bit of casting room. At this rather vigorous range you can reach the mixed slick and broken water at the top of a long break in the river. Between your casting position and this ledge are many submerged rocks and an intricate skein of currents and submerged rips. Salmon will hold right out in this hard water; deep, fast, even broken, it is not too much for them, especially these fierce far-northern fish of the Whale.

I worked methodically through the upper part of this water, as methodically as the broken footing allowed. Sometimes it was necessary to wriggle through the current around a chest-high boulder, then to brace myself against it with one hand and somehow manufacture a cast. The Whale seems to particularly favor the riffled hitch, so it's not just a matter of making a presentation from an awkward place and fishing it out. You have to make sure the fly continues to behave itself, by which I mean proper fly speed.

Of the many views as to how the riffled fly should be fished, I'm certain that finding a personal comfort level is first among equals, comfort level in this case being whatever produces conviction in the angler. I have a clear picture of what I want to see in order to facilitate the feeling that a take is imminent. I want the fly to be breaking the surface in such a way that it pulls a long, narrow, and serpentine V in the water, the effect of a little water snake making its way toward the shore. It does not sparkle along like a mackeral bait; it does not spit water; it does not sink and reappear. Instead, its movement ought to be seductive, which requires mending and back mending, line control to keep it working properly in various current speeds. One of my Whale River companions showed me how on my first trip. Nat demonstrated the whole business on a short line in about ten minutes. Though it's not all that difficult, it does require a high degree of vigilance over long hours to make the most of it. When fishing is slow and one's daydreaming escalates, it is sometimes more agreeable to return to the more conventional across-and-down presentation, the metronomic, two-step consumption of the river.

I found myself at the end of Price's, the end I liked best. Here the fish, having come up through wild white water, pause in currents which have slowed enough to clear, forming a rapid slick. I made a cast and watched the progress of the riffled fly as it swung down and crossed this inviting patch. A salmon surged up under it and stopped without taking the fly. The boil appeared with something of the shape of a large fish visible within it, then opened and rolled into the white water.

Now the slick, until recently one of many spots that offered the mild likeliness of potential holding water throughout the river, was water which specifically held an Atlantic salmon. There was a difference. You feel all your senses training on this bit of moving water. There is a kind of anxiety that comes of knowing an interested fish awaits. The general unlikeliness of good hookups becomes theoretical even before you've had a take. You sense that fate has spoken: You asked for it, here it is. There is a slight feeling of dread.

Any tightening or interruption in the track of the fly results in a missed fish. This can be so subtle that I now asked myself if this boil might have been a take I had somehow fouled up. In this kind of fishing, as with fishing waking flies for steelhead, there is sometimes entirely too much visual information during the take. If the fish doesn't come back, there is reason to assume I have been at fault; if it returns, I'm absolved.

I rested the fish, an interval which for me amounts to a painful refusal to make another cast for as long as I can bear it. Others have borne this same trying experience before me and described the pause as one full cigarette, counting to such-and-such a number, saying rosaries, et cetera. And some good anglers go straight back with the experience-hardened take-it-or-leave-it attitude of tired shopkeepers. No one knows for sure if you should rest the fish. For example, what if the fish moves upriver during the "rest"? All things considered, I think the pause clears the air a bit, freshens the salmon's mind for another look. When you do resume, there is new pressure to make a good cast and a heightened alertness about what could happen. Once the mend has been made, I hold the rod by my side, sometimes circling thumb and forefinger in front of the grip so that the rod swings freely as it tracks the line. I try not to hold my rod in a striking position in case my resolve gets overpowered by a violent and visible take. I am in no position to make a reactive strike. Few things in life are more painful than taking a fly out of the mouth of a salmon or steelhead, especially, as is sometimes the case, after days of fruitless casting. Suddenly the angler is tired of living. If a fish takes, there will be ample opportunity for the tightening and securing lift. In fast, wild, broken rivers with great races of fish like those of the Whale, things will soon enough be out of control; the angler mustn't add to that.

I removed the size 6 Rusty Rat, replaced it with a size 8 Green Highlander, and kept the original length of line. Then it was just a matter of a roll, a pickup, and a cast before I was swinging through the slot again. This time the refusal was slow and considered, amazingly so in view of the current speed. I could more clearly see the size of the fish and knew it much bigger than the typical twelve-pound fish of the Whale. While these salmon are not large, their strength is such that they could drag the twenty-pounders of other rivers to death. In this kind of situation, you are aware that you have unsuccessfully played another card and that the number of remaining cards is uncertain but not unlimited. I made another cast with the Green Highlander and saw no sign of the fish.

I took my time tying on another fly, a Black Bear Green Butt, the fly I would fish if I were reduced to a single pattern, another number 8. While smoking down the imaginary cigarette, I thought about our host Stanley Karbosky, a member of Darby's Rangers who had fought the Nazis virtually hand-to-hand everywhere they went, finally getting machine-gunned himself in Italy. After a long recovery he came to

Labrador as a professional explorer. And it was Stanley who discovered the salmon fishery of the Whale. Such thoughts made my fish-resting lull feel both brief and painless.

I had absolute faith, close to a hunch, in the latest change of fly. I tracked it toward the salmon's lie with hypnotic attention and was expecting the sight of the fish, which came as a leisurely inspection and refusal. The fly trailed on past the fish into the slow water against the bank before I picked it up and held its soggy shape between my thumb and forefinger, feeling that this dismissal was perhaps final. When I tried it again the fish's nonappearance seemed emphatic.

For the first time in this episode I gave in to impatience and a kind of annoyance at my fortunes, and promptly marched through six more fly changes, all the Rats and a small black General Practitioner, without getting another response. My attempts to engage the mind of this fish to my advantage had failed utterly. Using my own tackle, this simple creature had turned the tables and driven me crazy. When I looked out at the river and imagined beginning another long search for a fish, I was discouraged. So, like an old and chronic sinner gazing into his Bible in hopes of a last-minute reconsideration by God, I once more opened my fly book and peered within. It was a phenomenal mess of used and replaced flies, a week's worth of arguing with fate, flies once in neat rows now pointing every which way, some with bits of leader still attached or riffle knots embedded at their throats, heads once lacquer bright now milky and dull, hair-and-feather brainstorms from Norway, Russia, Ireland, Iceland, Scotland, and Canada. All I wanted was one fish to bite one fly!

I took off the ten-pound tippet and tied on a six pound, determined to break out of the chain of logic that was causing me to miss this fish. My next challenge to the fish was to say, "Here's one that's way too small for your feeble eyes." My inspiration was a tiny Blue Charm, an insectlike speck of wizardry on a single hook. I tied it to the tippet with a loop to assure maximum wiggle and cast it much closer to the lie than I'd been doing, so as to subject my small offering to fewer vagaries of current and fewer needs to be mended, fewer chances of refusal.

The fish went straight to it in a deep-bodied swirl. The line tightened on the water before me and I felt the weight in my left hand. I lifted the rod and the fish was hooked. I remember only my conviction that things were completely out of control. I had waded deep among large, submerged boulders, then wedged my feet for the long time I had been casting. Behind me was a high bank. It was not possible to get to better ground where I could control the angles. The fish controlled the angles. I had to just stand there during the violent runs and ferocious, heedless jumps. It seemed marvelous that all the quasi-reasoning behind the fly changes, the fussiness over the line mending and the constant revision of my views as the fish and I moved toward closure would end in such an uproar. Though we were well inland here, this struggle had the power of the northern ocean. I wanted to cry out, Fook! Wot spawt!

Finally I worked the tired fish toward me, leading it through boulders and finally to the beach and the net. She was a powerful, heavy hen not long out of the sea, with subdued black dots on gunmetal and silver. I held her around the tail into the current, feeling the deep curve of belly and fat shoulders, running a finger over the small wonderfully shaped head. When I released her, she picked her way out among the boulders in an unhurried progress to deep water. I found myself at a great altitude yet with all of my life in which to come down. Indeed, as I write this years later, those moments are inescapable and vivid. What a thing to own.

ONE OF THE CHARMS of any trip to the Whale was the annual evening of ghost stories in which the anglers tried to frighten the staff with accounts of the supernatural. Many of the people helping things to go 'round are inhabitants of tiny, unchanged towns on the rocky North Shore of the St. Lawrence. Their traditions and innocence are remarkably preserved, if overlaid by information and images that fly through the air into their TVs and radios. But their culture allows them, it seems, an astonishing ability to suspend disbelief and enjoy stories told them, no matter how implausible. My observation was that *all* the stories were implausible and yet absorbed with a kind of thrilled and grateful credulity. Jackie, one of our country's most outstanding architects, delivered a dizzily mechanical version of the old chestnut *Skyborg*, which had the staff screaming with terror. When our host, who insists on being called "the Benevolent One," came to tell his story, I noted that it was entirely plotless. Clearly the Benevolent One had little in mind when he set out, but in the growing awareness that he had an expectant audience he rather desperately, I thought, began to punch up the plot details of his feeble narrative with the sinisterly intoned repetition of the word "evil." The staff, having listened to his maunderings in wild surmise, now invested all their energy into irrationally reacting to the repitition of this disconnected word. *"Evil,"* came the muttered imprecation, and the kitchen girls, guides, and cook screamed in terror. Few noticed that the Benevolent One had nowhere to go from here and indeed revealed, even through his mutterings, a look of hangdog creative defeat. *"Evil,"* he croaked once more to manifest success.

But the best came last. John, a New York merchant banker, told a ghost story meant to be heightened at its denouement by the sudden rise of flames in the fireplace behind him. Achieved by covertly tossing a snifter of Calvados into the glowing coals, this had the unfortunate effect of introducing real terror into both staff and cynical anglers when the chimney caught fire. Fearing the worst, we all ran outside into the Labrador night. The chimney was blowing sparks and fire fifteen feet into the night sky. Fascinated, I watched John detach himself from these events and take a purely objective interest in what threatened to destroy our housing in the arctic. But gradually the fire subsided and as our evening wound down I heard our architect friend inquire of the Benevolent One, once the chief financial officer of a large movie company, as to the prospects of a film sale of the *Skyborg* project. While the B.O. refrained from throwing cold water on his hopes, he later confided to me that he thought an experienced studio executive like Sherry Lansing would find *Skyborg* "thin."

NAT'S FISH was going berserk, not so much jumping as bouncing angrily off the water as though it were stone. Nat ran down the river past me, reel squalling, and said rather calmly, "Number ten light wire

Icelandic shrimp. I'll never land this fish." But I saw him a while later, bending to make his release. I photographed Nat with his fish but again the pictures came back with the high-latitude hoodoo, and Nat was transformed into an incubus holding a glowing reptile.

At the end of the day we picked up Dr. Hobie, who recited a rather morose saga. He had waded out to a thin spit of bottom where one could barely stand up and hooked the biggest fish he had ever seen on the Whale. After a long battle, the fish was within a rod's length but would not accompany Dr. Hobie ashore, nor could he bring it to hand. At this stalemate, the man and fish faced off for a long time, the latter making no further bid for escape and the former unable to cross the deep trough to the beach. A prolonged acquaintanceship ensued, at the end of which the hook pulled and the fish went on to its next appointment. If there was a philosophical overview to grant this moment of closure, it was lost on Dr. Hobie. Fate had dealt him a heavy blow.

"Fook, wot spawt."

Izaak Walton

THE COMPLEAT ANGLER owes much of its interest to cycles of turbulence, starting with the one within which Walton wrote. In the years shortly before the Restoration, social discord, especially among the literate classes, rose to a genuinely dangerous level. The austerities of Cromwell were undertones of an ominously gathering future. Quietist dreaming, gentleness and contemplation, rusticity and the ceremonies of country life, including fishing, beckoned compellingly. From the Restoration until now, *The Compleat Angler* has been renewed by turmoil, none more conspicuous than the Industrial Revolution, which produced an explosion in the popularity of angling and an idealization of the pastoral life. Its cousins, Gilbert White's *Natural History of Selbourne* and Thoreau's *Walden* and *A Week on the Concord and Merrimack Rivers*, profited similarly. Armchair anglers and the various harried people of the western world have elevated these books to scripture.

Today's faithless reader will be somewhat baffled by the long shelf-life of this unreliable fishing manual, until he realizes that it's not about how to fish but how to be. Of this fact even Walton was unaware; thus its inescapable persuasiveness and the bright, objective picture the author has left of himself, without which all quickly deteriorates into the quaint or, worse, the picturesque.

Anglers, above all, have given this book a long life. Its lore and advice are largely obsolete. Its spiritual origins, drawn contradictorily from pagan and Christian sources, may well appeal to the instinctive pantheism of bucolic dreamers, but anglers tend to be more persistently interested in methods. The greater number of them are less about capturing a truth than capturing a fish and eating it. Still, the sport demands immersion, from air to water, from warm blood to cold, to a view of the racing universe and all its stars through a river's flowing lens.

Two things from Walton seem contemporary: the flies and the recipes. The first, hooks wrapped in bits of silk and songbird wings, reveal a poetic intuition for breaking down the watery walls. The recipes seem the product of avid reflection as to what a predator ought to do with his prey in a manner complimentary to the destiny of each. The sense of a holy sacrifice, benign and undoubted, subtends the making of these innocent meals in honest alehouses where the angler could expect to find "a cleanly room, lavender in the windows, and twenty ballads stuck about the wall."

Walton is one of our principal literary sojourners, with White and Thoreau. By comparison with White, he is unscientific; and by comparison with Thoreau, discursive and confident about his world, less challenging of his fellow man but also less wintry and intolerant.

Walton is the leading player in his own book and is helpless to be otherwise. Unlike the rather alpine, punctilious, and detached Thoreau, or the hyperkinetic White, Walton's persona is one of equitability and such serenity of faith that his journey, in the view of one contemporary, from sepulcher of the Holy Ghost to pinch of Christian dust, spoke of an amiable mortality and rightness on the earth that has been envied by his readers for three-hundred years. But the three do share a conviction that the elements of the natural world are Platonic shadows to be studied in search of eternity, a medium in which man was presumed to float as opposed to sink, as in the present when eternity has been replaced by the abyss.

All three make note of the vast share of their fellows, getting, spending, and laying waste their powers, "men that are condemned to be rich," in Walton's words. He observes, "there be as many miseries beyond riches, as on this side of them." The rich man, he thinks, is like the silkworm which, while seeming to play, is spinning her own bowels and consuming them. One thinks of Thoreau "owning" the farms by knowing them better than their tenants; it is less that the meek shall possess the earth than that "they enjoy what others possess and enjoy not." The subject of *The Compleat Angler* is, really, everyday miracles, friends, a dry, warm house, remembered verse, hope. Walton reserves but one spot for envy and invidious comparison: "I envy not him that eats better meat than I do, nor him that is richer, or that wears better clothes than I do; I envy nobody but him, and him only that catches more fish than I do." I think of gentle, forgiving Anton Chekhov, who could not bear the slightest criticism of his angling.

It is not given to every soul pining for the natural world to be a naturalist. Most of us require a game to play, whether hunting, bird-watching, angling, or sailing, and each create superb opportunities to observe the weather, the land under changing light, the movement of water. In Walton's century, man went from one of God's creations to being an actor who might undertake the management of nature, whose "activism" has grown catastrophically worse ever since. This was part of the seventeenth century uproar, and part of the wedge Puritanism was driving between man and nature. Walton, with his many resonances in Roman literature, is often most serene when he is most medieval. The angler preparing his wiles for the capture of fish is closer to the fish themselves than that husbandman cited by Walton who manages fish ponds as though they were extensions of his farm. The angler's skies are wilder, his cycles as deeply circadian as the migratory birds he encounters during the seasons of the river, his perils on earth less those of a few pinches of Christian dust than a ray of fortuitous light in the heart of creation itself.

Walton tells us that "angling is an art" that, like "mathematics, can never be fully learnt." However, "as no man is born an artist, so no man is born an angler." Therefore, some instruction is in order. In general, fishermen should conduct themselves as "primitive Christians, who were, as most anglers are, quiet men and followers of peace." He excuses his contemporaries slightly by adding that primitive Christians were "such simple men as lived in those times when there were fewer lawyers."

Today's reader, who is himself three-fourths river water, can accept that the world of fish is the "eldest daughter of the creation, the element upon which the Spirit of God did first move," and from whose abundance all living creatures originally proceed. We can live with this. It is close to factual as we currently understand the world. The angler deep in a river intuits his nearness to the primary things of the earth. And Walton tells us that while God spoke to a fish, He never spoke to a beast, and that when He wished to prepare man for a revelation, He first removed him from the hurly-burly of cities so that his mind might be made fit through repose. A learned Spaniard is quoted as saying that "rivers and the inhabitants of the watery element were made for wise men to contemplate and fools to pass by." There are rivers of every kind on earth, he says, even one which runs six days and rests on the Sabbath. And of course, four of the Apostles were fishermen. Walton adds with some prescience that if we would live on herbs, salads, and fish we would be saved from "putrid, shaking, intermittent agues." Indeed, he who has the urge to angle would do well to set out both physically and spiritually, not just with rod and creel but with "wit . . . hope and patience, and a love and propensity to the art itself." The angler has everything to gain. He cannot even lose a fish, "for no man can lose what he never had." But by skill and observation he might still hope for success—first by becoming enough of a naturalist to make a dozen imitation insects to see him through the seasons of the year. And if he is sufficiently skillful and observant, he will own "a jury of flies, likely to betray and condemn all the trouts in the river." He may also carry with him a bag containing the hooks and silks and feathers to imitate unforeseen insects, or to pass time of a "smoking shower" under the nearest sycamore. He is after all seeking a fish "so wholesome that physicians allow him to be eaten by wounded men, or by men in fevers, or by women in childbed." In fact, Walton's fish regularly pass in and out of mythology with their enameled spots and colors, "march together in troops" like the perch; pike hunt like wolves and tench minister to other fish which are ailing. Some are driven by hatred of frogs, others, like the old trout, possess a mournful intelligence and acute sense of mortality. The angler who understands such things may betake himself to steepletops and, with his rod and line, angle for swallows.

Walton reminds us, as we daily remind ourselves, that it is terrible to resolve whether happiness consists in contemplation or in action. But he contents himself in telling the reader "that both of these meet together, and do most properly belong to the most honest, ingenious, quiet and harmless act of angling." Walton anticipates modern riparian conservation in recognizing the need for controlling weirs and illegal nets by public policy with the forceful reservation that "that which is everybody's business is nobody's business." This is, of course, the tragedy of the commons, which deprives us daily of our window on nature.

As modern naturalists have come to do, Walton relates the lives of various fish to all the things around them: weather, insects, worms, the seasonal habits of townspeople, the tides of the sea, the budding and blossoming of plants, the dispersion of cities during plagues or religious wars, the follies of anglers themselves. Most of all, angling, to Walton, is about being fully alive: "I was for that time lifted above earth, and possess'd joys not promised in my birth." Beside rivers, we seldom fill our minds with "fears of many things that will never be." Here, "honest, civil, quiet men" are free from dread.

The angler's day begins humbly, wherein he differentiates between the various dung—cow's, hog's, horse's—as he searches for "a lively, quick, stirring worm," perhaps in old bark from a tanner's yard. Or, competing with crows, he may follow the plough through heaths and greenswards. Finally, he may cultivate a dead cat or raid a wasp nest for its grubs. But his day becomes a soaring event in the mysteries of sea and stream, milkmaids reciting Christopher Marlowe, hours among the "little living creatures with which the sun and summer adorn and beautify the river banks and meadows." At times, *The Compleat Angler* resembles Pliny, or a medieval bestiary, so ravishing and inexplicable does our author find his microcosm. What is this grand beast? "His lips and mouth somewhat yellow; his eyes black as jet; his forehead purple, his feet and hinder parts green, his tail two-forked and black; the whole body stained with a kind of red spots, which run along the neck and shoulder blade, not unlike the form of St. Andrew's cross, or the letter x made thus crosswise, and a white line drawn down his back to his tail; all of which add much beauty to his whole body." Answer: caterpillar.

The technocracy of modern angling has not been conducive to the actual reading of Walton. Today's fisherman may own *The Compleat Angler* as an adornment, but turns to his burgeoning gadgets for real twentieth-century consolation, staring at the forms of fish on the gas plasma screen of his fathometer or applying his micrometer to the nearly invisible copolymers of his leader. In Walton's words, his heart is no longer fitted for quietness and contemplation. Even in the seventeenth century there was need of a handbook for those who would overcome their alienation from nature. In our day, when this condition is almost endemic, it requires a *Silent Spring* or *The End of Nature* to penetrate our stupefaction. The evolution of angling has reached a precipice beyond which the solace, exuberance, and absorption that has sustained fishermen from the beginning will have to come from the way the art is perceived. And here, learned, equitable Izaak Walton, by demonstrating how watchfulness and awe may be taken within from the natural world, has much to tell us; that is, less about how to catch fish than about how to be thankful that we may catch fish. He tells us how to live.

Iceland

THE VOLCANIC LANDSCAPE, the cool fog from the sea . . . this must be Iceland. I walked out of my small hotel on the northeast coast of the country. A large river, milky with glacier melt, flowed beneath us in a shallow canyon. From among a church and some houses around the hotel, an old man appeared, hobbling toward the estuary on ski poles and following a small black hen. They traveled at the same speed and eventually disappeared over a low hill, first the hen, then the old man, to the edge of the sea.

Another fellow came out of the hotel and struck up a conversation with me in English. A nervous sort, he kept touching his lips. "Of fish, I prefer their heads. I go to the store, I buy only the heads. I cook them and then I suck out all the little parts."

That night, I found myself dining with some English salmon anglers. One, a florid, lively man in his sixties, was telling me of the recent death of his mother who had always been bored by salmon fishing. On the Alta, where his father had persuaded her to fish for one day, she caught a fifty-pounder and never fished again. This year, as she lay on her deathbed, her son sat by her side. She was only occasionally conscious as her life ebbed away. At the end, she opened her eyes and gazed at him. "You'll never catch a fifty-pound salmon," she said, and died.

The buildings of the town were rugged and pretty, sided with brightly painted corrugated iron, the windows and fascia of the roofs decorated with fanciful designs and ornamental carpentry. Streetside windows had their shades drawn for privacy but the window ledges were filled with small objects and souvenirs their owners thought might amuse pedestrians: a little horse, a soldier, a German postcard, magnets in the shape of small black-and-white-dogs.

We stopped to bring a couple of salmon to a priest, a popular man, perhaps forty years old, who served four congregations in old rural churches whose steeples pointed sharply in this big green landscape. The stated passion of this man of God is salmon. My host inquired of the priest and his jolly, bohemian-looking wife as to the well-being of their son. Very well, very happy, apparently. Does he still have the bright blue Mohawk haircut? Yes, yes, says the priest. The son was in a band and that, somehow, was part of it—his eyes playing continuously over the bright sea fish. Yes, all the lads in the band had Mohawks, what a lovely fish. Leaving the vicarage, we stopped on a narrow bridge high over the stream to look at salmon. This is still something of a miracle to me, peering from country bridges at sea-run fish. We used to have more of these fish in America than anyone so we killed them off. In the bend below us, a pair of swans sailed along slowly. The fish held steady. Sooner or later, something would make them move decisively but we are not sure what that was. Without doubt, a specific moment of departure would register and the salmon would move up.

I was fishing with a young man named Steini on the Haffjardara River. Early in the season, he had had a hard time being away from the Internet. Most of his friends are out in cyberspace and he hated leaving them. When I first asked him about himself, he said, "I'm a Knicks fan."

We talked about the agonies of Karl Malone, the helplessness of the Utah Jazz in the face of Michael Jordan. I told him about a new biography of Isaiah Thomas just out and he made a note to himself to order it when he got back to Reykjavik.

The evening was quiet, the beautiful river whispering in its rocky banks. We were fishing at a narrows where one of the heroes of the Icelandic sagas, Grettir, a sort of Viking outlaw, leapt the Haffjardara to make his escape. The Sagas, the NBA, the Internet, and the thousand years of trying to catch a salmon, all had the effect—and a rather cheerful one—of making these disparate times seem simultaneous.

Steini, I learned, had just broken up with his girlfriend of many years. In fact, she had driven up to our salmon camp to inform him of her decision. He was unashamed of his sadness and Ludwig, one of the older guides, took him for long walks to discuss his heartbreak. There was in this a human simplicity I noted in many things Icelandic. That and a widespread competence. Ludwig disliked paying expensive gas bills for his old Land Rover, so he plucked out its engine and installed a Nissan diesel. "What about all the fittings between the Japanese engine and the English drivetrain?" I asked.

"We machined new ones."

"Have you had any problems with it?"

"I've only put thirty thousand miles on it since we changed the motor. We'll have to wait and see."

Ludwig and I fished a couple of long and unproductive sessions, one in the pools below a beautiful falls, a beat that had not been fishing well. You stood on a sliver of rock, deep water on either side, and fished to the left and the right. I didn't like the kind of drifts I was getting but the fish were there. The falls was just to my left a few feet and every so often a salmon went airborne burying himself in the curtain of falling water, making it impossible to determine whether he made it over the top or not. Less often a sea-run char, resplendently colored and resembling a huge brook trout, would make the same heedless vault at the face of the falls. They either surmount it or vanish at the base, you never really know which; but the magic of these pure sparks of marine life is acute.

Ludwig was formerly a schoolmaster. He had once been a Fulbright Fellow in the States. He was a fine-boned, handsome, weathered man of around seventy, a fly fisherman and ptarmigan hunter, a driven golfer, and a navigation instructor. When I asked where he sailed, he said Greenland, Poland, different places. He taught for thirty years beneath the glacier to our north, and when he moved into Reykjavik to be near his six grandchildren, he chose a house with a view of the glacier in the distance. Ludwig loved every season of Iceland, even the long, dark winter. The weather seemed to me to be remarkably varied,

impacted as it was by many seas, the Gulf Stream, and the high latitudes. "In Iceland," said Ludwig, "we don't have weather. We have
examples."

Our cook, a man of rare talents who presented us with marvels of
local provender—langoustine, sea fish, lamb with wild icelandic berries, still-living scallops, regal salmon, char gravlax—had a very short
fuse and was intolerant of things going wrong at any level. "Our cook
explodes," said Ludwig, "and we love him for it!"

We took in all this fishing with the blithe purity available only to
those who are guests. We were guests of my dear friend Bo Ivanovic,
who too often impedes his superb angling abilities by looking after
his friends. At a fleeting moment of semidespair, he allowed that it
was hard to "keep these gears and wheels turning." This looking after
other people is trying to anglers as serious as Bo, who are happiest as
solitary wolves intent on enmeshing themselves in the skein of signals
and intuitions that tie the angler to the fish. Triangulating wind, tide,
and weather isn't made easier when a guest totters up in his robe and
asks if you "haven't a little something for the Hershey's squirts." The
social savagery of anglers is such that they are liable to point out to
the very host who has seen to their food, shelter, and transportation
that they've caught more fish than he has. That the host rarely passes
among his guests with a heavy sword is a testament to the depth of
character in those who take on this role. The day comes, however,
when they tire of all this and tell some repeater-sponge, unhappy that
the staff is late in changing his sheets, to go fuck himself. One instance
of this, after years of benevolence, and the host necessarily acquires an
indelible reputation for being a short-fused spoilsport. By now, most
any host realizes that he can turn this to his advantage. Fish camps
are filled with dour former hosts who stay to themselves, read in their
rooms, and push off early for the best pools.

My luck might have been better had I quit plying Ludwig with
questions. I may have been more interested in him than in the fishing.
But I did want to catch a salmon, and he was anxious that I succeed.
We went to a beat where low water had almost brought the current to
a stop. While there were plenty of fish, it was necessary to stay well
back, lengthen and lighten the leader, and strip the fly. As I fished,

Ludwig told me the story of his childhood. His mother died when he was a boy, and since it wasn't possible for his father to keep him at home, he was sent to his uncle's farm on the north coast of Iceland. He and his father missed each other tremendously and throughout Ludwig's boyhood they wrote to each other at every opportunity. His father saved Ludwig's letters and years later gave them to him. We talked about his idea of using them to write a biography of the boy who wrote them, the boy he'd been, tilting this idea around a good bit but then, still without a fish, drifted off into a chat about Pablo Neruda.

A gyrfalcon—Ludwig called it an Icelandic falcon—appeared in the distance, coursing over the land with extraordinary power, certainly the most impressive bird of prey I'd ever seen. It intersected the river about a quarter of a mile above us and turned down the bank, searching. I could hardly believe my luck as the bird rode right down the bank opposite me, the heroic falcon of dreams, a stark medieval-looking raptor, every bit of its shape refined to heraldic extremity. It hovered slightly as it passed us, swept downstream thirty yards or so, banked up to slow the velocity of its turn, then came right up the same bank. Directly in front of me, the falcon crashed into the deep grass of the far bank. A bleak cry issued from some creature and the falcon lifted off with a duckling in its talons. When it soared off to a spire of rock with its prize, the mother duck tumbled into the stream and, pushing her two remaining babies ahead of her with urgent, plaintive, heartbroken quacks, paddled away. Ludwig was holding his heart; it was really very sad. I felt an ache until that night when our English companion, David Hoare, said, "That falcon has a nest of babies to feed."

Time was running out and I didn't have a fish. I suppose that, technically, this was a streak of bad luck, several half-day sessions without a take, when all others in camp were doing fine. I was even mourning the duckling who would never be a duck and its mother, by now down to two babies out of what had probably been eight.

I tied on a Red Francis, a horrible tube fly that looks like a carrot with feelers on one end. Certainly it is a shrimp imitation but fish react to it strangely. Often they ignore it, yet sometimes it seems to drive them crazy. In the last minutes of daylight, the latter obtained. Every fish in the pool ran around violently—if it's supposed to be a shrimp, why would they do that?—and one large fish won the race. A bite! I fought this very strong fish in a most gingerly manner up and down the pool and landed him, a fifteen-pounder, with the clear understanding that my bad luck streak was over. I don't know how you know this, but you do. Ludwig's pent-up emotion boiled over too as he, at about 150 pounds, lifted me, at about 190, into the air with my fourteen-foot double-handed rod waving overhead. I had played this fish so carefully that reviving him took a bit of time. I was glad to be back in a realm in which I greedily put green fish on the bank with all their strength intact. One swipe with the hemostat and they were free to go.

Bo wanted me to see several other rivers in Iceland and took me next to the Selá River in the northeast. There I spent a day with Orri Visguffson who grew up in a family of herring fishermen but now leads the effort to save the North Atlantic salmon. We discussed Halldór Laxness, the great Icelandic novelist, whose *Independent People* everyone in camp seemed to be reading. "He lived just outside Reykjavik," said Orri. "We saw him often. At some point, he began to think of himself as something of a gentleman. There was an ascot tie, a house in the country. But we never held this against him. We had no idea why he did these things. Certainly he had his reasons." In Iceland, a thousand years of freeholding farmers have created a specific culture within what is the world's oldest democracy. Taking on airs is perceived as fabulously exotic and inventive. In Orri's patient account, Laxness's ascot tie floated like an enigmatic object in a surrealist painting.

Orri was helping me to fish a run that was not easily understood. A stream flowed into the main body of the Selá, which flowed from right to left. Orri had me stand in the stream thirty yards above the juncture and cast to the outside of the seam caused by the stream. He continuously adjusted my position with push-pull gestures of his hands and monosyllabic instructions about the cast itself. Then he had me wade across to the inside of the small stream, changing my angle slightly on the drift, then directed me downstream for a cast or two until I had reached the beach, the stream now entering the river to my right and the drift swinging acrosss the seam of the incoming water. Orri watched the drift, indicated that I must move several inches to my left, then returned his hand to its sweater pocket. He nodded solemnly and the salmon struck.

No expression crossed his face as I fought and landed a very hardy eight-pounder fresh from the sea. I released the fish and stood up, enormously pleased with everything. Orri made a forward motion with the back of his hand. "Back to work. This is not a vacation."

Jack Hemingway joined us for a day. He was going from river to river and would continue to do so, he said, until every source of funds had dried up. Few people who were parachuted behind German lines in World War II would've thought to bring a fly rod, but Jack did. To this superficial observer he seemed a happy man. In any case, something contributed to giving a seventy-five-year-old the enthusiasm and energy of a boy. I kept thinking of Jack as "Bumby," the infant of his father's *Moveable Feast*, baby-sat by F. Puss, the cat, and imagining the tempestuous times in which he'd grown up in France among the century's most evolved characters. Jack turned out great, and a real fisherman. He called his most recent birthday party The Son Also Rises. It was a pleasure to sit near one splendid river and talk about others with someone who had lived so fully for such a long time. We each have Gordon setters who are related to one another, so we tried to fathom their clownish and not entirely comprehensible personalities. Jack trained his on chukars in southeastern Washington; I trained mine on huns in Montana sagebrush; but we both could marvel at the cooperation we'd had from these grouse dogs. So many things you love to do: the best combination, we here decided, was hitting the Bulkley in British Columbia for steelhead at daybreak and sundown, and hunting roughed grouse through the day, with a little nap somewhere in between. But now we were in Iceland. How good. How utterly good.

My companions, David, Bo, and Tarquin, were well acquainted with the Selá and went to each day's fishing with a purpose. I went forth rather more uncertainly with my tiny map of the river. Bo usually sent me off with a small disquisition about the nature of my beat, and then I was on my own. It is surprising how much a steady current of the unknown adds to the excitement of angling. One knows what salmon-holding water looks like, generally. But "generally" doesn't get it. In streambed hydrology the fabulous secrets known to the fish are revealed to us only by experience. On the Selá I fished with continuous puzzlement but a kind of excitement that may not survive familiarity. I walked among small bands of sheep very unlike the bland animals of my home country. These are more wild, more alert, and probably haven't had the brains bred out of them in the genetic search of some economic edge like thicker wool or leaner mutton. I clambered down through a shattered granite slope among wildflowers and deep grass to a long run beneath a falls where the sparkling slicks and runs, ledges and boulders, were thrown before me like a complex hand laid down by a demonic bridge player. For a long moment, rod at my side, I was overcome by the richness of the possibilities and the sense that this opportunity could be wasted in the many beckoning but probably fishless runs.

There were wading maneuvers that enabled one to fish the pool which involved following rocky ridges out into the torrent and covering the water in a series of overlapping casts. I'd had good coaching on this from my companions, but a river, once you are out in it, has several kinds of sorcery that make you wonder if you are truly doing things as you should. Further, you cannot follow instructions very well, except to make a beginning, because it shuts off the faint pulse of intuition, the cutting for sign, the queer alertness that comes when you are fishing suitably. Coming to know water offers the prospect of crossing what Conrad called a "shadow line," beyond which a profoundly satisfying sense of where you are, even *what* you are, enters your soul, and you begin to fish with such simplicity and doubtlessness that it is of little consequence if you fail to catch something.

I remember a conversation with Bo when we were in Argentina, the inevitable contention as to what makes a good fisherman. I think Bo had grown tired of anecdotes about effective fishermen, anglers on what the permit wizard Marshall Cutchin calls the "production end" of the sport. Perversely, I took the position that a good fishermen should be an effective catcher of fish, citing, as an analogy, the case of a man at a driven shoot who, though enjoying himself, never hit any-thing. Would we call him a great shot anyway? At this Bo politely folded his tent with the gracious comment, "I see I'm going to lose this one." But actually I prefer his argument. My analogy would have held up if it had concerned hunting rather than shooting, where the feathered targets and other aspects of the malady obscure the very real differences. Shooting has more in common with golf than it does with hunting. There are great hunters who kill very little and great fisher-men who never kill anything. And it's a kind of greatness that not only doesn't require recognition but one which recognition tends to discredit. A great fisherman should strive for equanimity in the face of achievement, and this cannot be trafficked. Probably all who write about fishing should be disqualified, except those who, like Walton, Haig-Brown, Kingsmill-Moore, Aksakov, Plunket-Greene, are cele-brants. Most fishing writers have tried to show us how much smarter they are than everybody else, creating an atmosphere of argument and competitition.

So, having fished my way through the enchantments of perfectly clear Icelandic sea-bound water and the myriad puzzles of its move-ment among submerged boulders and right down to the tailout with-out so much as a pull, I retreated to the shore and took the spit of raised bottom out to the last position in the lower pool. Against the pale yellow of the slabrock in the tail, I could see two small salmon holding. They were at the end of a long cast, and to get a good mend it was necessary to make the cast and then immediately strip the slack for the mend. I covered these fish for a good while, several changes of fly, and failed to interest them. I reeled up and tried to decide if I should fish the run through again or go downstream. Leaving such good-looking water is never easy. As I looked at the two uncoopera-tive grilse in the tailout, I noticed a dark shape slightly below them. I tried to recall if the bottom was discolored there but the shape moved up beside the grilse, which it dwarfed. This was a terrific salmon.

I went right back to what I had been doing on behalf of the smaller fish and had as much success. I was really feeling driven about this, not having seen a fish anything like this one all trip long. There was no shift of movement, no ardent elevation, much less a boil, when my fly crossed the fish's window. I did note that the grilse were getting agitated, either to move up into deeper water or to simply depart this atmosphere of disturbance I'd created. Perhaps the big fish would go with them, too.

I decided to change the game entirely, before I wore out my welcome. I put on a 120-grain sink tip and tied a small, black Madeleine to the end of my leader. I made the same presentation, except that the whole ensemble was a couple of feet down, slap in front of the fish. He moved slightly. I had to assume something had happened, so I lifted the rod and concluded I was either into the fish or the bottom. My line bellied out downstream briefly, then tightened as the leader sheared upstream.

The salmon took a hard left onto the shallows where he made a fearful uproar. I told myself that I would never land this fish and I was right. Ploughing around in the rocks, flinging water everywhere, he liberated himself as decisively as he had taken my silly little fly.

But I was so jubilant because for a moment at least we had agreed about something! It was like a brief truce in a marriage, following which one partner says, "I'm out of here."

I felt oddly content as I sat at the bottom of the canyon, and willing to wait to fish again until I absorbed it all, the idea of the streamlined shapes coming in from the sea, by the moon, by the tide, by whatever mystery, up through the sheep pastures, bent on some eternal genetic strategy. They know what they're doing.

Roderick Haig-Brown

For many who regard angling as the symptom of a way of living rather than a series of mechanical procedures, the writing of Roderick Haig-Brown serves as scripture. He is a genuinely famous fisherman in an era when famous fishermen scramble to name flies and knots after themselves with a self-aggrandizing ardor unknown since the Borgia popes. Anyone who has sat in on the bad-mouth sessions at fly shops and guides' docks will welcome the serene observations of a man more interested in fish than fishing, and in the whole kingdom of nature rather than holding water and hot spots.

There is scarcely an angler so avid that he doesn't spend most of his time not angling; much of the time, because of the inclemency of weather or the demands of work or the inferiority of actuality to fantasy, he pursues his sport in what is called "the armchair." There are any number of armchair anglers who do not own armchairs and often are harmless creatures whose minds have beaten out everything else for the control of things, and for them the theory of the sport lies heavily upon the sport itself.

Others use the armchair, actual or not, selectively, to read and to think, and at such times they're susceptible to the guidance of men who have written about this peerless sport which affects the world's fortunes not at all. For them there is no better place to turn than to the work of Roderick Haig-Brown.

That much has been clear for some time: Haig-Brown's prominence in this fugitive literature is seldom doubted. His series *Fisherman's Spring*, *Summer*, *Fall*, and *Winter* is an integral part of the bookshelf of every angler who thinks about what he is doing. *Measure of the Year*, *Return to the River*, and *The Western Angler* amplify that great series and lead to increasingly broad preoccupations within his sport, until the reader shares with Haig-Brown a continuity of perceptions from the tying of small brilliant flies to the immeasurable and celestial movements of fish in migration. Finally, he accounts for the ways the angler holds his fishing grounds in trust, because I suppose before anything else Haig-Brown is a conservationist.

He lived in Campbell River, British Columbia, and one summer I decided to pay him a visit, not, I hasten to admit, without some trepidation. Sportsman, magistrate, prose stylist of weight, Haig-Brown seems artfully contrived to make me feel in need of a haircut and refurbished credentials. I wanted to withdraw my novels from publication and extirpate the bad words, reduce the number of compliant ladies by as much as 96 percent.

As I winged my way north, the Rockies, in my present mood, unrolled themselves beneath me like skin trouble. A drunk boarded the plane in Spokane and was assigned the seat next to mine. He wore a shiny FBI drip-dry summer suit and a pair of armadillo cowboy boots. He told me he couldn't fly sober and that since he was doing emergency heart surgery in Seattle that afternoon, he certainly didn't have time to drive.

"At three o'clock," he explained, "I'm going to thwack open a guy's heart and I'm already half in the bag. I may have to farm this mother out. I'm totaled." He leaned over to look out the window. "Aw, hell," he said, "I'll end up doing it. It's my dedication. Think about this: when the hero of Kafka's *Metamorphosis* wakes up and discovers that he's been transformed into a giant beetle, the first thing he does is call the office and tell his boss he's going to be delayed. Where are you headed?"

I explained about my trip. As a reply, I suppose, my seatmate told me he'd seen matadors in the Plaza de Toros fighting a giant Coca-Cola bottle as it blew around the arena in the wind; ultimately it was drawn from the ring behind two horses and to resonant olés, just like a recently dispatched bull. "Tell that to your buddy Haig-Brown. He's a writer. He'll like that story."

At this point, my companion confessed that he wasn't a doctor. He was an inventor. He'd come up with an aluminum ring that you put over the exhaust pipe of your automobile; stretched across the ring was a piece of cheesecloth. An antipollution device, it was already patented in twelve states. "If you kick in twenty thousand," he said, "I can let you have half the action when we go public."

"Well, I don't know—"

"I've got a friend who sold ten million smackers' worth of phony stock and got a slap on the wrist from the Securities Commission. This is free enterprise, pal. Shit or get off the pot."

"I just don't see how I—"

"How about your friend Haig-Brown? Maybe he can buy in. Maybe he can stake you and the two of you can split the action. What say?"

In Vancouver, I spent a long layover waiting for the small plane to Campbell River. There were a number of people whose small luggage suggested a weekend trip to Vancouver, an enormously muscular girl in hot pants, and a number of loggers. At one point I looked up from the book I was reading to see a familiar face. It was Roderick Haig-Brown, lost in conversation with the ordinary people around me, many of whom seemed to know him.

I introduced myself and we flew north together, Haig-Brown describing the country of mountain ranges and fjordlike inlets beneath us with great specificity. Everything we saw provoked further instances of his local knowledge, and despite his modesty as a storyteller (and he is a meticulous listener), I was reminded of his two great strengths as a writer: his command of anecdote and his ability to reason.

When I told him about the surgeon-inventor I'd just escaped in Seattle, his chin dropped to his chest and he laughed convulsively. I began to be able to see him.

Haig-Brown is British-born and somehow looks it. Though the great share of his life has been spent as a Canadian, you think instead of the "county" English for whom culture and sport are not mutually exclusive. To say that he is a youthful sixty-three suggests nothing to those who know him; he is neither sixty-three nor, it would seem, any other age. He is rather tall, strong, and thin. He is bald on top, and the prelate's band of hair that he retains sticks out behind like a merganser in profile. His eyes are intent and clear and suggest such seriousness that it is surprising how quickly he laughs. He has a keen appreciation of genuine wit, but will accept whatever is going. He relished *Mister Hulot's Holiday*.

By the time we approached Campbell River, Haig-Brown was at my urging describing his origin as a lay magistrate in the British Columbia courts. "Well, my predecessor as magistrate was a teetotaler and didn't drive an automobile, and he was hard on the loggers and fishermen who were my friends."

We landed on the edge of the forest and Haig-Brown's wife, Ann, met us in a car that said on its bumper: LET'S BLOW UP THE WORLD. WE'LL START WITH AMCHITKA. Both Haig-Browns, I was to see, had a sense of belonging to a distinct political and cultural entity that seems so fresh among Canadians today as to be something of a discovery both for them and for the Americans who see it. The inherent optimism—this was back in the seventies—was in some ways painful for an American to observe. But to a man like Haig-Brown, whose formal judicial district is some ten thousand square miles of mostly wilderness, it would be difficult not to be inspired by the frontier.

The Haig-Browns headed home, caught up in their own talk, while I waited for my rented car. Later Ann Haig-Brown would ask me quite ingenuously, "Isn't Roddy wonderful?"

I was raised two miles from Canada, but this seemed to be the interior. Most of my trip from Vancouver to Campbell River had been over grizzly country, yet in those noble ranges I had seen some of the ugliest clear-cut logging. The woman who brought me my car had moved to Campbell River from the Yukon. My spirits rose. How did she like it here? Very well, she replied, but the shopping plaza in the Yukon was better. I wondered if she would have the same chance to marvel at decimation's speed as we'd had at home.

From the largest seaplane base in North America, poised to survey the roadless country around us, to the hockey hints in the newspaper and the handsome salmon boats with names like *Skeena Cloud* and *Departure Bay* (despite the odd pleasure boat with *Costa Lotsa* on its transom), I knew I was in another country.

During my week of visiting Roderick Haig-Brown, at some inconvenience to his intensely filled schedule, I began to see that I had little chance of discovering that precise suppurating angst, that dismal or craven psychosis so indispensable to the author of short biographies.

I had fantasized a good deal about Haig-Brown's life; angler, frontiersman, and man of letters, he seemed to have wrested a utopian situation for himself. So it was with some shock that I perceived his immersion in the core problems of our difficult portion of the twentieth century.

I knew that his work with the Pacific Salmon Commission represented an almost symbolically tortuous struggle for balanced use of a powerful resource among explosive political factions. But the hours I spent in his court did as much as anything to disabuse me of any cheerful notions that Haig-Brown's clarity as a writer was the result of a well-larded sinecure.

A man brought before him for reckless and drunken driving allowed that he did not feel he was "speeding too awful much." His speed was established by the arresting officer as something like 300 percent of the limit. The officer mentioned that the motorist had been impaired by drink and described the man's spectacular condition. "I wasn't all that impaired." The numerical figure from the Breathalyzer test suggested utter saturation. The accused had heard these numbers against himself before, yet reiterated doggedly that he hadn't been "impaired that awful much," before giving up.

A young logger and his girlfriend who had run out on a hotel bill were the next to appear. What did he do, Haig-Brown inquired, referring to the specifics of the young man's profession. Boomed and set chokers. Haig-Brown nodded; he, too, had been a logger, and one who'd blown up his inherited Jeffries shotgun trying to make fireworks in camp on New Year's Eve.

"You are addicted to heroin, aren't you?" Haig-Brown asked the sturdy young man. The logger replied that he was; so was his girlfriend. He had always lived between here and Powell River, had only had eight dollars the last time he got out of jail, and so on. He and his girlfriend wanted to help each other get on the methadone program and feared their chances of doing so would be reduced if he went to jail.

The prosecutor wanted just that, but Haig-Brown released the young man on promise of restitution to the hotelkeeper and adjourned to his chambers, where his mongrel dog slept in front of the desk. I asked what he thought about the young logger. "He's probably conning me," Haig-Brown said, then added with admiration, "but he's a marvelous talker, isn't he?" Haig-Brown believes that a magistrate who risks an accused man's liberty risks his own honor as well.

Haig-Brown feels himself in the presence of the potentially ridiculous at all times, yet does not seem to feel that his position as magistrate or as chancellor of the University of Victoria separates him by nature from the people who come before his court. And when he talks about the scheme to dam the Fraser River and wipe out the major run of Pacific salmon, a toothy smile forms around the stem of his pipe and he says, "Bastards!"

After court one day, we stopped to buy some wine. While he shopped, I wandered through the store and discovered some curious booze called (I think) Hoopoe Schnapps. I brought it up to the cash register to show Haig-Brown. "Bring it." He grinned. "We'll take it home and try it."

We spent a number of evenings in his study and library, where I prodded him to talk about himself. He would stand with one foot tipped forward like a cavalier in an English painting, knocking his pipe on his heel from time to time, trying to talk about anything besides himself: his children; Thomas Hardy, whom as a child he'd actually seen; his literary heroes like Richard Jeffries and Henry Fielding; the great First Nations people of the Pacific Northwest.

Eventually my persistence led him to sketch his schooling at Charterhouse; his attempts to get into the shrinking colonial service; his emigration to Canada; his experience during the Second World War as a major in the Canadian Army on loan to the Mounted Police; his life as a logger, angler, conservationist, university administrator, and writer. As he stood amid an Edwardian expanse of well-bound books, sipping brandy and wearing a cowboy belt buckle with a bighorn ram on it, the gift of the Alberta Fish and Game Department, I began to visualize that powerful amalgamation and coherence of a successful frontiersman. In Haig-Brown, a Western Canadian with roots in Thomas Hardy's England, I imagined I saw a pure instance of the genre.

He had just made his first trip back to wander the streams he had fished and the places of his childhood unseen in forty years. I asked how it had been.

"It was like being psychoanalyzed," he said.

Such a life does not produce sentimentalists.

AS TIME GOES BY, Roderick Haig-Brown seems to rise higher in our esteem. Not many years after I visited him, he died. It's clear there was no one around to replace him.

At that time, fishing was still enjoying its last esoteric days, and had neither been invaded by the current numbers of people nor tormented by the new technologies. We were still in the reassuring hands of fine old generalists like Ray Bergman and Ted Trueblood.

Haig-Brown began as an Englishman, a European, looking at the rapidly disappearing empire with colonial habits of mind, a thoroughly democratic disposition and the matter-of-fact sense that he would have to make a life for himself. He settled in the Canadian Northwest for a while, very much an emigrant. During World War II, his thoroughgoing travel in all of Canada while on secondement to the Royal Canadian Mounted Police, was, I remember Ann Haig-Brown saying, "the making of a Canadian." I think by then he felt quite detached from his British origins—perhaps on purpose—and had not particularly enjoyed a recent visit to his first home. Happily, I believe he retained his English view of amateur sport and its importance in everyday life. His many confirming expressions seemed a real tonic in the face of the professionalization of American sport at every level. One pictures a logo-festooned Haig-Brown with enormous difficulty. Americans and probably Canadians are sufficiently tainted by Calvinism to feel that to play is to sin or waste time, so we assuage our guilt by associating ourselves with manufacturers so that our days afield reveal the higher purposes of product research, promotion, and development.

Haig-Brown was after different game. He was trying to define the space we give to angling in our lives, and to determine its value, by finding its meaning in his own life. Most fishermen do this, remembering their first waters, their mentors, their graduation through various methods; there is for each of us a need to understand and often to tell our own story in fishing. It is this that gives Haig-Brown's work its lasting quality, despite writing that is often quite impromptu, ranging from absentminded and repetitious to sublime, like life. It is this *plein air* quality, with triumphs accorded no greater emphasis than failure and boredom, that spares so much of his work the calamitous mustiness that afflicts most fishing writing after a while, particularly that which tells us how to fish.

Frankly, revealing what a day astream means is a good bit harder than describing an eight-part nymph leader or showing the reader where to place his feet when sneaking up on an undercut bank. Fishing is infinitely subjective and we sense, I think rightly, that all instruction is unreliable. After a century of science in materials and the design of fly rods, no generally accepted set of tapers for a trout rod exists. There is more objective agreement about cellos, fiber optics, and nuclear submarines. Haig-Brown's work rests most firmly on those subjective issues that seem to last better.

Haig-Brown discovered that the meaning of fishing lies more in its context than its practice: a day alone on a remote steelhead river; floating with your child; fishing a lake with your family when picnic preparations overpower the angler's concentration; seeking a fish whose race is threatened by your own or whose ancestral breeding grounds have been lost to town crooks. Fishing is sometimes about a disinclination to go fishing at all. An important part of life, maybe the *most* important part, is the quest by each of us to discover something we believe to be more worthy and permanent than we are individually. Haig-Brown persuades us that the truth which angling can lead to about our place in nature is one such greater thing.

In generic fishing literature, the angler is always raring to go. Fishing is forever a challenging problem the angler usually solves. In the end, he admits it was tough but knows he will try again, for that's the kind of stuff he's made of; in short, group attitudes, as in a fraternity. We float the river, rain or shine; we always use antelope fur; we always stop for a big bag of doughnuts and hot coffee on our way to the stream; and so forth. By comparison, Haig-Brown is a lone wolf. Not that he's antisocial. My most pressing memory of my visit to Campbell River was of someone embedded in a community, a wizard at making diverse people comfortable in his presence. He was a natural leader and probably never thought about it. In person, he was considerably more presidential than our last five presidents, and if he had possessed just a sliver of vigorous fraudulence, he might well have risen to great political prominence. Forgoing such shortcuts, he was nevertheless chancellor of the University of Victoria, a member of the International Pacific Salmon Fisheries Commission, and the magistrate for a vast area larded with wilderness, seacoast, and often perfunctory human settlements.

Does all this high-mindedness imply a detachment from the intriguing minutiae of fishing? Hardly. He was as unscientific and prone to voodoo in selecting a fly as you and I; in youth as vulnerable to booze-fueled miscalculation as any young bachelor; and in adulthood, according to one biographer who coiled himself around a man in every way his superior, prone to marvelous and imaginative follies supposed to discredit him in the eyes of frowning Christians. Indeed, Haig-Brown lived a life as any other except that it was richer than most and, from his bohemian stint in London to his logging days on Vancouver Island, higher in risk. Still, he found intimations of immortality in fishing and along rivers where ancient human instincts encounter nature at its most profoundly cyclical and mysterious, where human behavior is so clearly part of nature, where our detachment, even from the brevity of our own lives, is consoling.

Down Under

THE RIVERS of the world translate high-country snows to the salty rollers of mid-ocean. Some, like the Makarora of New Zealand or the Whale of Labrador, are images of perfection; the Nile and the Mississippi, images of deep history and civilization. Too often, the rivers we grow up with are like the Rouge or the Cuyahoga, rivers which catch fire or take the paint off the bottoms of ships. But even the worst ones are quite wonderful. I live among the smaller headwaters of the Missouri, crystal cabinets of moving trout water that begin in watercress. Eventually their waters move thousands of miles, ending in drifting sludge, syringes, and condoms before debauching into the Gulf of Mexico. These intimate by-products of man-the-party-animal are the most appalling things transported by moving water in its several manifestations. But if you love rivers you have to take the good with the bad.

I was flying low over the sheep pastures of New Zealand in a small helicopter whose doors had been removed to facilitate jumping on red deer which had been detained by a net gun. The man who leaps onto the backs of frantic and dangerous creatures wears motorcycle leathers in bleak anticipation of the tossings and abrasions he may reasonably expect. Generally, if he wasn't the town bum, he would not have gotten himself in this position. But for some it is an awful thing to run out of beer, and stranger things than jumping out of aircraft upon wild animals to cover bar tabs have perhaps been done, but not many.

Today I'd taken his seat, and such meager room had been allotted this luckless individual that my right buttock was hanging over thousands of feet of clear antipodal space, so charging my senses that, half a decade later, I intently remember the brand-new green of that country, the pale and eerie sheep trails and the cedar forests where the kia bird, a knee-high alpine parrot, whiles away his evenings pulling nails out of the roofs of sheep stations. Everywhere there were rivers, and though I never quite feel I've seen or fished enough of them, this was certainly a vast supply.

These flights over the South Island of New Zealand jarred me out of my routine perceptions, especially those I'd acquired as an angler. When my friends and I settled in at a small and comfortable lodge in Makarora, I was almost surprised to find Americans there: specifically, an emergency room doctor, Monte Downs, and his father, Wil, a man in his seventies who had dedicated his life to tropical medicine and fly-fishing. The two men were on a month-long trip together and you sensed a great catch-up devised fairly late in the game; in the glow around them was an almost palpable relief. They sang antique harmonies, they discussed dengue fever and trout, and they fished very hard. Old Wil seemed to drive the guides like rented mules. And at dinner, if conversation flagged, he dropped his chin to his chest and went to sleep. He often grabbed insects out of the air or, apparently, when he was shaving, off the bathroom mirror. At the end of his stay, he presented to the proprietor, pinned on a sheet of Styrofoam, a neatly organized and labeled collection of these bugs, and recommended the display as a training aid for the guides. Of this stay in Makarora, I recall one riverbank aircraft landing sufficiently in doubt that the Kiwi pilot was moved to remark, "Chaps, it looks a bit rough. We're going to have to thumb it in soft." No one compares to New Zealanders when it comes to bestowing stupendous vulgarities on delicate subjects.

Mostly I think of that father and son, a month of fishing together; that is, days and nights spent in active intimacy at what might have been inflexible ages, late in life in a country where we were all strangers. The rest of us, men with fathers, either living or dead, caught this out of the corners of our eyes.

Six years later, a big box arrived at my house in Montana, filled with fishing books—first editions beautifully bound in fragrant leather—along with a letter from Monte Downs which confirmed what the rest of us had suspected, that the month the two men had shared was the best time of their lives together and a permanent resource to this surviving son.

Wil Downs died the past January 26 after returning from two weeks fishing in Patagonia. Monte said Wil had often mentioned our good times and comic evenings in New Zealand, and Monte wanted to commemorate that with this gift of books from his father's library. I put the books on my shelf thinking that they somehow told me something I would one day have to understand, something about all that has come to me through rivers and fishing, memories of people who were spending the best of themselves in time.

Wil Downs, though, stuck out. In an obituary by his colleague Thomas Aitken, Downs was described as one of the most accomplished tropical medicine authorities in the world, a malariologist, a virologist, a parasitologist and epidemiologist, an entomologist and an ecologist. From our dinners in New Zealand I knew his sharply focused and intimate views of literature. But his love of rivers and fishing seemed to overarch it all, a music as deep as his love of the world.

I also have in hand Wil Downs's New Year's letter for 1991, wherein he begins dispensing various accumulations preparatory to moving into a rest home. Simultaneously, he announces a trip to South America to fish some rivers that have aroused his curiosity. Departure is soon. "This causes immediate stress and a desire to unload. My suspicion is that the Argentine fishermen largely fish with wet-fly, streamer, Matuka flies and when they do the dry-fly, fish a large fly. I hope to make a serious study of the susceptibility of Argentine trout to the small dry-fly."

Afterward he planned to go to his ranch in Colorado where, aided by his teenaged great-nephew, he meant to fish and to study "the relationship of the abundant Culicoides of the Upper North Platte River Basin, altitude 8000' or higher with vector-borne viruses infecting livestock, wild animals and birds, and maybe even human beings." Then on to the Skeena drainage of wonderful steelhead rivers in British Columbia, followed by a visit to a daughter in England. There was a piano to ship, a pool table to ship, books to ship; a chapter to write on yellow fever for an Oxford practitioner's manual of diagnosis. Splendid fighting cock necks had arrived from Monte in Kauai and must be shared among fellow fly-tyers. At this point, describing the colors of the necks—furnace, ginger, black, cree—Wil conjures fishing friends over the years, a rain of small, generous biographies, amounting to a "pantheon," he says, "major and minor saints."

About this time I must introduce my son, Monte Downs. We had a heartwarming experience several years ago when the two of us went to New Zealand and spent the best part of a month together. On one memorable occasion, when we were fishing together on the South Island, with a New Zealand hardy guide, 15 years Mont's junior, and showing the guide's usual poorly concealed opinion of his patrons' prowess, Monte hooked a big trout in Siberia. The trout ran him under a big rock at the top of the pool, in deep water, Mont tried to disengage it, with no success and finally broke it off. Not long afterward, he hooked another large trout in the same pool. This fish also ran upstream and deep and got under that big rock. Mont, from below, walked into the frigid stream, deep, deeper, with tight line on the fish all the time. Deeper still, over his waders, deeper still nearing the rock, and his hat floated off downstream, and Mont's head disappeared under the water. He was under for half a minute, and then his head reappeared. And wonder of wonders, he was still onto the fish and the fish was free and a few minutes later, Mont, soaking wet and shivering, beached a 26-inch brown trout. The guide murmured, "I'll be damned!" My heart swelled with pride. Indeed, I had fathered a fisherman.

Wil, considering the rich companionship he had from angling, wondered how could he reconcile it with his love of the solitude of rivers.

He hoped to fish with each of his cherished angling companions, "but please, not all at one time."

ONCE IN A WHILE during fishing season, Craig Fellin gets a day or two off from his guiding business in Montana's Big Hole and invites me to join him for some low-pressure, semi-exploratory fishing. This summer, when he invited me and our friend Mike right before the mayhem of the salmon fly hatch began, we tried an old tailing pond left behind half a century ago by a mining company. With banks of raw gravel, it's a lunar place to fish, and the heavy metals–laden trout living there are protected by their carcinogenic flesh. They grow to tremendous size.

I caught only one fish that day but it was a good one, a cutthroat which rose to a size 16 Parachute Adams and weighed between four and five pounds, a short, cold, and animated slab that felt wonderfully substantial in my hands before I released it and saw its golden shape sink into the green depths of this weird fish pond.

Then things got so slow and the air so warm that we took a long snooze on the bank. When we awoke, encouraged by the ants crawling on our faces, we had completely lost track of our original momentum and perhaps couldn't even remember what brought us to this strange locale in the first place.

We went back to Craig's camp that night and talked about his winter guiding on the Malleo River, at the base of the Chilean Andes on the Estancia San Huberto. There he'd met a remarkable man, an old man who wanted to fish twelve hours at a stretch, who sometimes had to be carried up the bank at day's end. Craig had found a man who, once he saw the water, held nothing back. They fished every day for two weeks. As they drove to the river, the old man recited Civil War poems, interpreted the landscape, identified the birds, and rhapsodized about the burgeoning life he saw. He and Craig had once corresponded before they'd ever met, and the man sent him jars in which to catch and transport insects. Craig dutifully stood under his porch light at Wise River, Montana, snatching caddises out of the air to fulfill this request.

"He not only fished hard," Craig said, "he took everything in, everything. It was just so wonderful being with this guy. You'd get to a run and he was in touch with everything in it. If fish quit feeding, he could wait. He could wait 'til they started again. He was always watching.

"On the last day at the corral pool, he took a nap. There were some big fish on the bank. We crawled up and marked those fish and crossed the river so he could cast to them. He hooked a great big fish and landed it. I guess it was maybe the biggest fish he ever caught in his life. It was only four o'clock. But he said, 'Let's call it a day.' That was so unlike him." Craig paused. "He flew out the next morning."

Craig brought out a beautiful collection of necks, enough hackles to last out the millennium. A tributary of the Big Hole River roared just beyond the window. "Maybe we fished too hard," Craig said. "He admitted that himself. Because when he went home . . . he didn't feel well. And, well, he died." Craig looked at the fly-tying materials. "He sent me this stuff, to remember our trip by, I guess." Craig was struggling with something. He said, "He was a doctor of tropical medicine."

Unfounded Opinions,
Rants, and Miscellany

E VERY FLY FISHERMAN has an unreasonable view of fly rods, and
I am no different. Generally, we're united in the belief that all
rod design has been progressive and that the thinking about fly rods in
the past was so bad as to make it amazing that people were able to fish
at all. This is based in good American fashion on the belief that angling
is perfectable and chiefly concerned with efficiency. "I stepped into
the water," a fly fisherman was recently heard to say, "and proceeded
to empty the pool." We, his listeners, were bowled over. The trout
stream as modern toilet. Now I understand that this sort of hyperbole
is part of the fun, but its humor is based on a crackpot idea.

I don't think bamboo rods, for example, are as efficient as glass and
graphite. But I like the smell of varnish when I open the rod tube! I like
the human hands that made them. I had a graphite tarpon rod whose
hook keeper wouldn't take anything larger than a number 10 dry-fly
hook, an understandable mistake when you realize it wasn't made by
a fisherman but someone who looked with equal interest upon golf
shafts, tennis rackets, riding crops, skis, and umbrella handles. Yet
I dearly love graphite for helping me put some poetry in my loop and
for relieving the tennis elbow I acquired from steer roping.

Anglers have begun to crave conformity. This has not always
been the case. Now some of us long for leadership, someone to tell us

whether we should have a fast action rod or one that loads with less line. Fast was the mantra until recently, but slower, softer rods have claimed the moral high ground.

Evaluation is subjective. The dream is of the perfect rod and there is no such thing. A fly rod has to meet too many criteria, of which many are contradictory. Think of a rod for western rivers that require delicate presentations in high winds. Is the rod matched to the fish, the fly being cast or the atmospheric conditions? The rod suited to casting large streamers in the fall is as big as some people use for tarpon. But the fish haven't gotten any bigger since August. A five-weight easily handles the sparsely dressed flies we use on bright sand bottoms for tarpon, but it would never land the fish. Though the perfect distance for a trout rod to load is probably around twenty-five feet, who wants to try out a rod down at the fly shop with twenty-five feet of line? And while no rod casts nicely with split shot, some tolerate it better than others. In a perfect world, fishing with split shot on the leader wouldn't be fly-fishing at all. Neither would monofilament nymphing, and maybe even shooting heads. Lee Wulff said that the fish is entitled to the sanctuary of deep water. That's where most of us used to set the bar in trout fishing. We fished on top and tried to devise ways of catching big fish that way, fishing at night, fishing with greater stealth, hunting remote places that rarely saw an angler.

So many rods are now designed for micro-niches, with extreme line sizes and weird lengths. It is a great pleasure to use some of these rods when the conditions for which they were designed are perfect. Unless we begin using caddies, it would be useful to remember that conditions are rarely perfect in angling. Long ago, when I started fly-fishing, the standard trout rod was an HCH, a six weight, eight to eight-and-a-half feet long. After four decades of evolution in material and ideas, I have concluded this is still the case, especially when you consider what it takes to make an all-day rod in most places. The rod might have grown to nine feet. A full day in one of my local rivers might require the angler to go through five sizes of dry-flies and three of wet. The wind will range from zero to forty. A five-weight rod is not enough and a seven is too much. For predictable, shorter sessions, like the evening rise, the three-, four-, or five-weight rods might be fine.

In my view, fly rods have some mysterious ergonometric range of length that is hard to explain. The same is true of hammer handles, oars, tennis rackets, and golf clubs: the variations in length are surprisingly small. A trout rod significantly under eight feet is too short, and significantly over nine, too long. If it's too short, it leaves too much line on the water for good drag control and speeds up the casting cycle. Too long and the rod becomes a handful in the wind and helps produce tailing loops. I had a ten-foot summer steelhead rod that I loved until the wind came up, then I wanted to swap it with someone unwitting enough to obsess about line control, just as I had. A rod better have a great reason for being over nine feet or under eight. Nine is a wonderful length for trout, tarpon, or billfish. It's a length the human body likes. Just today I got out an old favorite, a seven-and-a-half foot trout rod, and fished half a day with it. I hadn't used anything shorter than eight-and-a-half for so long that I was unpleasantly surprised to discover the extra drag problems posed by the lower angle between rod, line, and water, not to mention the hurried casting cycle. The speeding technology of fly rods has finally just emphasized some basic truths. Even in the days when bamboo was king, light and fast were the ideals, sometimes called "dry-fly action." Describing a rod as having a "wet-fly action" was tantamount to admitting that it was a clunker.

I know that I'm not going to stop anyone out there from acquiring a bunch of overly specific niche rods. I'm probably not even going to stop myself. I sure haven't so far. The dream of fly-fishing is one of simplicity, and most of us pursue it in the same way: acquire a blizzard of flies and gear in the belief that you are casting a wide net and that, at some point, you will get rid of all but the few perfect items and angle in the dreamed-of simplicity. For most, this pile grows until death brings it to a stop. If fly-fishing weren't still more or less esoteric, yard sales would never recover from this epidemic.

The biggest problem with fly rods is that they must not only meet all the physical criteria for the fishing you do but also inspire "love." For example, I have a six-weight rod that is far and away the best trout rod I have ever owned. It is fast, light, and has the quickest damping stroke imaginable. It was designed by probably the greatest fly caster of all time. It is also cheesily built, with porous cork in the handles, disco guide wraps, and decal graphics that include bar codes to distinguish this rod from other recreational products from the same company. I'm going to have to work at loving this, the best trout rod I've ever had. I'm going to have to almost wear it out. Its ultramodern decor will have to sink into history and become sort of campy. I may have to break it, or use it to defend myself during a holdup or to stand off a bear. Right now it's a yuppie artifact with as much soul as a paper clip. It casts a thousand times better than the beautiful old Garrison I have which takes the same line.

I think we can work it out. But this great new rod is made of materials that are part of a rapidly evolving technology and thus might be obsolete by Thanksgiving. I could be given cause to worry that its modulus of elasticity may be trailing the next generation of rods. I'm actually capable of thinking about crap like that; I kind of like it. The other day, I put this soulless wand away and, instead, fished with that fine old bamboo I've had for several decades. By comparison, this beautiful wooden shaft with highly individualized handwork and matchless esthetics was a dog, and I was reminded that someone likened the classic action of a bamboo rod to a cow pulling its foot out of deep mud.

Gough Thomas, the English gun writer, warns against the vice of "polygunning," which means using too many guns and becoming master of none. I could point out that this same malady afflicts anglers, but what's the use? We'll always have too many rods.

Returning to my topic: a trout fisherman can do it all with a nine foot for a six line. A nine foot for an eight-weight line will cover most of the rest, including bonefish and small tarpon. I've seen tarpon of more than 125 pounds landed on eight weights, also ideal for snook and redfish. For repetitive casting, as demanded in steelhead and salmon fishing, it's as much as most of us want to cast all day long, and plenty of people use their six-weight rods for steelhead.

I know, nobody's listening to this excellent advice. Is it because I have about twenty fly rods?

Let's see what my excuses are. I have an eight-foot Garrison for a size-six line. I keep this and still use it because it is so full of fishing memories. It was owned for years in the middle of its life by my former brother-in-law; I had to buy it back and he did well in the transaction. I also keep it because I remember my consultations with the builder and the giddiness of those years when there were relatively so few of us fly-fishing.

I have a six-foot three-inch Bob Summers Midge because it reminds me of my first significant fly shop, Paul Young's, where Bob originally did his beautiful work. Also, recalling the follies of A. J. McLane and Arnold Gingrich and Lee Wulff when they were promoting these impractical "flea rods," it suggests that even great men are prone to foolishness.

I have a four-weight nine-foot Light Line Sage, which is the most exquisite use of graphite I'm familiar with in a spring creek rod. With this one I caught my best public water dry-fly trout, after forty-five years on the job: a twenty-five-and-a-half-inch male brown, on a size-20 Pale Morning Dun, from Silver Creek near Ketchum, Idaho. I'm convinced the rod kept me from breaking the 6X tippet and from suffering an avalanche of grief.

I have an eight-and-a-half foot Winston for a number-five line, a rod I've followed throughout its evolution of materials. This one is of IM6 graphite and in my view is the five-weight trout rod against which all others are measured, although the Scott of the same size is right in there. These are the best for the small freestone rivers of the kind that I often fish.

I have a seven-and-a-half foot bamboo rod for a five line built by John Long, a gift from a builder I've never met. A fine piece of work and an extremely pleasant small-stream rod.

I have a seven-and-a-half foot Payne, two-piece, for a five line because I always wanted a Payne and even named the hero of one of my novels after this maker. I consider Payne to be the finest cane rod builder of all time. When you pick this rod up you can tell everything you need to know; it's startlingly good.

Now, the rod I discussed earlier: a nine-foot six-weight Loomis GLX, a tremendous fly rod designed by Steve Rajeff and otherwise a thoroughly impersonal artifact. The guides are single-footed; there is glitter thread in the windings; the reel seat is air weight spun nylon. It's the fly rod as pure idea. It tracks perfectly, dampens perfectly; the action seems to progress through infinity without ever hitting bottom. You forget about the rod and think about the line. I don't believe it weighs three ounces. I can fish big western rivers for ten-hour days and never want for another rod.

I have an eight-foot nine-inch Russ Peak Zenith for a seven line. Russ Peak was a genius who understood better than anyone what could be done with glass. He was the ne plus ultra rodmaker in the seventies, when I was fishing two hundred days a year, so there is sentimental value. By today's standards it's a deliberate number that requires the angler to recalibrate his timing somewhat. But once I'm actually fishing with it, usually on the Yellowstone in the fall, I quickly fall back into its rhythms. It is perfectly built.

I have an eight-foot nine-inch Winston cane rod, for a seven, goes best with a Wulff 7/8, that was built by the great Glenn Brackett and was a gift of the Winston Rod company. I enjoy fishing this rod enormously, for it is entirely in the spirit of the West Coast glory days in steelheading when Winston and Powell were kings. I can accept the extra weight of the rod because of the time between casts in steelheading. It is a great roll casting or single-handed Spey casting rod.

I just traded for a nine-foot two-piece Payne light salmon rod for an eight line, beautiful with a detachable fighting butt, ferrule plugs, case, and canvas overcase. It weighs the same as a thirteen-weight billfish rod. What will I do with it? I'm bound to come up with something.

The eight-weights and the age of excess: my Sage eight-foot nine, an outstanding, wind-penetrating bonefish rod, doesn't seem much good for anything else I do. My Sage nine-foot for an eight-weight, the 890 RPL, as much of a classic as the old Fenwick FF85. My Loomis four-piece nine-foot for an eight, designed by Steve Rajeff and Mel Krieger, is an outstanding travel rod, the only rod I know of better in the multipiece than in the two-piece.

My faithful permit rod, a nine-foot for a ten-line Winston graphite, though somewhat sluggish by current standards, seems to absorb the vagaries of big, heavy permit flies better than stiffer rods. It's a good all-around striped bass rod, too.

A nine-foot for eleven-weight Sage built for me as a gift by George Anderson. I use a twelve-weight line on this rod and it is a rod which,

when used carefully, is adequate for big tarpon. It won't wear me out
on active days the way the twelve does. It is simply built, no fighting grip, and full of happy memories. I couldn't retire this rod, even
though the twelves and thirteens are nicer once the fish is hooked.

Perhaps it would be wise to leave out my three Spey rods. I have
good single-handed steelhead and salmon rods but I may never go
back to them. The Spey rods just work too well. The English are not
pleased that we call them "Spey rods" at all, in the conviction that
"double-handed rods" is the correct form. All the English anglers I
know feel this way and all are using American-made rods. It perfectly
symbolizes the relationship between the two nations.

I subject the reader to my inventory for two reasons. First, I myself
love to read this sort of thing, sniffing around the author's tackle
room; and second, to suggest that what's at work here has nothing to
do with necessity but rather with the elaboration of the dream that is
fishing. And as I look back at these remarks, I see that they are period
pieces. The technology has moved on without me.

MOST REELS are sold to the public by suggesting some unheard-of
emergency involving a running fish and guaranteeing that this reel is
the only available product capable of bringing the trophy to a standstill before it changes area codes. Right now, a large variety of magnificent reels is available to choose from. Most have one thing in
common: they're far better than they need to be. Reels evolve slowly:
the ninety-year-old Vom Hofes are still among the best. I have a number of Pfleuger Medalists made in Ohio, and even in the most awful
conditions they have never failed me. There were Japanese knockoffs
of these reels, and they're great, too. Though built to appalling toler-
ances, they keep on ticking.

The backing on a trout reel usually dies of old age before it sees the
light of day. Rarely does a salmon or steelhead go a hundred yards,
yet most reels designed for this purpose carry a quarter-mile of backing. If a tarpon, permit, or bonefish gets more than a hundred yards
from you, your problems have nothing to do with your backing. The
last time I got spooled was on the Henry's Fork when a big rainbow

got downstream where I couldn't wade after it. It didn't matter how much backing I had, I was meant to view the spindle.

I'm not sure about the great drag systems, either. I don't believe any freshwater reel needs a drag at all. A good, strong click will suffice. Anyone who is not enough of a hand to palm the reel or put a couple of fingers through the arbor is already fighting a fish too big for him.

Leader strength is based as much on margin of error for nicks and abrasions as it is on real breaking strength. Many anglers feel that the ultrathin leader materials now available do not equal their breaking-strength counterparts because the thin stuff weakens steeply if at all abraded. There is a very long list of things which can quickly change the breaking strength of tippets; touching bottom, hinging at the knots, scraping on teeth and gill plates, and so on. The real reason why many anglers, especially steelheaders and salmon anglers who cast a lot between bites, stick with the low-tech stuff is this: it doesn't have to be terribly heavy because there are few rods which are comfortable to cast that can break anything over a ten-pound test at all.

As to flies, I asked the greatest trout fisherman of my era, who is himself an out-of-control proliferator of equipment and technical doodads, what percentage of his annual catch would remain if he were reduced to Adamses and Gold-Ribbed Hare's Ear nymphs. His answer: "Certainly over ninety percent." When pressed about the staggering variety of patterns available in his fly shop, he said, "I don't sell flies to fish."

I've become fairly avid about my fly-tying because it is, as I do it, a modest craft that I can master. More importantly, it enables me to tie flies that look exactly right to me, which means I will fish them with conviction. For example, my usual searching pattern combines several favorite traits: moosehair tail, because there's something that feels right about those crisp black fibers; the body is wrapped turkey quill barbs as on my first favorite fly, the Borcher Special, a Michigan favorite; white calf-body hair wings, à la the Wulff flies; brown and grizzly palmered hackle as on an Adams. When looking at it, I believe I'm going to catch a fish. That feeling affects the way I cast and read water. You have to have that feeling, wait-and-see being an approach preferred by losers. If you are anxious to kick major butt on your local stream or lake, try my fabulous fly. It turns blank days into bonanzas, depression into jubilation.

In fishing, many traits separate the men from the boys, but in my opinion, one thing we should all work toward is what I would call, for want of a better term, "smoothness." Many of the great anglers I have fished with have had this trait above all others and it is the one thing that I continually strive for. This is the trait that unites sportsmen as diverse as the Grand Prix driver Juan Fangio, who was so smooth he rarely strained the cars he drove, golfers like Bobby Jones, and baseball players like Ted Williams and Joe DiMaggio. There are always a few anglers blessed with genius and inspiration: towering casters, leadfooted deep river waders, anglers with astounding vision, and so on. But the angler who accepts both his gifts and limitations, who recognizes the importance of keeping his fly in the water, who abjures tackle tinkering once he reaches the river, and who strives to fish coherently throughout the day will usually, finally, succeed. Steelhead and salmon fishing exaggerate the importance of this. And sometimes, relatively unskilled anglers who are otherwise persistent and capable of sustained focus will outfish flashier types, better casters and even more experienced companions. I have seen steelhead rivers act with great leveling effect, rewarding the scrupulous-if-limited anglers and penalizing mere technicians, tackle nuts, distance casters, and fishing experts. A great angler like Bill Schaadt was a tremendous caster, an outstanding schemer and intimate with the rivers he fished, but what impressed me about him the few times we fished together was that he was tougher and more persistent than anybody I'd ever seen. He kept the fly in the water longer than anyone, ever. He was smooth and efficient. All of his strength and talent—indeed the overall design of his life—was at the service of keeping the fly fishing, which begins with casting a straight line. There are armchair anglers who can cast four kinds of curve but never a straight line except in dead still conditions. A late start in the morning prevents the fly from fishing; a crooked cast delays a fly from fishing; fly changing, leisurely meals and a forgotten bailing can all play a part in separating the fly from its job. Schaadt's term was "lost motion." Every angler should strive for its elimination, not so as to become an automaton but to facilitate *smoothness*.

Why do fishermen lie? This interesting question ought to be dealt with because it's the single thing we are most famous for among the general public. I have a hunch that most anglers do not wish to compete but have found no successful way to avoid competition when fishing with others. I, for example, do not wish to compete and therefore do most of my fishing alone so that I may better absorb its mysteries, poetry, and intimations of mortality. On many occasions, however, I find myself fishing with others and it is then that I helplessly find myself competing, crowing at hookups, admiring some great thing about my tackle when I really mean myself. The lone angler, or even the one who just scooted around the bend from his companions, may fish and dawdle as he pleases, take in the migratory birds, the soaring hawk, the hunting mink, the glancing light on the riffle, the sound of a hollow bank. He may even catch fish. Moreover, upon meeting up with his retinue, he may dispense with matters of competition by lying about his results. How did he do? "Major poundage. A semi-load." The most incredulous of his comrades have probably come by their disbelief honestly: they've been lying, too. So, all is well. A day in the life has been suitably taken in, and in this avalanche of lies, a kind of truth has been served. The only people any the wiser are the general public.

ALLOW ME TO ADD a few more rants and I'm outta here.

Barbless hooks: all flies and especially flies bought in fly shops should be barbless in the *first* place. "Pinching" the barb is not good enough and either weakens the hook or leaves a small lump that disfigures and hurts fish, tears mandibles, damages gills, and creates fatal bleeding. I have no idea in this era of catch-and-release why fly shops continue to sell these abominations.

Don't scrimp on tippets: the usual eighteen-inch tippet is, after a few fly changes, too short. And while you have striven to keep it from becoming too short, you have been tying bad knots. While sticking to a leader that will turn over properly, use a very long tippet—two to three feet is not unreasonable, especially on flat water. Beware in the case of knotless leaders that, as you have been changing flies and shortening the portion of the leader allocated to tippet, you may have moved up sizes without knowing it, as the change is gradual.

The fewer the ferrules the better. A one-piece nine weight weighs the same as a four-piece six weight. I once compared the one-piece Hardy Zenith five weight to the four-piece version: They were completely unalike; the one-piece rod was a much better rod. The four-piece fly rod is a concession to the decline of local fishing in America: your rod must go on an airplane. My tarpon rods are all one-piece. An experienced angling friend saw them in my boat and asked how I could travel with them. I told him I don't: they stay in the boat. We fished for many years before we needed an airplane to get to good water. Kiss those days good-bye.

Through no fault of their own, guides are a mixed blessing. On unfamiliar water, they are a necessity. Fishermen are often advised to hire a guide to learn new water. Better not tell the guide that's why you hired him or he won't show you jack shit. Guides are drawn to one another, not to their clients. A guide will fish the same client a hundred days straight at tremendous cost to the client and on a free day take another guide rather than treat the client. Most guides are excellent anglers; in fact, the guide *is* the angler and you, dear friend, are the caster. After all the work of finding and setting up on fish, it's no wonder that when you blow the cast the guide feels strongly that you're an unpleasant presence in his boat. You may be read the riot act as he hangs on the push pole and looks up at the sky. Your only defense is to offer to pay the guide his fee and ask to be taken in. This gets you out of an uncomfortable situation and makes the guide feel terrible. Hunched over his drink that night, the guide may feel remorse and this is good for him. He may improve—not as a fisherman as he is already excellent at that—but as a human being.

A SECTION OF ONE of my local rivers containing almost all the long pools was a guest ranch, of interest mostly to visiting anglers and available to us locals on Sunday, known as "changeover day." I frequently fished it on this once-a-week opportunity. It has since been acquired by an out-of-state group and is no longer available on changeover day.

Since I know some of the members, I am invited once a summer or so, much less than formerly. One member hosts a pleasant Fourth of July party on the property and this year I noticed the eloquent portable defibrillators. It put a smile on my face.

There are, as elsewhere, a good many celebrities moving to the West, for the season, generally. There are so many that the feeling that it will be necessary to store the B-listers in abandoned Nebraska corn towers has occupied the regional imagination. If you live and fish in the West, there is a good chance a celebrity will be among your acquaintances. A kind of distant hostility to these people preoccupies the locals; "distant" because close range reduces them to gooberish attempts at ingratiating themselves with the exalted soul who may recently have been parking cars in an overhead public garage. I have even seen a ranch listing that promised the property was at least a hundred miles from the nearest celebrity. It is reckless to go on a guided trip with a celebrity because many—not all—guides will find their panties in a wad at the sight of the famous and ignore your needs— that may include drowning or animal attack—as inconsequential pestering. Years ago, a small group of us that included a well-known entertainer planned a trip to western Montana to fish; I thought to call ahead to secure our permission and received from the ranch wife, who had no idea who was in our group, a *rant* about celebrities ruining the West with their cohorts in "the media," who had reported the unquestionable drought that she dismissed as fake news. We were concerned with extreme low water, but I thought better of mentioning the real and present drought.

We arrived at the ranch and gathered on the front lawn; our celebrity seemed radioactive at the moment the ranch wife emerged and spotted him. She froze, then ran back into the house, a move we found hard to understand until she came back out bearing a ball cap with the ranch logo, which she offered to our celebrity while the rest of us stood by and shuffled. Our guy is a good sport and put the hat on, raised open hands, and asked how he looked with what seemed to be touching affection for his new hat. He's an experienced entertainer but his act encouraged us to compliment him on his capacity for bullshit.

·   ·   ·

WHEN I WAS A BOY I told my friends about a beautiful brook trout I had seen swimming in a tiny pool in the woods. I described everything, spots, fins, the works. It wasn't until years later that I admitted to myself that the fish never existed other than in my imagination. I just longed to see it. The desire to see fish is a big part of the angler's enterprise. We want to see them because they are emblems of the broad perfection of nature. They help us to know that everything in nature is *perfect* and we have to start somewhere, with something that calls to us, like trout or birds or rain. E. O. Wilson feels this way about *ants* and it has taken him a long way into profound understanding of both himself and the earth.

Is there a way to persuade people that difficult fishing is good fishing, that there is mortality even with catch-and-release fishing, and that crowing about your thirty-fish day is nothing to be proud of, especially if you put all thirty on social media? Social media kills a lot of fish.

WE SHOULD TRY TO understand where we fish. We could learn from Native Americans who did not view rivers the same way we do, that is, *as boundaries*—like the Ohio River dividing slave from non-slave states, the east-west division of the Missouri, the Río Grande that divides Mexico from the United States. They thought in terms of watersheds, in which the river was but one component. They also viewed different sections of rivers as entities within them, what we might call "beats."

I MET BILL SCHAADT in San Francisco, his hometown, in the sixties. It was the Summer of Love and Russ Chatham and I had already painted flowers on our Pflueger Medalist reels. Bill was one of the greatest anglers who ever lived. Those with double-sided Wheatley boxes with a hundred compartments will be interested to know that Bill kept his flies in the cellophane sleeve from his pack of cigarettes.

When he came to visit me later in Key West, I had a chance to see what he considered a fishing day filled with meaning. He wanted to try permit fishing, with which I was then obsessed, and climbed into my skiff one early spring morning, bringing with him his peculiar tackle: fiberglass rod, unshaped cork grip, taped-on guides, and an assortment of shooting heads. We ran straight west from Key West and I poled Bill around behind Woman Key. I found one tailing fish. Bill raised his rod at about seventy feet and the permit flushed. Bill turned to look at me. *Huh?* Time to move. I ran to the northwest where I had a favorite finger flat, long, narrow, covered with crunchy staghorn corral. The tide was falling obliquely across it. We had the light, and the conditions seemed ideal. We found tailing permit from one end of the flat to the other. (Remember that we really didn't have good permit flies then.) Bill probably had thirty good shots, firing those shooting heads with pinpoint accuracy. The permit would swim right over the top of his fly looking for something better. Finally, as Bill threw down his rod in the bottom of my skiff, I got to hear his famous booming voice firsthand. "These goddamn things are not game fish! A game fish has to have a mouth!"

I didn't know what to do. We lost the tide; the fish were gone; I cranked up and ran around the end of Boca Grande Key where a cold and unseasonable north wind was blowing and migrating warblers stopped by the wind were falling into the sea on spread wings. Bill saw them first and yelled that we had to do something. So I motored around on the ocean while Bill, hanging off the bow, captured dozens of half-drowned warblers in a net. When we'd gathered the last we could find, we headed back to the beach on Boca Grande Key and spread them out on the warm sand. One by one, they dried out, took wing, and resumed their migration. Sitting in the sand, we watched them fly away. Bill said it was one of the best fishing days he had ever had.

Years later when Bill died surrounded by friends, he said, "I can't believe how much fun I've had."

Does "fun" suggest that Bill Schaadt had led a frivolous life?

Let me bring in my favorite authority on such things: Johan Huizinga, the author of *Homo Ludens*, which translates roughly as "man at play." Huizinga wrote that no other modern language has quite the sense of the English word "fun" and he associates the word "fun" with play, while claiming profound aesthetic qualities for it. All field sports, he said, ventilate our monotony and produce a longing for the past as a time when the importance of play was self-evident and relieved its practitioners of the need to account for themselves. Huizinga added that "the great instinctive forces of civilized life have their origin: law and order, commerce and profit, craft and art, poetry, wisdom and science. All are rooted in the primeval soil of play." He says that its first characteristic is "freedom," a word that shines for every fisherman, and man's imperishable need to live in beauty.

Therefore, nothing frivolous about Bill Schaadt.

ONCE I GAVE A TALK: "Does Fishing Mean Anything?" A local wag commented, "Yes, it does, but it's a secret."

A GROUP DEDICATED TO helping injured veterans was in our river valley. They believed that fishing could get some terribly injured men to quit staring at the road for IEDs or scanning the ridge tops for snipers, which was nearly all they had been doing. I thought that fishing might offer little more than a distraction or a hobby to men in the extremity of need. It seemed entirely farfetched to me, but it worked—maybe not in all cases, but it worked.

MULTIPOCKET FLY-FISHING VESTS have been style leaders for generations now, with festooning bags and attachments; over time the clever angler learned that some of those pockets he's carried so many miles have not been opened since he was younger and looked better. Please welcome the "minimalist" vest and a new market for those who used to carry more but now wish to carry less. With inflation, the new minimalist vests, easily confused with brassieres, cost as much as the old cargo-based torture garments. Last summer I tried to see how far this might go and carried the flies I expected to use in a Band-Aid tin, and a spool of 5X and a floatant in my shirt. I monitored my suffering throughout several days and found that my condition at the end was survivable. And there was a new intimacy sprinkling flies into my palm and musing over their comparative virtues.

THERE ARE MANY WAYS anglers manage time when they can't fish. Tying flies is my default waste of time; but I also make a space in my life for fly-box feng shui. I can always look into those compartments and conclude there is a better arrangement than the one I see before my eyes, especially if there are nymphs, as there is never a good place for nymphs in an old gentleman's kit. Scuds lie just at the margin of acceptable; but the proud compartments belong to dry flies, with the honored holes going to flies in the Catskill style with divided wings. There remains the matter of sorting out the chi that can arise between such individuals as the Adams or Cahill and such modern nuisances as the Chubby Chernobyl.

WE WERE PREPARING TO fish a trico hatch and these irritating little bugs were everywhere. Two of us were garden-variety trout nuts and had rigged up fifteen-foot 7X leaders and tiny imitations that we tied on by putting our reading glasses over the top of our flip focals. The third member of our group was Bob, a six-and-a-half-foot Mormon cowboy friend of mine who fished once in a while and had brought along his older glass rod, his short leader, and a large rubber-legged floaty toy for a fly. Bob had a big night. We had tough going. Our knots could have been better. Maybe something more impressionistic in the fly department instead of our too-literal offerings. Because Bob is a cowboy, he made no secret of his triumph or his pleasure at the insincerity of our smiles. "Why, fellows," said Bob, "that stuff is too small for a fish to see. They think it's pollen!"

LIVING NEXT TO A CREEK or a river as I have done for many decades is instructive. You begin to sense when it rises and falls, and why.

People in the north have watched winter come and their rivers just stop. Once I heard a rumbling in the cottonwood trees upstream from my house. It was January and a huge plug of ice broke loose, stopped the river, turned it brown, then scoured the bottom for a quarter of a mile, groaning and breaking things as it went. These unexpected stirrings of the natural world move us toward a better understanding of our place in it.

THERE IS NO REASON to believe a higher power will help you catch more fish. I tested this theory on the Bulkley River in British Columbia. I had hooked a big, bright steelhead that was cartwheeling in the middle of the river a hundred yards away. I said aloud, "I will never land this fish." Why did I say this aloud when there was no corporeal presence nearby to hear me? I must have been hoping the gods would see that I was in a difficult situation, would pity me, and I would land the fish, something I desperately wanted. The fish got off faster than the words left my mouth. Fly fishermen are alone in the universe.

I SAT WITH A FELLOW ANGLER and a local Argentinian. My companion offered the humblebrag that he had been coming to southern Argentina to fish for over forty years.

"Forty years!" exclaimed the Argentinian.

"Yes," replied my companion.

"It's unbelievable!" said the Argentinian.

My friend nodded modestly. "Mm, a long time."

"Coming to Argentina for forty years," said the Argentinian, bumping his forehead with the heel of his hand, "and still can't speak Spanish!"

After many trips to Argentina, an acquaintance wrote a book about fishing there. One year he went to Argentina without his fishing tackle and announced his discovery: "Jeez, Argentina's a great country!"

A case could be made that fishing home water and taking good care of it is what an angler should do.

Sons

BOTH MY PARENTS were Irish Catholics from Massachusetts. My father had had enough of the Harp Way and was glad to get out of there and move to Michigan. My mother never accepted it and would have been happy to raise a nest of Micks anywhere between Boston and New Bedford. Every summer she did the next best thing and packed us children up and took us "home" to Fall River. My father seemed glad to watch us go. I still see him in our driveway with the parakeet in its cage, trying unsuccessfully to get my mother to take the bird, too, so he wouldn't even have to hang around long enough to feed it. At the end of the summer, when we returned from Massachusetts, the bird would be perched in there but it was never the same bird. It was another $3.95 blue parakeet but without the gentleness of our old bird. When we reached into the cage to get our friend, we usually got bitten.

We traveled on one of the wonderful lake boats that crossed Lake Erie to Buffalo, and I remember the broad interior staircases and the brassbound window through which one contemplated the terrific paddlewheels. I hoped intensely that a fish would be swept up from deep in the lake and brought to my view but it never happened. Then we took the train, I guess it must've been to Boston. I mostly recall my rapture as we swept through the eastern countryside over brooks and rivers that I knew were the watery world of the fish and turtles I cared so madly about. One of these trips must have been made during hard times, because my mother emphasized that there was only enough money for us children to eat; and it is true that we had wild highs and lows as my father tried to build a business.

Many wonderful things happened during my endless summers with my grandmother, aunts, and uncles in Fall River, but for present purposes, I am thinking only of fishing. Those original images are still so burning that I struggle to find a proper syntax for them. In the first, my father arrived and took me up to see some shirttail cousins up in Townsend. A little brook passed through their backyard and, lying on my stomach, I could look into one of its pools and see tiny brook trout swimming. It was something close to the ecstasy I felt when I held my ear against the slots of the toaster and heard a supernal music from heaven ringing through the toaster springs. The brook trout were water angels and part of the first America, the one owned by the Native Americans, whose music I'd listened to in the toaster. I had seen the old trails, their burial mounds and the graves of settlers killed in the French and Indian wars. For some reason, I understood the brook trout had belonged to the paradise the Native Americans had fought to keep. I knew King Phillip—or Metacomet, as they called him—had eaten them.

All this seemed to be part of a lost world, like the world I was losing as my father became more absorbed in his work. We had good times together only when fish were present, and those brook trout are the first memories. It was casually easy for us to get along fishing; the rest was a bomb. I think of the fathers-and-sons day at his athletic club with particular loathing, as it was an annual ordeal. Silver dollars were hurled into the swimming pool for the boys to vie for. Each father stood by the pool, gazing at the writhing young divers and waiting for his silver-laden son to surface. Rarely coming up with a coin, I was conscious of appearing to be less than an altogether hale boy and hardly worth bringing to this generational fête, with its ventriloquists and Irish tenors or, more usually, the maniacal Eddie Peabody on the banjo. All of this was an aspect of the big dust we were meant to make in our mid-American boom town where sport of the most refined sort quickly sank into alcoholic mayhem. Steaks in the backyard, pill-popping housewives, and golf were the order of the day, and many youngsters sought to get their fathers away somewhere in search of a fish. Most of our fathers were just off the farm or out of small towns and heading vertically upward into a new world. We didn't want them to go and we didn't want to go with them.

I thought that if I devised a way to free my father from his rigorous job, we could fish more. I saw an ad for a Hart, Shaffner and Marx suit that said it was for the man who wanted to look like he would make ten thousand a year before he was thirty. (Remember, this was many years ago.) I told my father that he ought to make ten thousand a year, then ten thousand a year in eleven months, then ten thousand a year in ten months and so on, and with this properly earned free time, he and I would go fishing together more often. "With an attitude like that," my father boomed, "you'd never make ten thousand a year in the first place."

None of this mattered in Massachusetts. Across Brownell Street from my grandmother, between Main and Almy, lived Jimmy McDermott, an elegant Irish bachelor, and his spinster sister, Alice. They seemed very sophisticated and witty, especially compared to their immediate neighbors, the Sullivans, who were unreconstructed Irish, with a scowling mother in a black shawl and an impenetrable brogue. Jimmy McDermott took me fishing and bought me my first reel, a beautiful Penn Senator surf-casting reel whose black density seemed to weigh coolly in my hands. Jimmy McDermott detected that I needed someone to take me fishing.

He thought it was crazy for a boy who loved to fish to be hanging around Brownell Street in Fall River in August, so he packed a lunch and we went fishing for tautog along some small and lonely beach with its granite outcroppings and sunshot salty fog and tidal aromas. We caught several fish on the fierce green crabs we used for bait and I heard about several more, because Jimmy was the sort of person who made sure at such a sacramental moment as angling that the full timbre of the thing must be appreciated by the recounting of such holy incidents in time, of striped bass and flounders, the gloomy conger eel who filled three skillets with grease or the rich sports in the old days who baited their bass rigs with small lobsters. A Portuguese family picnicked on the nearby strand, and in my somewhat more global view today I think of us amusing ourselves on that *mare nostrum*, the Atlantic Ocean, casting our hopes on those ancestral waters toward Ireland, the Azores, toward the Old World. The sea heaved up around our rocks, pulling a white train of foam from mid-ocean along with its mysteries of distance and language, drownings, caravels, unwitnessed thousand-foot thunderheads, phosphorous and fish by the square mile.

IT IS A GREAT TRIUMPH over something—biology, maybe, or whatever part of modern history has prolonged adolescence to the threshold of senility—for a father to view his son without skepticism. I have not quite achieved this state but at least have identified the problem. Therefore, when I stood at the airport in Cancún and watched my frequently carefree son emerge with several disintegrating carry-on bags and his shirt hanging out of his pants, I did not take this altogether as a sign of complete disorganization.

When we hugged, because he's so much stronger, he rather knocked the wind out of me. And when we made our way to the small aircraft that would take us to Ascension Bay, I asked if he had practiced his casting. "Once," he said.

"These aren't trout," I said. "A thirty-foot cast doesn't get it."

"Don't worry about it," he smiled. "I don't expect to have any problem with bonefish."

"How can you say that?" I asked. "You've never seen one before, you don't know how tough they can be." He smiled again, knowing exactly how to drive me crazy.

We had a comfortable, really wonderful cottage with cool concrete walls and a roof of thatched monkey palm. Birds were everywhere and the blue Caribbean breakers rose high enough that you could look right through them, then fell. Just past the line of breakers, the coral garden seemed like a submerged quilt.

Thomas was slow in getting ready to fish. He was bent over the sink, doing something and taking too long about it. I said we ought to hurry up and head for the boat. I said it twice and he straightened up from the sink holding a pale green scorpion he had just extracted from the drain. "In case you were thinking of brushing your teeth," he said, and grabbed his rod.

Our guide was a Mayan named Pedro, a solid fifty-year-old of easygoing authority. I thought of a Little Compton voice of yesteryear—"We've been here for generations"—Pedro's family had been on the shores of this bay since thousands of years before Christ. As Pedro was a mildly intolerant man, all business, one soon learned not to pester him with trifles. I did ask if he had ever visited the United States.

"I've never been to Mexico," he said coolly.

Walking to the boat, I was excited to see a lineated woodpecker who loves to eat Aztec ants from their home in the hollow pumpwood tree. A brave soul, he defends his nest against toucans. Ruddy ground doves scattered along our trail and we saw the splendid chacalaca on the edge of the jungle, noisy as a chicken in flight. When we set out in the skiff, mangrove swallows scattered across the narrow channels. My son explained to me that some birds had taken to flying upside down over New York City because "there was nothing worth shitting on." Birds have much to tell us.

Pedro ran the skiff through the shallow water wilderness with the air he seemed to bring to everything, an absence of ambiguity. There was no scanning the horizon or searching for signs. If a tremulous ridge of tidal movement betrayed a shoal in our path, Pedro adjusted his angle of travel without ever looking in the direction of the hazard.

When we emerged completely from the congestion of cays, remarkably similar bands of pale blue, of sky and sea, stretched before us at a sublime scale, white tropical clouds reaching upward to heavenly elevations. A scattering of small islands lay in the distance.

I was still thinking of Pedro's answer about never having been to Mexico. Quintana Roo was his country. In my minimal Spanish, I decided to pose a peculiar question. "Pedro, to us this is an extraordinary place, a beautiful place. But you have never been anywhere else. My question is this: Do you realize and appreciate that you live in one of the world's great places?" He pulled his head back and, pursing his lips to state the obvious, said in an impassioned growl, *"Sí, señor!"*

Thomas was in the bow of the boat, line stripped out, and Pedro was poling along a muddy bank near the mangroves. A squadron of bonefish had come out of the light, our blind side, and flushed in a starburst of wakes. It wasn't really a shot, so Thomas remained in the bow, ready. After a while, I felt Pedro kick the stem of the bow out to position him and declare, "*macabi*"—bonefish—in his quiet but insistent way that made it clear he expected no screw-ups. We stared hard, testing Pedro's patience, then made out the bonefish about seventy feet away. He was feeding slowly, his back out of water at times and his tail glittering when he swirled deliberately in the shallows to feed. The fish came almost to a stop, faced right, then moved steadily but imperceptibly forward. The bonefish seemed to be staring at the skiff.

This seemed like a tough prospect: the water was much too thin, the fish insufficiently occupied; and since he was alone, his green-and-silver shape all too clear, I couldn't imagine the bonefish would tolerate the slightest imperfection of technique.

Thomas was false-casting hard. Faced with such a good fish, his intensity was palpable throughout the boat. I told him he'd only get one shot at this fish, treading the parental thin line of reminding him of the present importance without exaggerating its difficulty. He released the cast. His loop reached out straight, turned over, and the fly fell about four inches in front of the bonefish.

The fish didn't spook. The fly sank to the bottom. Thomas moved the fly very slightly. The bonefish moved forward over it. I looked up and the bend of the rod extended all the way into the cork handle. The fish burned off through the mangrove shoots which bowed and sprang up obediently. When the fish headed out across the flat, Thomas turned to look at me over his shoulder and give me what I took to be a slightly superior grin. A short time later he boated the fish.

We were actually fishing in the middle of the Sian Ka'an biosphere reserve, over a million acres of the coast of Quintana Roo, savannas, lagoons, and seasonally flooded forest. Our simple camp met the Mexican requirement of integrating human use while preserving the complex and delicate ecosystem whose uniqueness derives not only from the phenomenon of a tropic sea inundating a vast limestone shelf, but from long human history. Every walk that Thomas and I took brought us past earthen mounds that covered Mayan structures. One superb small temple has been excavated and its inspired siting caused us, hunched under its low ceilings, gazing out on the blue sea with bones and pottery at our feet, to fall silent for a good while.

Since I have been unsuccessful in bringing any formality to the job of parenting, I wondered about the matter of generations, and whether or not this concept added much to the sense of cherished companionship I had with my son. And I thought of the vast time-scape implied by our immediate situation and the words of the leader of the French Huguenots when the terrible Menendez led his band of followers into a hollow in the dunes to slaughter them. "In the eyes of God," said the Huguenot, "what difference is twenty years, more or less?"

As we wandered through the barracks of an abandoned copra plantation, I saw a carved canoe paddle leaning against a wall—the kind of ancient design used to propel dugout canoes but probably the backup for an Evinrude. Inside, the walls were decorated with striking graffiti, ankle-grabbing stick ladies subjected to rear entry and the prodigious members of grinning stick hooligans, complete with rakish brimmed hats and cigarettes. There you have it.

MY ANXIETY about Thomas's bonefishing disappeared. He did just fine. Less obsessive about fishing than I am, he had to be harassed into organizing his tackle, showing up at the skiff on time, and fishing instead of crawling around the mangroves to see what was living in there. We began to catch plenty of bonefish in a variety of situations: schooling fish in deep water, generally small, easy prey; small bunches lined up along the edge of a flat, waiting for the tide to come in and help them over; singles and small bunches, tailing and feeding, on the inside flats. Several times I looked up and saw Thomas at a distance, his rod deeply bowed and his fly line shearing an arc toward deeper water. We were happy workers on a big bonefish farm.

"Pedro, are there many permit, *unas palomettas*?"

"Yes, of course."

"Have you had many caught from your skiff?"

"No one catches many *palomettas*."

"How many?"

"Maybe six this year."

Pedro stared in the direction he was poling, getting remarkable progress from the short hardwood crook with which he pushed us along. Florida guides with their graphite eighteen-footers would refuse to leave the dock with an item like this. Pedro had a faint smirk on his face, as though reading my thoughts; more likely he was feeling that the hopelessness of predictably catching a permit was his own secret. The look challenged you to try, but declined to subdue skepticism.

I feel, when searching for permit, as a bird dog must when the unsearched country ahead turns into a binary universe of sign and absence of sign. Now, I certainly couldn't expect my son to feel the same way; here in the Sian Ka'an his attention was trained on *all* the wonders around us, the sea creatures scooting out in front of the skiff in response to Pedro's skillful poling, the spectacular flying squid that sailed across our bow, the cacophonous waterfowl that addressed our passage from the secrecy of the mangroves, the superb aerobatics of frigate birds trying to rob royal terns of their catch. Graciously, Thomas offered me the first cast.

The little bay had a bottom too soft for wading. We were at a relatively low tide and the hermit crabs could be seen clinging to the exposed mangrove roots. A reddish egret made its way along the verge of thin water, head forward, legs back, then legs forward, head back until the sudden release, invisible in its speed, and the little silver fish wriggling crossways in its bill.

"*Palometta*," Pedro said, and we looked back to see which way his phenomenal eyes were directed. A school of permit was coming onto the sandbar that edged the flat. Once noticed, the dark shape of the school seemed busy and its underwater presence was frequently enlarged as the angular shapes of fins and tails pierced the surface. I checked to see if I was standing on my line, then tried to estimate again how much of it I had stripped out. I held the crab fly by the hook between my left thumb and forefinger and checked the loop of line.

Now trailing alongside the boat, that would be my first false-cast. We were closing the distance fast and the permit were far clearer than they had been moments before. In fact, if they hadn't been so busy scouring around the bottom and competing with one another, they could have seen us right now. The skiff ground to a halt in the sand. Pedro said that I was going to have to wade to these fish. Well, that was fine, but the few permit I have ever hooked wading had spooled me while I stood and watched them go. Furthermore, the freshwater reel I was using had lots of backing but no drag. That I'd picked it for the sporting enhancement it provided now seemed plain silly.

I climbed out, eyes locked on the fish.

"Dad!" came my son's voice. "I've got to try for these fish, too!"

"Thomas, damn it, it's my shot!"

"Let me give it a try!"

"They're not going to take that bonefish fly anyway."

How could I concentrate? But now I was nearly in casting position, then heard something behind me. Thomas had bailed out of the boat and was stripping line from his reel. He was defying his father! Pedro was celebrating three thousand years of Mayan family life on this bay by holding his sides and laughing. For all I knew, he had suggested my son dive into the fray.

Once in casting range, I was able to make a decent presentation and the crab landed without disturbance in front of the school. They swam right over the top of it. They ignored it. Another cast, I moved the fly one good strip. They inspected it and again refused. A third cast and a gingerly retrieve. One fish peeled off, tipped up on the fly and ate. I hooked him and he seared down the flat a short distance, then shot back into the school. Now the whole bunch was running down the flat with my fish in their midst. Thomas waded to cut them off and began to false-cast. I saw disaster staring at me as his loop turned over in front of the school and his fly dropped quietly.

"Got one!" he said amiably as his permit burned its way toward open water. Palming my whirling reel miserably, I realized why he had never been interested in a literary career. Not sick enough to issue slim volumes from the interior dark, he instead would content himself with life. He seemed to be enjoying the long runs his fish made; mine made me ill. He was still in diapers when I caught my first permit but my anxiety over a hookup had never abated.

Pedro netted my son's fish, his first permit, and waited, holding it underwater until mine was landed. Thomas came over with the net. When the fish was close, I began to issue a stream of last-minute instructions about the correct landing of a permit. He just ignored them and scooped it up.

This was unbelievable, a doubleheader on fly-caught permit. I was stunned. We had to have a picture. I asked Pedro to look in my kit for the camera. Pedro admitted that he had only had this happen once before. He groped deeper in my kit.

But I had forgotten the camera, and when Thomas saw my disappointment he grabbed my shoulders. He was grinning at me. All my children grin at me, as if I was crazy in an amusing sort of way.

"Dad," he said, "it's a classic. Don't you get it?" He watched for it to sink in. "It's better without a picture."

The permit swam away like they'd known all along that we weren't going to keep them.

Later, I stewed over his use of the word "classic." It was like the day he buried a bonefish fly in the calf of my leg. My expression then was "timeless," he had said. I would have to think about that.

Unintended Consequences

PART OF THE ALLURE of angling is the unexpected. That's why we follow sports when so much else is curated generally on behalf of sales. We are offended by cheating in sports because it is an attempt to make sports predictable. We've all experienced predictable fishing: it's not interesting. At the same time, not all surprises are welcome. A friend invited me to fish his wonderful spring creek, several hours' drive from my home, and I accepted eagerly. At streamside, I strung up my rod while watching a couple of bank feeders pick off drowned mayfly spinners. When the time came to make my first cast, I slid down the bank and broke my ankle. Instead of stalking big, wild trout in pristine surroundings, I lay in a bed of thistles trying to reach the ranch manager on my cell phone. There are better unexpected outcomes, and the annoying first-love-while-angling stories are all too abundant, but they are unexpected and positive, at least at first, before the love object becomes devious or loco. As I reminisced about a lifetime of angling, my thoughts turned to the surprises. Here are a few.

A Surprise Encounter

Early season is all impatience. You scrutinize the USGS streamflow data for your home fishery. Perhaps you know the magic current stream flow number is when you won't be swept off your feet or you won't have to bolo three BB split shots under a pompom indicator. At length, you think you know when it will be, barring unexpected heat or rain on snowfields. Perhaps low country runoff is finished—a long wait: Montana is a snow-based ecosystem. You come to know the patterns of melt to which your passion is beholden, the ones where you live and the ones on rivers a hundred miles away. When big Western rivers blow out, experienced locals know by color which headwater is guilty and how long that color takes to clear.

But then it happens: the cliff-face runs gather familiar luminous green light. Golden Stones are just starting their clumsy flights, the Yellow Sallies vivid as they rise against the pale stone of the cliff. But the river is marginal, flying past. The aspens and cottonwoods are newly leafed and there are birds everywhere, mocking the nuthatches and chickadees who'd stayed all winter. The redtails, our most companionable hawks, beseech one another in screeches and build nests. The ringing calls and drumming of northern flickers say that everything implied by summer at the forty-fifth parallel is still ahead. A few items of human occupancy upstream show up: a retriever dummy, an irrigation canvas, a red-and-white bobber.

The first real fishing days were at hand, at least by my standards, which are those of someone who tries to fish with dry flies even when it is unreasonable. Dividing a stretch of water into a grid to be systematically scoured with my Czech nymphing rig has not engaged my sense of angling romance. But this early hour entailed creeping through brush along a rocketing river, albeit on a warm and sunny day, looking for spots where bits of hydrology had slowed it into slicks where I could float a fly for a few feet.

As I clambered through the vegetation, something caught around my left foot. I tried to kick it free, then felt a sharp pain in my right calf. I was standing on a rattlesnake. I watched him slither down the riverbank, and as I walked toward my house, I tried not to obsess about that fat diamondback, mouth opened flat against my leg.

My friend Dave, a doctor, has a summer cabin up the road. I told him what had happened, and he drove down to view me where I lay on the sofa. We looked at the fang punctures, and as we waited for something to happen, Dave regaled me with snakebite stories from his practice on the West Coast. He explained that most people who are bitten by venomous snakes in his district are either drunk or on drugs. He had some grisly things to share and one of them helped me forget my present plight: the clever fellow who held a rattlesnake in one hand and imitated its flicking black tongue. The reptile rewarded the comedian by biting him in his own tongue.

After an hour, Dave announced "dry strike," and we were free to resume our day. When I told my wife what had happened, she said, "Get a hearing aid."

Most people living around here accept rattlesnakes, but there is a trend among summer people toward eradicating them by attaching GPS locaters to captured snakes and following them to their dens in order to wipe them out wholesale. I understand the impulse and when you come from a place where wildlife is gone altogether, an unpleasant denizen like a rattlesnake probably seems more ominous than it does to those who live with them. You never get all the snakes and a false security reduces your vigilance. In any case, it's a slippery slope. Once you decide that some form of indigenous wildlife is not to your liking and should be eliminated, then you invite others to think alike. Wolves and grizzly bears can be quite naughty and their extermination has a large constituency. Some of the West's most disgraceful activities fly under the banner of predator control.

Technology Plays a Trick

We can't hide from technology, and when I'm fishing with someone who tells me I'm at a huge disadvantage with a down-locking reel seat, I really feel it. But one approaches this new world with hard-earned wariness. Last spring, I was tarpon fishing on the west coast of Florida. I was having a good day and decided to tell a few pals. I sent text messages to my friends staked up around Pine Island Sound and Bokeelia to tell of them of my good luck. But every time I used the word *tarpon*, autocorrect changed it to *Tampon* and my most fervid speeches came out as "3 Tampons in the air," "tail walking Tampons," and so on. Anyway, I recommend vigilance while embracing technology in your quest for meaning, and be prepared for it to surprise you. We don't know who is behind these tricks; they live somewhere in "technology."

A Young Angler Experiences an Unintended Consequence

My cousin Fred, my oldest fishing partner, lives in Little Compton, Rhode Island, where as boys we fished from the rocks and checked the incoming fishing boats offloading at the pier, especially the swordfish boats back when swordfish lived long enough to reach heroic sizes. Their bills adorned the doorways of fishing shacks throughout town. Fred remembers one consequence of fishing by another little boy.

The nurse's problem began with twelve-year-old Cap Phillips fishing for stripers up the shore from our summer house. Cap hooked into a good-size striper and managed to get it to shore where he was perched on a rock. As he was taking the fish off the plug, it thrashed and Cap wound up with a hook deeply embedded in his hand. "Mister!" called Cap, as he came around the corner of our house. "I need help!"

We took him to the fire station at the Commons, hoping the medic on duty would withdraw the hook, but greater medical skill was required. His father, Bud, a local fishing guide, took him by car to Saint Anne's Hospital in Fall River. In the emergency room, the nurse giving him a tetanus shot pricked herself with the needle, and by doing so, set off the AIDS protocol. Cap was then questioned about his sex life and drug history. Finally, he exclaimed, "I'm twelve years old! I've never even kissed a girl!"

When Someone Indifferent to Fishing Damages Our Hopes

The increasing number of women coming to fly-fishing should be instructive to the rest of us. They fish differently. It has long been a mystery that most of the biggest Atlantic salmon have been caught by women. One conjecture is that they aren't so fixated on casting a straight line or moving on too quickly. I met an Englishman at dinner in Reykjavik who had fished the Alta all his life, where the Holy Grail is a fifty pounder. I don't know how I ended up at that meal and the guests seemed baffled by my presence, too. All I could do was eat and listen. In the 1940s, the father of this Englishman persuaded his mother to try fishing—just once—instead of reading under a tree, as she preferred. She went for one day and caught a fifty-pound Atlantic salmon. A half century later, on her death bed, in and out of a coma, she looked up at her son, the baleful Englishman telling the story sitting by her side, and said, "You'll never get a fifty pounder." And with that she died.

Familiar Misbehavior of Floridians Near Water Can Still Surprise
Waterborne hostility in Florida is even more acute than formerly, when routine abuse of clients by their guides was the limit of hostility, and such was the meekness of anglers in those days that retaliatory measures were rarely taken. First prize at last year's Boca Grande tarpon tournament, an emblem of the new order, was an AR15 assault rifle.

At many of the larger Florida boat ramps, people sometimes pull up lawn chairs to watch for mistakes and accidents. Not everyone is handy at backing bumper-hitch trailers and so exciting humiliations may be on view and the goobers in lawn chairs look on with undiminished hopes for disaster.

I was waiting to splash my own boat and ahead of me a man was preparing to launch an old Hewes skiff from his Mercedes SUV. I watched from the side of the ramp on an elevated dock that gave me a good view of the operation. Next to me was a lawyer from West Palm Beach, tall, in a rust-colored leisure suit, dark circles under eyes nearly concealed by rainbow-frame Oakley sunglasses, a weary face that had seen it all, and an odd hairdo that combined a slight pompadour and over-the-ears sides. My attempts to talk to him didn't go far beyond the information that he was a lawyer, delivered in a languid New South accent. He lit a cigarette from a well-worn Zippo and watched the launch with minimum interest.

The best procedure is to back down until the stern of the boat is sufficiently immersed to float it slightly, set the emergency brake, block up a rear tire, and launch the boat. That's not what the driver, a chubby fellow with a white goatee, did. He backed to the right spot to pause, and then I suppose, reaching his foot for the brake, found the accelerator and launched boat, trailer, and automobile straight back into the bayou, where the boat floated to the top and the car went to the bottom.

There was a moment when tragedy seemed at hand, a moment to which the lawyer in his leisure suit failed to react: I glanced to him anxiously but my gaze went unreturned. The pale roof of the SUV glowed from underwater.

The driver swam to the surface. He was wearing a Dallas Cowboys blue windbreaker, filled with air. This caught the lawyer's interest, and he slowly raised the cigarette to his mouth for a puff as he watched the swimming driver. His words seemed to come from deep thought as he watched.

"That's cool," he said. "I hate the fucking Cowboys."

WTF!

Jim was an avid young fisherman from the hills of Oklahoma, a real angler who had worked out some remote and difficult places to fly-fish for bass or anything else that looked like a serious opportunity. He'd had several jobs, selected for their compatibility with fishing, but the last one, telemarketing, had put him on the road to Florida. "I got tired of people hanging up after telling me to eat shit and die." The abuse seemed to linger in the distant gaze that accompanied these memories of the direct speaking style of Oklahoma telephone customers.

I don't know where Jim is now, but when I last heard, he was headed for the Keys and there is no evidence that he has emerged. During the time I knew him, he was visited by various friends from home, rough-and-ready fellows towing battered jon boats who really knew how to catch fish.

We left in my skiff on a sweet morning of southeast winds and nearly cloudless sky to a small basin fed by salty creeks, one of which led for a considerable distance to a circular pond that may have been excavated by the Calusa, who built the tall, distinct mound near it. The bar at the mouth of the creek had enough oysters on it that I thought it best to shut down and pole into the creek with Jim on the bow and ready. Small snappers scattered at our arrival—you could already tell this was a lively place—and as I moved along, I could see just enough tidal movement to assure us that ambush feeders like snook would be active, as well as assurance we'd be able to get back out. This was not a place you would want to get stuck for a full tidal cycle while the infinite biting insects had their way with you. From time to time, Jim took a picture of one thing or another as part of drinking in this lovely place, setting his phone on the deck between shots and scanning the ledges of shadow beneath the mangrove walls where snook liked to plot. They plot against other species and they plot against us.

In this windless place, a clear tide was moving gently, the very thing that would keep us from stranding but the same thing that would keep fish looking in the wrong direction; that is, away from us, a difficult opportunity for presenting the fly. Not that any cast would be easy in this narrow corridor where any variation from a straight backcast would have the fly in the mangroves.

I saw the snook from just a bit out of casting range. It was a big fish turned into the tide and to our advantage, as it was facing our way. It was picking off glass minnows that were carried toward it, requiring very little effort. I was most concerned that I would bump the boat with the push pole and really didn't dare lift it from the water, risking a splash. I made a small unnecessary grunt to alert Jim, who nodded slightly and glanced down to make sure no line was under his feet. We managed to get into casting range without disturbing the snook, and Jim began a few careful, low false casts.

On the deck, his cell phone, set to vibrate, buzzed to life. The snook burst off in a cloud of sand and disappeared. Jim cried out, bent to grab the phone, glared at the screen as he checked the caller's identification. "I told her to never call me again!" He sat on the foredeck and cradled his head in his arms. It was not clear what I should say. I actually remembered her. She drove a red Saab, worked at Southern Commerce Bank in Punta Gorda, and always seemed to be in a bad mood. I hoped Jim would never tell her about her success.

Ingenuity of Florida Developers versus Women's Eternal Traits

For many, marriage is an adversarial arrangement with a commonly renegotiated détente at its center. Because of associated surveillance, few activities fail to arouse suspicion; same-sex golf groups would be an example, unless a member wears a wire and exposes the lurid dialogue. Fishing looks fairly innocent, and mostly is, but an affluent old fellow teaching his "niece" to fish in a remote locale is not unheard of. I recently learned of a vastly wealthy Florida developer whose wife was justifiably in the condition of perpetually smelling a rat. His enormous yacht was an obvious site for misbehavior, and so his wife oversaw all loading and departures for Caribbean waters. She failed to discover that he was bringing women aboard in empty fuel barrels. True story. Another group of Florida developers arranged a private jet trip to remote waters, again with departure supervised by spouses. A stopover in Costa Rica facilitated boarding by sex workers. Once established on the remote island, the sportsmen failed to anticipate the boredom of the sex workers with island life when our sportsmen were at sea trying to catch fish. The anglers returned to extremely disgruntled company, and the women shunned them for the rest of the trip, refusing to dine with them and demanding specialized cuisine from the compliant lodge staff.

An Unexpected Shadow Falls on My Best Fish

It's a familiar picture to lifelong fisherfolk who have read electrifying stories about their beloved sport in the hook-and-bullet press: a tiny rise, a dimple, a blush of subsurface movement signals the start of a long and punishing battle. I was on the New Fork of the Green River in Wyoming. A foul-up at the fly shop meant that I had two licenses for each day I fished, which gives rise to a split personality, one self fly-fishing and the other sunbathing.

I was fishing with Ben Brennan, who has long experience on the New Fork and an undiminished love of the sport, plants, wildlife, and the intricate realm of aquatic insects. Combining his extraordinarily quiet speech with my poor hearing, we learned to emphasize the sights. We saw wonderful things during our day, most of all a breeding pair of goshawks coursing slowly over the river, the clearest view I'd ever had of these forest birds, normally seen hurtling through trees, dark and mysterious as bats. The New Fork is an odd place, a sweet, sinuous river bottom, full of life and big trout, surrounded by abandoned subsistence ranches, fracking facilities, and overgrazed land. Each of our companions said independently at one time or another,

"How would you like to live around here?" It was a first-rate opportunity to learn what the energy industry thinks of landscape.

Wyoming has very restrictive riparian laws, meaning the landowner also owns the bottom of the river: you can't wade, you can't get out of the boat, and you can't anchor. Here, where land values are high and the Jackson metroplex within striking distance, these laws are enforced. The owner himself may occasionally be viewed in his new hat and on his horse. In remoter parts of Wyoming, where good fishing also exists and where the riparian laws are the same, the landowners are working too hard ranching to worry about somebody going fishing.

I fished some attractor dry fly or another; the green and gray drakes never quite happened but a smattering of Golden Stones and Pale Morning Duns kept the fish looking up. The fishing was very good, and in the middle of the day, the cast I mentioned earlier, a fish made a mere dimple of a rise. I told Ben I thought it was a tiny fish and Ben agreed, but then I felt the serious weight of a big fish churning deep in the river. I really wanted to see this fish most of all and to land it, of course; but losing a fish is not so bitter if you have seen it. I fought on as Ben stood by with the net.

After several powerful runs, the trout was almost next to the boat, a big male brown, not quite close enough but Ben tried for it anyway. The fish teetered out of the net. I decided that there was no sense prolonging things. I had a strong leader, and accepting the risk, I pulled hard to lead the fish closer.

At that point, the fish I had in fact hooked, the five-inch fish of the storied "dimpled" rise, still holding my fly, flew out of the brute's mouth. The big trout swam in furious circles to have lost a sure meal.

Ben shouted to put the small fish back in play. I stripped line until I could feel its weight on my leader and launched it. The sprat landed with a splash and the big trout found it quickly, gulped it, and held on hard until Ben could net it.

It was my biggest fish of the trip and, so far, my only venture into live-bait fishing for trout. I look askance at those stories that begin, "At first I thought it was a snag." I will want it to *still* be a snag at the end of the tale; I don't care how long the fight lasts, preferably a very long time with a genuine moment of self-loathing at the end, as a committed dry-fly fisherman resorts to bait.

The Lesson

As with the anglers who have preceded you, when you go fishing, you are committed to the idea that you don't know what will happen. It's possible you are tired of living a life in which you seem always to know what to expect, but there is risk. A frontier story says that if you twist a mule's tail, you won't be as pretty as you once were but you will know more.

Sasha and the Salmon

I WAS ASKED TO BE A GUEST at the Atlantic Salmon Reserve in Russia, a princely invitation, except that first I had to get to Murmansk, which is a long way from my house. Jet lag is different every time. In Helsinki, I wandered the hotel corridors blearily greeting the chambermaids. I staggered into the parking lot to stare at cars. I climbed a viewing tower to watch planes take off. Finally I met my new friends, Bruce and Kurt, sitting side by side at a long desk in their hotel room, an avalanche of fly-tying materials spread from one end to the other, reading glasses in place. The doodads in their vises suggested they were suffering jet lag, too. I ordered a cheeseburger from the jackals of the Hilton, who wanted thirty dollars for it, plus a tip to the lad in the platinum Mohawk who brought it, wringing his hands and staring at my wallet.

In the morning we flew to Russia. It had seemed remarkable that we were on such a recreational junket, flying over the waters that had sustained the great Murmansk Run during WWII, convoys that brought one hundred fifty thousand American aircraft to our Soviet allies, soon our enemies, now our friends again—and our fishing hosts! All in my lifetime. The U-boats, newly situated in conquered Norway's Nazi submarine pens, devastated the shipping. The German battleships had fared less well and after successful Allied landings of tanks, fighters, bombers, and fuel, an infuriated Hitler withdrew them. The British minesweeper *Bramble* sank with all hands, as did the German destroyer *Friedrich Eckboldt*. These sailors rested on the bottom of the sea beneath us. The convoys of the Murmansk Run and German attempts at interception were prosecuted in winter, or "arctic night," once the Allies learned that summer runs of twenty-four-hour daylight exposed them excessively to enemy predation. The battle on the Barents Sea took place in pitch-dark, with the participants hunting one another in unlighted warships. A former U-boat captain had recently made this same trip to fish for salmon. The aging captain was still proud of all the ships he'd sent to the bottom.

The Murmansk airport serves a city of four hundred thousand: a vast Soviet mural in concrete on one wall, a collapsing luggage conveyor that hadn't worked in years, customs officials in what looked like unpainted phone booths, when off the plane came the luggage, dominated by fishing gear, a mountain of duffels with rod cases sticking out, deposited unceremoniously into a huge orange dump truck and driven from the plane to the terminal. The Russian women working around the airfield in hot green safety vests tottered on the broken pavement in stiletto heels.

I would soon catch the fish of a lifetime, I mean, *so far*. The event, when it finally rolled around, presented such a complexity of meaning that I'm still thinking about it and what "fish of a lifetime" actually means. I had long thought that the twenty-six-pound sea-run brown on a Bomber was that fish, but I don't think so anymore. I think it's this one. I can still remember when it was a bullhead on a worm, a gar on a spear, a carp on an arrow, a walleye on a Lazy Ike, or a snook on a Zara Spook. I could go back through my whole life this way, fish to fish, and that's what my future looks like, too. But a new one was waiting for me in the Rynda River.

Since the Barents Sea is closed to all use except that of the Russian military, principally its submarine fleet, there has been no commercial fishing; the runs of sea trout and salmon go about their business uniquely unmolested unless their travels take them to Norway, whose fisheries management practices are greatly to the disadvantage of the fish. Norway, with her oil wealth, could do better by her natural resources but has declined. Her salmon interceptions are brutal to say the least. That said, the rivers of the Kola are as pristine as can be found anywhere on Earth.

We were soon bound for the Atlantic Salmon Reserve in an angler-filled helicopter, a congeries of great rivers that includes the Kharlovka, the Rynda, and the Zolotaya. Beneath us a landscape of tundra, blue lakes, white patches of remaining snow, a community of Sami people collectivized under the Soviets, some of whom will still drift north with the reindeer as the summer progresses—a frankly inhospitable-looking landscape and obvious bonanza for mosquitoes. Like indigenous people elsewhere, the Sami have had their subsistence practices greatly curtailed by encroaching civilization, and even our sport fishing has interfered with their rights.

Siberia is not known for its wholesome climate, and imagining your needs from half a planet away results in colossal overpacking: packing for heat, packing for cold, packing for dry, packing for wet. The salmon reels with various lines weigh like lead. Even four-piece Spey rods fit nowhere in normal interiors. Since we are now slaves to electronics, we must be prepared to plug them in all over the world where all the plugs are different. Another five pounds of adapters helps with the load. The current practice of putting wheels and tow handles on luggage encourages unreasonable excess. I encountered a Kharlovka-bound angler towing three of these as well as a two-hundred-pound Alaskan adviser who was teaching him how to fish.

I fished my week with a guide named Alexander Duschenko—"Sasha"—a fifty-two-year-old man with a well-trimmed mustache and an infectiously cheerful demeanor. All the guides were exceptionally sure-footed as they carried heavy packs over rough, boulder-filled terrain. You begin any new river by slipping and stumbling while the feet learn and gradually adjust their expectations, until you are sailing along far better than those first days when you appeared to be drunk. You don't bound from boulder to boulder as your guide does with his big pack, but you spend less time flooding your waders. If I ever seemed to be flagging, Sasha offered me my choice of either a Mars Bar or a Snickers. This came out as "Mozsneekiz?" and I would answer "Moz" or "Sneekiz." I was adapting. There were Moz days and Sneekiz days but seldom both on the same day.

Fishing by helicopter took some getting used to. The Rynda is a long river and can accommodate many anglers if they can be distributed. This takes a big chopper, in this case, the MI-8 Russian workhorse. The door of the chopper opens and an aluminum staircase is thrown down. Holding hats with one hand and with rods pressed against chests, the anglers scramble aboard, clutching at the red ear-protection muffs hanging in a cluster from the ceiling. We sit on the floor of the helicopter, a friendly group, who tries and fails to talk over the noise, resorting to hand signals that don't work, ending with hopeful thumbs-ups at each drop off. The helicopter lands; you and your fellows are crouched on the ground, rods broken down and held in a cluster with rubber bands. If you aren't on your knees but instead on the balls of your feet as you crouch, you will possibly be sent tumbling by prop wash. I saw this happen a couple of times, quite harmlessly and with all the dignity of a Three Stooges sight gag. At the end of the day, the guide fires a pocket flare into the sky when he hears the helicopter in the area. It streams a thin crimson band toward the earth and the sound of the chopper shifts as it turns to your location.

When the helicopter leaves and you and your guide are alone by the river, the silence and isolation seem acute. I thought that modern warfare must feel like this: sophisticated equipment, complete communication with home base, and then isolation in a lonely place, back to basics. In my generation you invariably know people who have been dropped off in lonely places with a more somber "Good luck," gazing at the departing helicopter from a squatting position.

Sasha liked to use English expressions in an ironic way, unique in that he knew little English to begin with. Thus when fishing was frustratingly slow, he liked to call out in a hopeless voice, "Tight lines!" His exuberant manner of travel over broken ground with his big pack, his wise nod at fresh bear scat in the trail as though to confirm that of course we are about to be eaten, an especially large hooked salmon in midair, "Nothing to worry about." My persistent cough brought from the States reminds him that I'm not smoking enough cigarettes (I don't smoke). I was surprised when I asked him about his years of service in the war in Chechnya, when a cigarette must have been a pleasant distraction. He turned away from me and I could see his shoulders shaking with muffled sobs: he had lost many friends. Chechnya seems to have been Russia's Vietnam, a stalemate never supported by the Russian people, that left many of its veterans psychologically abandoned.

As to the Chechens, said Sasha, "They are the same people." I did my best to comfort him and soon he was calm again, if quieter than before. "I have been given a second life," he said, and pointed to the beautiful Rynda. "This is my life now." Sasha does not hunt; he says he doesn't understand why anyone would shoot an animal or anything else that was alive.

We caught fish early on, strong fish not long out of the ocean. It was a thrill to catch these hard, fast fish. But it was less about capture, less even than about releasing fish. You begin as a predator, end as a stakeholder. I was using a fourteen-foot Spey rod and a floating line. I had more than enough flies, most on Ken Sawada double hooks; but each morning Sasha got up, made coffee, lit a cigarette, put on his earphones and Russian music—and tied a single fly. That's what we used. The flies were inevitably small, size twelves, well tied and based on something in Sasha's mind. My flies stayed in my coat.

The Rynda was a beautiful river, one rapid and pool after another, inevitably tangled currents everywhere. I fished with accustomed attention to line speed, and Sasha watched the water. His eyes were remarkably attuned to any movement of salmon, and when a fish moved, however subtly, he reacted as though struck on the chin. I began to know what this meant. My eyes might wander to a mink on the riverbank or a string of reindeer crossing the bluffs, but Sasha was intent on the water.

We hiked from one pool to another, occasionally passing through a little copse of trees, birches with crooked trunks. Out of the wind, you noticed the birds, the feeling of shelter the trees made in a hostile landscape. Because of the presence of trees and the absence of permafrost, this was taiga, not tundra. At a bare minimum, taiga seemed habitable. As we sat near these trees eating our bowls of borscht, I asked Sasha about his life when the Kola Peninsula was in the midst of the arctic winter. I had seen the Soviet-style apartment buildings in Murmansk, towering featureless slabs with laundry drying outside the perforations that stood for windows. Sasha lived on the ninth floor of such a building and took various jobs through the winter, fending off attempts by his wife to make him give up smoking. When not working he slept, smoked, watched TV, or went ice fishing. "It's dark all the time." His hometown was a village on the Volga, thousands of miles away. He visited his mother there in summertime and seemed to delight in the world of his childhood: backyard vegetable gardens and chickens running in the street. Nothing in Russia is nearby: it has eleven time zones.

Sasha kept a jar in his shirt so that he wouldn't leave so much as a cigarette butt on the taiga. He was a long way from Chechnya and this was another way the Atlantic Salmon Reserve strove to occupy the place without leaving a footprint. Boardwalks between buildings kept us from crushing the plants, and the tagging program revealed a remarkable rate of return for the fish as we fishermen drove up their value. The lodge was comfortable and familiar to a traveling angler: guests showing you fish on their iPads, clouds of cigar smoke, enthusiasm that rose to a howl by midnight. The odd burst of away-from-home silliness: we had ice cream for dessert, two small white globes. A guest asked the attractive serving girl, "Do you find these erotic?"

"These?"

"Yes, do you find them erotic?"

"I do what?"

"Never mind."

Pretty Katya greeted the returning anglers each day with excellent English she learned at school in Murmansk. I asked if she traveled, especially in what must be the long, very dark winters here at the edge of the arctic. She said that it was nice to go to the beach when her budget allowed. "Egypt or Thailand, but Egypt is kind of a problem for going to the beach just now." Those pesky revolutions.

So we now move on to the "fish of a lifetime." Sasha led me to a pool called Horse Shoe, I'm not quite sure why. It is one of those runs whose current causes you to stare for a long time trying to understand the drift. From the left bank, it runs toward you, a swinging undercut that corrects itself in time to run straight to the rim of the next break, an even bevel of water falling away into the subsequent rapids.

The right corner of the break is a split and a small countercurrent: the swinging fly tends to linger there, and mine did. It stopped more emphatically than the swing should have indicated. It was the fish of a lifetime: just stopped the fly. Then it moved deliberately back to the middle of the pool and stopped with such conviction that after a long moment I asked Sasha if I still had the fish since it felt more and more like bottom. Then the salmon erupted and hung in midair, the biggest salmon I'd ever hooked. Sasha said—I think this is Russian humor— "Don't worry, it's a small one."

Once salmon are in the river a few days, they are reluctant to go back downstream. That was not true of this fish: it bolted down through the rapids, my size-twelve double still attached, and I began to run, through boulders, down a reindeer trail, around birch trees, to another set of rapids. I wanted to stand and fight, but the fish blasted down the next set of rapids, and Sasha kept running and urging me to do the same through huge granite boulders. Again, I wanted to stop but Sasha wouldn't allow it. I was seriously out of breath, and when I thought this was the last trip through rapids, the fish set out again through another. I honestly wondered if I could follow but Sasha beseeched me. After the third rapids, the salmon stopped and we had a more conventional fight. Because this was such an exceptional fish, the likelihood of losing it seemed dreadful, and I began to prepare myself. I wanted to be able to accept the loss and not feel just sick.

Twice the fish came almost to Sasha's net and bolted. Sasha tried to get under it on the second bolt but ended up sliding into the river up to his waist. On the third try, he had the fish in the net, and for this angler, seeing the great silver arc suspended in the net was simply overwhelming. My lungs were burning and a steady stream of perspiration ran down my sides and back: a big, beautiful, bright male, so recently in the Barents Sea.

Was this the fish of a lifetime? Not yet. Sasha wanted to weigh the fish but the scale was back where we'd eaten lunch, on the other side of the river. He asked me to keep the fish in the water until he returned; then he set out and would be gone nearly a half hour. I sat on the edge of the river, the fish submerged and close at hand: it, like me, was gasping for oxygen. We seemed to be recovering at about the same speed. I touched the slightly frayed dorsal, then the big pectorals, which were unexpectedly rigid, like parts of an airplane. The lenticular spots on the thick shoulders gave the fish the beauty of a leopard. All the two of us wanted to do was breathe. The salmon made no effort to escape, just steadily faced into the current, pumped water through its gills with the movement of its jaws. Such a beautiful fish. I kept thinking: *my God, what a beautiful fish.*

Sasha returned and we weighed the salmon: thirty pounds, caught wading along a lovely river. So, was it now the fish of a lifetime? It was time to release the fish, to watch it return to its journey. Sasha lowered the net, and the salmon, having rested for half an hour, swam a few strokes and sank to the bottom on its side, trying to die. Sasha seized my arm, then waded out and was able to reach deep and tail the salmon and bring it back to shore. I took it from him and sat in the river, water lapping over the top of my waders. I held the fish by the thick wrist of its tail and supported it facing into the current with my right hand under its belly. We stayed there for a very long time as my feeling for this fish deepened. After a while, the salmon began to kick, at first tentatively and then with more powerful thrusts of its tail until I heard myself say, "Want to give it a try?" I lowered the hand that was under the salmon's belly and it kicked harder. I released the tail. With real strength, the fish swam out then into the hard current at the middle. When it disappeared it became the fish of a lifetime.

I'd found a message in the river.

Steelhead

I STOOD IN THE NEAR DARK at the top of the trail that led down a
series of switchbacks to the river. A neighbor had told me that for
several days there'd been grizzly tracks all down the trail. I thought
that grizzlies probably liked these low light levels and could see well
enough to take your face off with a swipe. I was certain that if I could
pass this test, I would catch a least one steelhead almost on arrival.
That was strong incentive and a steelhead had a better chance of forcing my move than a channel cat, perch, or horned pout. I fingered the
bear spray and thought the sliding cap was awkward considering
the speed of a bear. A friend of mine was attacked by a grizzly while
he carried a rifle. He shot from the hip as there wasn't enough time to
raise the gun to his shoulder and dispatch the airborne carnivore.

An acquaintance had given me a tin of After the Rapture Mints
that you could use to sweeten your breath. Moreover, I'd had a disqui-
eting dream: in it I strolled a small, luxurious mall filled with flowers
in hanging baskets and boutique stores whose fragrances filled the air.
I stopped at a small bakery to buy a croissant. The pretty girl wearing a French apron, her hair in a French twist, speaking with a French
accent asked me if I was a steelheader. I said that I was and she asked if
I would like to see the last steelhead on Earth: "*Zee* last steelhead." As
a dream, so far, kind of moronic. She led me out behind the bakery and
there, in a concrete tank filled with dirty, slimy water slowly finned a
huge steelhead, nearly blind and covered with barnacles. "It's the last

steelhead?!" I cried, and woke up, liberated from the satanic French bakery and what it foretold of a terrible future. Angling has its characteristic memories and probably they are different for every angler. When I think of steelheading, I imagine myself about to come over the bank or out of the brush at first light to see if someone I would like to kill is in the tailout. When hiking to the railroad tracks south of Moricetown on the Bulkley, it is sheer torment to hear the whine of a jet boat coming through the trees. I once clambered down a steep bank on one of the Skeena headwaters to find Dick Cheney's helicopter parked on the gravel bar. Oy!

When you start down a narrow, forested footpath imprinted with grizzly tracks, it's important to keep your motivation clear; in this case, catching steelhead. I carried my bear spray in my right hand with my thumb on the slide release. In the interest of making my bear bells ring out with authority, I discovered myself adopting a springy gait emphasizing the balls of my feet. I noted that when walking flat-footed the bells fell silent. I considered that seeing someone with a pole in one hand, a can in the other, festooned with bells, and bouncing on the balls of his feet would incite an attack in most cities of the world. Why would a bear feel differently? I thought about the big cattle-killing grizzly mounted in the Smithers airport that I had examined, standing next to a tall German holding a huge set of moose antlers, its tips encased in protective Styrofoam. We glanced at each other and nodded grimly, then went back to contemplating the bear.

Once I reached the river, I felt relieved. At the base of the trail I made out the bear's tracks in the river sand, but being able to see farther than the wooded sides of the trail made the difference. And the brightening day. I walked the shoreline, old pink salmon carcasses strewn among the boulders, ravens awakening, until I found the ledge under the high banks where the long slot showed green, a place I understood—understanding being roughly equal to knowing when and where the drift changed, fly speed altered, and often enough, a bite ensued. It happened right away, a bright, pissed-off hen of twelve pounds. Her jumps were so violent she hardly penetrated the water, bouncing off it as though on concrete. Then nothing happened, and nothing happened for quite a while.

The big fish came at another place entirely. This place was a characteristic bend in the big Skeena tributaries: a long, hard seam, lots of frog water in the corner, a fast dry-line swing in the upper portion that changed speed as the fly tried to pull away and across the river—not a morning spot, not a tailout. And it was a typical big-fish take, like the moment in an old movie when someone with a cigarette dangling from his lips says, "Don't nobody move." The fish was . . . *on.* That was the prologue: no screaming run, no jumps. I just wasn't getting anywhere and I wanted to see the fish before it got away, which seemed likely. For a very long time, the steelhead did what he felt like, sometimes running upstream against hard current, sometimes just crossing the river with the big bow in my line pulling at the corner of his mouth. But he was tiring and when I thought I'd led him to shore, he eddied up behind a boulder at the edge of the fast current and just stopped. I realized he needed to swim no harder than the inhabitant of a koi pond to keep me from landing him. I went downstream and pulled, stood perpendicular to the fish and pulled, tried a slacker line: no dice.

I was going to have to go out to him, but I couldn't quite get there before my waders threatened to fill. I did have a fourteen-foot rod and with it I reached across the eddy, which encouraged the fish to move slightly toward mid-river and out of the slipstream that had so far defeated me. With this we sashayed downstream together until I had him on the beach, my biggest steelhead, a wolfish male, thick throughout his length. Just looking at fish is a big part of this, but mainly I thought of that melancholy dream of the last steelhead and, as he slipped from my hand and disappeared into deeper water, I hoped that neither this one, nor any other, would be the last.

Seeing Snook

I STARTED FISHING around Boca Grande as a boy. My father brought me here when I was eleven years old to fish for tarpon: I caught my first one in Boca Grande Pass. For years my father and brother fished here with a redheaded guide who died from complications of skin cancer. My father and his friends, all clients of the redheaded guide, came to pay their last respects. The old guide was laid out in the living room of his small clapboard house, surrounded by family and friends. In the middle of it all, supported by her sisters, was his grief-stricken widow. When my father and his friends walked in, she looked up blearily, adjusted her focus, and cried, "There's the sonsabitches that killed my husband!" My father and his pals, in coats and Countess Mara ties, clutching Dobbs hats, made humble obeisance until escape was possible. "I thought those crackers would jump us," my father commented in a grave voice, as his group headed for the Pink Elephant bar for an eye-opener.

You reach a point at which you have to view your life through the things you've spent so much time doing. The alternative is a perilous feeling of waste. Cancer and gulag survivors alike treasure their experiences for reasons best known to them. The rest of us have logged more platitudinous days, and it takes an effort to assign their place and value. I've spent as much of my life fishing as decency allowed, and sometimes I don't let even that get in my way. Especially when it comes to snook.

Snook remind me of brown trout—something in their covert nature, their eccentric choices in safe harbors, their sensitivity that seems designed to humiliate the angler when less dramatic options would get the job done. In short, snook are sleazy.

They are also hard to see, hard to hook, hard to land, and, because they are so good to eat, hard to release. But release them we do. Cold weather reduces them to torpor; colder weather kills them. When they're at the threshold of death, a translucent window appears in the tops of their heads. Sometimes, when a snook follows your fly, then takes, you notice a quick roll up on its side, as though the fish were bringing the target in for close vision. The snook refusal has a quality of its own: a long cross-eyed follow, then a turn off. Snook just leave when suspicious, or change their swimming rhythm. They can also crash bait as well as jacks or bonito. There is something touching about snook, their funny-faced striving, their sneakiness, their lazy travel turning into serious speed. Their heedless jumps fill us with esthetic merriment.

The truth is, I have always had trouble catching them and felt that this was something I was going to have to work harder at. I decided to fish with a guide at least once a week, and I called on Austin Lowder, who guides here in the winter and in Montana, where he's from, in the summer. I'd heard he was effective but very demanding, and I thought I could stand a little embarrassment, as long as I learned something. I soon confirmed that Austin is not the guide for the angler who is comfortable with his bad habits or has lost the ability to learn. As we approached a group of redfish our first day together—brick-colored tails turning slowly, a pink, wavering shape below the surface, grubbing out baby blue crabs—I adjusted my stance to face them and cast. The tails disappeared, and I had no targets. "Don't move your feet," Austin grunted, and we looked for some new fish.

There was a single fish tailing at the edge of the mangroves. In the branches above him, a dozen wood storks watched my performance. This would take a long cast. As I began, Austin's cell phone rang in his pocket. I made the throw but a loop caught under my shoe. Fish gone.

I heard Austin say to the caller, "Just missed a fish. Guy with tennis shoes."

If you fish away from your home waters, guides are an excellent investment, although, after a pleasant day together, they will describe you to the other guides as a complete idiot. There are two kinds of clients: the meek and the proud. The former are happy to be insulted and abused; the latter regard guides as indentured servants. I'm a mixture of the two. I can accept a certain amount of abuse if I'm learning something; then indignation sets in and I become disagreeable. Austin's belief that a successful day on the water consists of doing a lot of little things right was a useful regimen for me. Among his assertions: don't move your feet when approaching fish; don't talk (they can hear you); don't trail a loop in the water; don't cast overhead unless you're a long way from the fish; watch all low-flying birds (they spook fish); and so on, in an ever-lengthening list.

Austin assumes you're trying to get better, but he's a strict instructor. Your first impression from fishing a few days with him is that you have lost the ability to pay sufficiently close attention.

Reaching into my tackle bag for my binoculars to look at a hooded warbler that had just appeared in the mangroves, I heard Austin say, "Put them back. You don't need binoculars." He dinged away at me for days on things like this, and eventually I conformed, though a few remarkable things stopped us both: a peregrine power-diving in perfectly still air, creating a searing sound of attack; an immense stork, a jabiru that had drifted away from its Central American home—from fifty yards away we could hear it crunching crabs with its colossal beak. In any case, back to work.

A big snook lay like a black arrow in the clear water atop an oyster bar that glowed yellow in the afternoon light. I was rigged for redfish but cast anyway. The fish rushed the fly, took hard, and ran. I was forced to play him gently to keep from breaking him. After a heedless jump, he made a run for the mangroves. I had to pull hard to stop him, and I got away with it. I landed the fish and kept him alongside long enough to admire the peculiar beauty of a grown snook—the upward cast of the eyes, the beautiful undershot mouth with its sandpaper interior, the boxlike shape of the body between its ventral fins, the slight greenish cast overall, and the amber fins.

Austin wanted a picture of this fish. "Hold him like a man!" he commanded.

The next day Austin and I fished together turned out to be when a stormy northwester was rolling down the Gulf Coast. I assumed we'd have to cancel, but Austin laughed at the suggestion. We tossed gear into the skiff while the north wind tore through the usually placid bayou, rattling the palms around us. As we got into our foul-weather gear, I found it hard to be optimistic. Austin called to Bill, the collector of ramp fees, "I know it's no fishing day! I just want to get paid!"

I hoped this was merely the grim joke it appeared to be, but I was ambivalent about our prospects, and my pessimism increased as Austin powered his Hell's Bay skiff over an angry gray chop. After repeated lashings of forty-mile-per-hour cold salt water, I moved back to the downwind side of the boat. I tried to look where we were going, but I was soon reduced to cowering in the noise of the two-stroke Yamaha, the hammering separations between the seat and my backside, and the sheets of wind-borne seawater.

We ran into a broad bay that narrowed and finally disappeared against a wall of mangrove swamp. Here there was no wind. Clouds scudded overhead, but we were in a place that was quiet as a church, and how very nice it seemed. Austin anchored the boat and we got out, entered a winding creek much like a prairie trout stream, with a sandbar on one side and an undercut bank on the other. I lost count of all the snook we caught and released.

It wasn't really a story you could tell without ruining your credibility. Angling often requires eluding your fellow anglers and discovering opportunities others don't want, and here is another lesson I'd learned from Austin: go fishing when only a fool leaves his house.

"You know, Austin, I'm thinking of writing about fishing this winter. I learned a lot. I suppose you'll be in it. Might do some good."

"I don't care. I've already got everything I want."

"Well, then, let's use a pseudonym for you."

"If you're going to do it, you might as well use my name."

"I was thinking of Captain Marvel."

"Captain Marvel . . . Hey, I like it!"

In the early years that I fished the shallows, we poled our boats from the bow; poler and angler were at the same level. Now the poler—the guide—is on an elevated platform and generally can see much farther than formerly. This should be an advantage to the team, not an opportunity for the guide to humiliate his angler, but this principle is frequently violated by a disorder known by its acronym PIMP—Platform-Induced Moronic Phaseout, and anyone who mounts a poling platform is in jeopardy of contracting it. I've had it several times. Standing up there with the graphite push pole in hand, with all its feeling of thrust and weaponry, you stare down at male-pattern baldness and sunburn and can't help but cry out, "What're you anyway, blind?"

"Big snook, nine o'clock, seventy feet going left!"

I looked all over the brown-and-gray-mottled bottom for a gray-and-mottled snook.

"I can't see him."

"He's right there!"

"I don't know where the fuck he is!"

"He's right in front of you! He's right next to that little island!"

"I don't see any little island!"

Austin's shoulders slumped. The push pole knocked against the platform. "He's gone."

"I just couldn't see him."

"He was right next to that little island."

I was getting hot. "What little island?"

"It was just this little floating island."

"Show me the little floating island."

Austin laughed, somewhat guiltily I thought. "Forget it," he said.

"I want to see the little floating island."

Austin ruefully poled the boat backward and pointed to a scrap of floating moss perhaps the size of my hand. I let on that it wasn't much of a landmark. I turned back to scan the water ahead.

"Let me offer this," said Austin from behind me in an abradable tone. "You didn't see the fish."

This left me speechless. But I was prepared to admit that I needed to work on seeing. Whether fishing with Austin or fishing alone, I strained to see better, and at the end of the day my eyes were worn out. Later, Austin, perhaps feeling he'd been a bit hard on me, said, "You need a prescription." I knew he wanted me to get glasses. He told me a kindly story about a citrus grower, a lifelong snook man, who had acquired prescription glasses. "Now, when I say nine o'clock, seventy feet"—a reference to my missed snook—"he says, 'Got 'im.'"

Seeing fish is the essence of shallow-water angling. Anglers who see fish exceptionally well can fish successfully in less productive water than anglers who don't. Fishermen love equipment and are always looking for mechanical advantages, but there is nothing to compare with learning to see well; if you see well enough, you can walk out in the mud with no boat and catch fish. I wasn't seeing well enough.

Not long ago, in response to a spell of insomnia, I learned some of the principles of meditation, to empty my mind piece by piece. It was like the old game of jacks—cautiously lifting each jack clear of its neighbor until only the empty background remained. I began to use this small skill to see better. Seeing fish well is usually assumed to be the result of concentration, but concentration bears too much of the deliberate—too much willpower and too little intuition about the way wild creatures use surroundings and how they exploit willpower into lies for the credulous predator.

Instead of longing for sleep, I longed to see better. I began to identify the things that kept me from seeing fish—motionless fish, slow-traveling fish, fish concealed in mangrove roots, fish up light, fish in glare, fish in shadows. I continued to scan ahead as the bottom flowed toward me in the gentle lap of the push pole, and when some thought about an unreturned phone call or e-mail tried to elbow its way in, the old insomniac let it all out the backdoor. I learned to sail through thoughts as though they were clouds, and this relieved me of direct combat with intrusion. I sailed through clouds and looked into the water.

Before any real progress, however, I had another prod from Austin. We were standing on Tarpon Street in front of my little railroad house, the sun glinting off the tin roof, through the grapefruit tree.

Leaning on his trailered skiff, Austin pointed down the street. "Read that sign. I think you need a prescription." It was a realtor's sign with enticements in small print. I read it aloud. He looked confused. "I still think you need a prescription." He got into his truck and drove off.

My wife said to me one evening after Austin and I had fished ten hours in a twenty-mile-per-hour wind, "This fishing you and Austin do just sounds like work." It gave me pause. My bones ached, my eyes were red, my tendinitis was aroused. There were no physical benefits—no aerobics, no stretching. It was actually probably bad for anyone who did it. Hemorrhoids, varicose veins, fallen arches come to mind. After a decade or two your dermatologist pleads with you to give it up. You consume a world of fossil fuel trying to get close to nature. A poet says to you, "I ask the fish permission to give herself to me, for I am hungry. I become the fish. The fish becomes me." The twisted sister within says, "I just want to kick fin."

I also have issues with the sun. It raises water temperatures to the point that snook want to come out of their winter hidey-holes and start busting bait. But snook are perhaps better suited to its effects than I. My wife found on the Internet some discounted bedsheets of "thousand-count cotton." I wasn't sure what that is, but they're right smooth, and we were right proud to have them, but by the morning my bleeding lips had ruined them. I moved from 45 SPF to white gobs of zinc oxide and then to a kind of tube sock for my whole head, surrounded by a broad straw sombrero from a saddle shop in Alpine, Texas. I had become a cross between a fool and a leper, staring at tide tables. When I ran the skiff at anything over half speed, the sombrero folded back and I became a child's nightmare of Deputy Dawg, a macabre heat-seeking cartoon of not-easily-understood motivation.

Mostly, I fished alone.

One of the last days Austin and I fished this spring, we ran down south in Pine Island Sound to a creek with several shallow bays appended to it; left the boat tied to the push pole, which was staked into the soft bottom; and walked a bay that was almost, at this tide, dry land. We stood there silently for a long time, and nothing happened; nothing could happen because there was no water for it to happen in. The wind rustled the mangroves; egrets came and went. Off by the boat, a group of pelicans had surrounded some bait and would flap forward without taking off to scoop up a meal; tucking their chins to swallow, they looked polite and bashful. However, nothing was going on at all as we gazed at little more than bare ground. I was using all my mind tricks to keep looking and to avoid potential commentary on my eyesight.

The flat began to moisten. Austin stood beside me with his unrelenting thousand-yard stare. What are we staring at? I wondered. Austin wasn't saying. The tide had turned, and over time the flat flooded, at first with an inch or two; at about half a foot of depth, the snook, lazy pikelike shapes, began to come. They came steadily, and we both caught them in a string of explosive battles. They came in such volume that it was soon necessary for us to stand back-to-back to manage the onslaught. We lost count of the fish we released, and Austin actually admitted it was the best day he'd ever had. My arm was lead.

I once had an episode of serious depression, and its onset was marked by a loss of interest in fishing. I gave away tackle. I sold cheap my cherished Bogdan reel, which was presented to me thirty years later at a usurious price.

I marvel at people discussing depression, gnawing the topic of their own malaise like dogs on a beef knuckle. My own experience of it was a disinclination to speak at all. I had the feeling of being locked in a very small and unpleasant room with no certainty of exit, and I recall thinking that it was the sickest you could possibly be and that my flesh had been changed to plaster. My business at the time was flight from expectations.

It was spring in Montana, and two old friends quite wisely arrived in my yard with a drift boat to take me to the river. I managed to say that I'd go if I didn't have to talk. As I was manifestly off my rocker, they were quick to agree, perhaps relieved at not having to hear my present thoughts. Once gliding silently down the Yellowstone, oars dripping, lines arcing out from either end of the boat, I began for the first time to picture better days, and it proved a turning point. I thought of incessant-angler pal and novelist Richard Brautigan, who relinquished his fly rod as he spooled up for suicide. Fishing, for many, is an indispensable connection to earth and life, and it matters little that the multitude that practices it is incapable of translating its ambiguities into another idiom.

A lingering, cool blow out of the northeast dropped water temperatures again, spread foam lines across green whitecapped waters, and shrank the broad pallet of local angling geometry to a gerrymandered world of lees around islands and oyster bars. Each jaunt meant donning oilies and the continuous sting of salt water on sunburned skin.

Mark Phillips—an Alaskan guide—and I went fishing anyway, taking a good spanking as we ran northeast to hide from the wind among the small mangrove keys scattered along the mainland. Mark told me a defining snook story as we poled out of the wind, staring into the water. He had cast to a huge snook, and the fish had followed his fly intently. Just at the moment he hoped for a strike, his cell phone, which he had set on vibrate and placed on the gunwale, went off, and the buzz put the fish to flight. He threw down his rod, answered the phone, and endured an unpleasant conversation with a despised ex-girlfriend. Another sleazy snook moment.

We caught a couple of small fish, anchored the boat in eight inches of water, and split up to wade, barefoot for maximum stealth. We had seen so many stingrays that I spent half the time watching the bottom in front of me and the remaining half looking for fish. A cluster of juvenile wood storks were scattered on a sandbar not far in front of me, and when I stopped to watch them, a snook blew up bait in the mangroves behind them. I stole over to look, but there was no sign of the fish, and the storks spooked nothing when they flew over the place I'd hoped to see him.

Then, farther back in a small bay, another blast. This time I was sure I could find the fish because the fish fed in a very shallow corner of mangrove shoots. I crept over without a ripple and looked into every crevice: no fish. So I waded out of the shallow bay and was looking for new water when I noticed a faint wake leaving the area I had just inspected. This time it headed for an isolated clump of mangrove shoots, which stood like a small, flooded island away from shore. Back into the bay on tiptoe and expecting only to be fooled again. Standing in perhaps six inches of water, I peered into the mangrove roots and there, nearly perfectly hidden, was my chameleon-green snook.

I could only stand motionless and flick the leader into the maze of shoots. It landed a couple of feet from the fish, and as it sank he turned and struck. After several moments of close-range snook pandemonium, I seized him by the lower jaw and the barbless fly fell out. I kept the fish in the water and ran my finger along his topside, feeling the thickness through the shoulders, the rigid upright fins. I then released him, and he swam off with cross-eyed, lazy insouciance. With the tops of the mangroves and wild palms tossing in the wind, the low-tide mudbanks plowed up by wild hogs, this one was special.

In the end, I occasionally saw fish before Austin saw them. "Good eyes," he even said once. "I didn't see that one." It had been weeks since he'd last told me I needed a prescription.

And then for the rest of the season, with new spring breezes arising in flowering trees, I fished alone, daily. I was catching more fish than I did formerly and getting a bit complacent about how much I'd improved. There was even time to crawl around and peer at the queer, nameless fauna of the shallows. I followed a scarce banded puffer fish, a piggy-looking football with a tiny propeller of a tail that motored him along at such a slow pace that only his spines, or his benign herbivore face, kept him from being chow for some apex predator.

I looked through my binoculars whenever I felt like it. I listened to the conversation of wild pigs, quit fishing to gather oysters, took naps in the skiff, and made more elaborate lunches in the morning, sometimes at the expense of an early start.

There was no doubt about it: I was getting worse.

Trails of Tarpon

RUNNING DOWN the sound in the dark, a three-quarter moon shining overhead and lighting a great path across the water, I pictured myself colliding with unlighted pilings, stone crab traps, or oyster bars that I couldn't see. Chains of islands to the east and west were just streaks in the night sky. I hoped I would recognize my destination, a small basin appended to a forked channel, when I got to it. There would be a row of fishermen's shacks on an oyster reef, an opening, then the resumption of the shallow bar. I knew I'd see the silhouettes of the shacks but was not so sure I'd see the opening. Indeed, I overran it, and only the sudden dark shapes in front of me made me know that I was about to go high and dry in a planning skiff, possibly wrecking the motor. By the time I shut down, I was floating in less than a foot of water. I got out my push pole and began to work my way in the presumed direction of the basin. If I had fetched up on some wide shallow, I would find no tarpon today. Fish were shooting off around me—redfish, I guessed—and it was interesting going, but uncertainty had taken away some of the pleasure. Then, at about the time I thought I would try a new angle, I pushed on until the pole dropped out from under me and I knew I was in the basin. I was confident that when the sun came up I'd be in the middle of a lot of innocent tarpon. If there were rollers, I'd see them in the moonlight or at daybreak, which was now less than an hour away. In any case, a bonanza was at hand. All I needed was a little light.

The sun came up, and I poled myself into an irritable sweat before admitting that the fish were not here. I was in the wrong place at the wrong time. I suppose if you can't take *this*, you can't take tarpon fishing. Only the vision of things going right, of fish this big that can run this far and jump this high, keeps tarpon fisherman knocking their heads against the mysteries. I had been immersed since the earliest fish showed in March, and despite some irregular success, I could think of little else. But the fuel bills were mounting, as miles by the thousands were accumulated on the log of my GPS.

THERE IS A HIDDEN BAY, five miles to the east of my dock, where tidal creeks enter, ridged with oyster bars that form a kind of corset at its middle, dividing it into two sub-basins attractive to tarpon. They should be there—they've always been there—but they're not there now. Each morning I run to the basin in the dark, to the unearthly music of awakening waterbirds. It's hard to believe that anything in South Florida could be this remote. Before the morning breezes from the east or the later sea breeze from the west, the basins lie as mirrors of salt water, marred only by the frivolous jumps of mullet or the deep pulling V of a hungry redfish. If the tide is low, I'll look for snook at first light, and I have often seen them emboldened by the hour, sometimes racing between the legs of wading birds in pursuit of mojarra minnows, glass minnows, and gobies. There is something funny about this, the tolerant birds trying to feed while the self-absorbed snook swim along their legs and shower them with their feeding rushes.

But this is about tarpon. When I've found them in years past, the fishing has had a classic quality: laid-up fish, floating, asleep but ready to be drawn into pursuit. This is exacting, addictive fishing; the casts must be accurate but from a distance. When the cast is right, and the fish stirs to track the fly, in all his great weight and pent-up exuberance, the excitement, the nearness to success feels like fear. This year, I can't find them. The fish are not in short supply in nearby water—thick, even—but they're not coming *here*, not many, anyway, not enough. But on each visit something happens that makes me come back for another look. It's a free jumper rocketing from the water, hanging in midair before the crash that seems to be the fish's object; or it is a fish feeding, perhaps on a mullet; once, it is an abrupt canyon in the tannic water that closes, overlapping waves gathering at the middle of a subsiding hole, gone. I come back that night, the next morning; I never catch them. This is the scene of subtle opportunity, and I seem not to be up to it. At night as I drift off, I picture a sustained time during which I stay in those coupled basins, risking time-consuming failure until I understand tide, wind, and migration. Of course, if I succeed, it will all be mine and perhaps I will be slow to share my secret.

At the lower basin, jacks marauded along the mangroves with their backs out of the water, a scattered front of stormtroopers killing and eating on the run. I made a cast, but before it landed, they settled and disappeared: they're not dumb. In fact, in this shallow water, not much is dumb.

Along the mangroves, a pair of dolphins hunted snook and redfish, and their predatory surges sent shock waves well down the shore. This is a much different picture of dolphins from the rolling, gamboling creatures we usually see; this is full of purpose, the controlled violence inescapable. Dolphins are, with sharks, the principal enemy of tarpon.

The sun was well up now, and the occasional boat appeared, probably fishing with popping corks for speckled trout. I have a collection of these popping corks that I've dug out of the mangroves, prettily weathered, some with rattles inside. These join my collections of battered white plastic buckets, which serve as the local fisherman's portmanteau, and of weathered net floats, all of which should be thrown away as they appear to others to be "crap." The howl of a rental boat going up on an oyster bar reminded me that I should be elsewhere if I hoped to catch a tarpon.

I had started the engine and was idling while I thought about what to do when I received one of the gifts that comes to anglers only when they fish unstintingly, especially in salt water, where tide goes from something you read from a tide chart and memorize to something in your blood, a tissue laid over intuitions of fish movement, especially migratory movement, teased about by the vagaries of weather, by winds that change water temperature or produce lees in specific places—from all of which comes the gift: a hunch.

Here was the hunch: a long grassy hump, almost black, in four feet of water with a round sand spot in the middle that would illuminate anything swimming over it. The falling tide crossed it at an acute angle. It would be an ideal checkpoint for tarpon moving on the tide to one of the three passes that open onto the Gulf of Mexico.

An angler who ignores his hunches discounts his opportunities by half. This one was strong, and I followed it, a long run in a steep quartering chop that kept me in stinging spray until I entered the quieter waters of the sound. When I reached my spot, the hunch transformed itself into real conviction as I savored the light on my pass point, light that seemed to illuminate a broad area of turtle grass and the nicely defined edge. I anchored my skiff and tied the rod off with a quick-release knot, its bitter end attached to an orange float from my crap collection.

I was not long awaiting my travelers. First came a string of smaller fish, rolling merrily and a bit out of range. They were followed by singles and others strings of fish, also out of range. Then, just as my conviction began to weaken and I thought of moving my anchor, five big fish cut across the grass toward the edge from an entirely new angle, one less advantageous to me—it would have my fly approaching them from behind, something tarpon will not tolerate. I suspected that there might be one more fish, though, coming after these five. I cast just behind the last fish I could see and let my fly float until an apparition appeared, moving over the grass, and I started my retrieve. The fish moved so quickly, I never saw it. Instead, the rod jolted in my hand, the fish was running, and I was clambering to the stern to pull the slipknot on my anchor line. The first jump was a twister that had the fish landing on its back; then one marlin style with a lot of horizontal distance covered; then several more until they became diminished efforts, only the upper part of the fish's body above the surface. Still, I had trouble moving it and had to go to the fish with the motor. I stopped and tried to turn the fish, which responded with shorter and shorter but still more powerful surges. We had gone a long way together, halfway across the sound. The tarpon was finning beside the boat now. The lower jaw makes a good grip for removing the hook, and I held on for a few more moments just to feel its weight, its remaining power.

The best part of fishing is watching a fish swim away, in no particular hurry. Now to hunt up the orange float, and perhaps have my beer and my ham sandwich. It was ninety degrees out, and I was imagining the big chunk of ice in my cooler, the lovely breeze as I ran home.

I WENT OUT TO the Gulf on a hot June evening to fish one tide. It was quiet, just a few swimmers on the beach in the distance and towering, pink, dark-bellied thunderheads over the mainland. I scared some tarpon as I maneuvered into my stakeout and was not waiting long before the first fish came along from the south—singles, pairs, strings, all moving quickly. I misunderstood the speed of the first fish; they overtook me before I could present my fly and flushed from the boat in whirlpools of turbulence. The next bunch came at a bad angle to my left, but I cast anyway, and to my surprise, the biggest fish turned out and tracked my fly for a long way, then lifted up in the deep shoveling take that no one gets accustomed to, and I hooked it. This, like most first jumps, seemed enraged, an attempt to knock me out with the first blow. Then came several more blows just as violent, followed by a burning run. The fight took us straight offshore in fading light. Trying to force the issue, I leaned into the eleven weight, faithful friend of over a decade, and broke it. The shattered tip traveled down the backing, the sharp edge of the broken butt cut the backing, and my fly line went over the horizon. If there is any weakness in your tackle, tarpon find out about it.

AUSTIN LOWDER was in my living room with the battered insulated coffee cup with which guides keep their bodies in motion during tarpon season. He looked discouraged. "I had my guy in fish all day. Nice guy. But stupid. IQ around fifty-five, but we got along great. Show him a hundred fish and he goes, 'Which one do I cast to?' He casts and I have to tell him to strip. 'Strip,' I tell him. *'STRIP! STRIP! STRIP!'*

It was hopeless. At the end of the day, still no fish. He asks me to tell him what he should do. I'm like, 'Dude! I can't take any more! Catch a tarpon! *I recommend that you catch a tarpon.*'"

My Montana friends George Anderson and Bill Hart show up, as well as a stream of other visitors, most with beer in hand. We have line burns in the crevices of our fingers. There are bits of eighty-pound fluorocarbon in the rug from building shock tippets. An argument breaks out as to whether the Slim Beauty knot is as strong as the Australian Plait or the Bimini Twist. Everyone is thinner than they were sixty days ago. Two-stroke engines have made us half-deaf. We try to remember the last time we read a book or a newspaper. One sport says the president was flying to France to meet with a bunch of cheese-eating surrender monkeys. The fishing guides seem embittered that when they finally get into fish, the clients have to go back for massages or manicures. There is some tension between the guides and us unguided "privateers."

Austin started his day at five in the morning, took a short nap at my house at midday, fished till nine at night, dropped the client, headed out to fish himself, came in at 3:30 a.m., made a peanut butter jelly sandwich in my kitchen, and picked up his client ninety minutes later for another day on the water. Some guides actually like to fish.

I really should catch up on the news: Here and there, we are advised to stay the course. Tests show that doctors' ties are full of germs. Most Americans are too busy to floss. Others have made "the ultimate sacrifice." Everything on the news seems so abstract, especially the pompous overviews of the talking heads. The fishing has become a parallel universe. It can't last, can it? Probably it shouldn't, but it seems so real next to the streaming nightmare on the news. Still, it's not right, either, to lament that you can fish only when you are awake—nothing realistic about that. I can get pretty abstract myself, too, explaining that I'm "trying to get to the bottom of this" by way of accounting for how it got so out of control for three unbroken months.

"When do you think you're coming home?" asked my wife.

"I have a ticket for Sunday," I assured her.

"Do you think you'll be on that plane?"

After a thoughtful pause, I said, "I wish I knew." I said that I was like the house cat that had been making love to a skunk.

"How's that, dear?"

"I haven't had enough but I've had all I can stand."

"Ha-ha," she said mirthlessly. "I think you can stand more. Yes, I think you can stand more. Have you learned anything?"

"Yes, I've learned that you cannot live entirely on Krispy Kreme doughnuts."

"Oh."

"You must have fiber. By combining Krispy Kremes with Metamucil and black coffee, I have a complete diet."

I actually had a nice meal that evening sitting on my poling platform in the rolling Gulf, where I looked for fish, rod in reach. I'd laid out cold sliced pineapple, slices of Fuji apples, a big piece of Black Diamond cheddar, a wedge of cold sirloin, and a green-glass bottle of beer. Sometimes I saw a manta ray jump, or a manatee bulge to the surface, or a shoal of bait go airborne, or frigate birds sortie forth on a twilight mission, the heedless plunges of pelicans, a sail on the horizon. . . . It was quite good. Yes, a pleasant way to dine. I had been less pleased in the smoky twilight of famous French restaurants.

Then, where the Pass met the deep flat, where the color changed from cobalt to foamy mid-Gulf pale green, right there, a string of playful tarpon was streaming north, the late light illuminating the frolic and the long bar of silver when several rolled at once. It was my job now to guess where they were going, to get there and shut down quietly. The line of travel was constant, and I had little difficulty moving into their path to wait. I began checking my equipment more urgently as the fish approached—checked the line, checked the loop in the water for flotsam of any kind, the fish now with separate bodies and those curious unseeing above-the-water eyes. Every few seconds a tail kicked clear as a fish fed; then they started to chain up, straightened again, and came my way. I looked once more to see if I was standing on line, then threw my reading glasses around behind my back on their lanyard. I had suddenly remembered how they've snagged line and robbed me of fish before. Now I began talking to myself: *They're not in range, they're not in range, please be cool.* The lead fish was bigger than the others, dorsal slicing the water and pulling a quarter wave behind him. These fish were going *fast.* As they bore off slightly to my left, I cast an interception, waited, then retrieved across the vision of the lead fish. Instead of taking as it crossed in front of him, the fish slowed and began to track it, for twenty feet, until I was thinking we were within a couple yards of the boat flushing the whole school. But the fish pushed up behind my fly, tilted, and that stupendous maw opened, and my fly went down. I continued to strip until I had contact, then, using only my stripping hand, I struck the fish and tightened, reaching with my line hand as far away from my side as I could. The coils were leaping toward the stripping guide and then I was clear, and in the words of Mike Tyson, "It's on."

The first jump often seems to express the greatest fury: the olive-brown fish in the water has become the plated silver fish in the air; his body twists violently, and again, he reaches for the sky. The reentry is a heedless crash, then a reorientation into a straightaway dash, the substantial line becoming the seemingly insubstantial backing when the run accelerates and I feel the elevation of line as another jump and another, each crazier than the last, marks several spots in the sea at once.

Why is it so thrilling? Why is it *incomparably* thrilling? It's the contest joined, but it's also a kind of euphoric admiration and—this is risky—it feels like love. You watch your fish and you are filled with admiration, transported by beauty. Isn't that love? It was in high school!

The jumping has proven costly and the fish must now slug it out with you and you don't necessarily want to slug it out with him. Barring tackle failure, you have every chance of winning this phase, but make it quick: learn every fish-fighting technique out there, because love and admiration are not the same as beating up the object of your desire. I have come to feel quite ambivalent about this side of angling. I delight in seducing fish, at insinuating myself into their private world, but defeating fish has less appeal—though I continue to boat tarpon from time to time, to remind us both that this is mortal combat. There comes a moment when your silver paladin is once again the brown and somewhat humbled but still potent fish that took your fly. But when he stands off at half the length of your line and tries to roll in exhaustion, it is time to quickly boat him and remove your fly or to break him off.

BY LATE MAY, a tarpon-fishing death march was in play. George Anderson was napping between sessions on a rolled-up tarp in my carport. Montana log builder Bill Hart tried sleeping on the porch, but soaking with sweat, adjourned to the dock, where he rested on the widely spaced planks. Austin snoozed in the guest room. Crushed ice in coolers didn't make it through the day, and we turned to blocks. Three guys and a Gordon setter from West Yellowstone never came ashore. It was part of the Montana hatch on the Gulf. My charge account at the fuel dock kept me at arm's length from reality, and we all fingered places on our bodies to speed up the dialogue with our dermatologists. Predawn runs were at fatalistically high rpms; the imagination that once conjured up hazards now only pictured the destination and its fish. The tarpon came in pulses from the south and we watched for them like herons, with the hope that our trails would cross on the pale green Gulf of Mexico.

A few times when a hunch placed me in some incongruous spot— a breach in the mangroves, the corner of a tidal bore—the tarpon appeared and it was enough to think, *There you are!* as the fish changed direction and swam out of range. A moment of recognition between two watchful beasts.

We like to think that we know things while animals are merely programmed. Tarpon know to spawn offshore, and their progeny know to head inshore to the brackish mangroves to grow up safely. They know to follow migrating baitfish, and they know at what stage of tide the crabs hatch. They know to go south in the spring and up rivers when it's cold, and when to return south in the fall. Some fish know their away around both coasts of Florida and the Gulf to Louisiana and Texas. They know which fish they can eat and which ones can eat them. They know man is a bad thing the first time they see him. They know when the palolo worm hatches and will travel for miles to arrive just as dinner is served. They know that a safe snooze can be had in the shade of a Gulfport or Key West shrimp trawler. By the time you can catch tarpon consistently, when you are convinced you know what they know, you think so much like them that your affection can create problems.

Marshall Cutchin, an old friend from Key West, and I were fishing with George one May evening on a long, sweet, curving shoreline that seemed to be a runway for inbound tarpon traffic. The fish were assembling in loose groups then stringing out in meandering lines, happy fish with one thing in common: they weren't biting. We threw everything at them, but they weren't even courteous enough to boil off in indignation. Each had that faraway look that is connected less to hunger than to destiny. This produces a new kind of effort from the angler: narcissistic casting based on no expectation of results. Tight loops! Casts so long no hook could be set. Another string of travelers came by, all average fish. I cast, and from the shadows beneath the string, a very different fish arose and wolfed my fly. I set the hook, and the fish jumped with magnificent hang time. "That's a big fish," George stated. Marshall said, "Tom, that's an awful big fish." The hook was firmly set, the fish began that run characteristic of big tarpon—reminiscent of expensive German automobiles—and *ping!* The reel froze. The three of us looked into the reel's arbor. I was sad and shaken.

"What was that all about?"

"What happened?"

"Could I have done something?"

"A trapped loop?"

"The reel malfunctioned. I wish I was dead."

"There'll be more."

"Like that?"

"Well . . ."

"Like *that?*"

The next day, things began going haywire for everybody. I put a lot of pressure on a straight-running, non-jumping fish, the Dacron backing stripped the coating off my fly line at the nail knot, and the fly line was gone with the leader fly and the fish. George reported that loose fly line jumping around the deck while a tarpon ran caught the keys to his boat, ripped them out of the ignition, and threw them overboard. I had just taken an early-morning jaunt with George, who believes that when it comes to a fast skiff, you should "drive it like you stole it." Indeed, while we hurtled along, I took a concerned look at the GPS to get a real idea of our speed. As we whined and skittered south toward Fort Myers, I determined we were pushing sixty and that not much of the boat was ever actually in the water. "The reason this thing is so slow," George explained, noting my alarmed stare at the speed indicator, "is I have the wrong prop on it."

I ADMIRED THE SUNSET, a fabulous peach meringue with towering thunderheads straight out of the *Arabian Nights*. It wasn't long before tarpon began to appear, pushing uptide in long strings. This was going to be perfect. I turned the boat around, bow to the tide, and anchored, then attached my buoy with a quick-release knot. Not long after, I was up on the bow, line stripped out and ready; I could see fish rolling on an undeviating course, and my heart began to pound.

A running guide boat slowed just offshore of me to see what I was doing. I hoped the tarpon wouldn't roll again, but they did and the guide started his electric motor and moved up an eighth of a mile to cut me off. My day was over. The guides' version is: we're trying to make a living. The privateers' version is: they're pimping our wildlife. I went back to the house to watch the Calgary Flames in the semifinals. The ice looked good, especially right after the Zamboni, when all is well with the world and the good air rises from the rink.

Once June came around, it was hot before the sun came up. Standing on the deck fueling my skiff, I could watch my sweat rain around my feet. Idling out of the canal, my eyes went to patches of shade and not to the glare of the Gulf beyond. Instead of thinking how many trout it would take to make a meal for a tarpon, I began to think how beautiful a trout looks when it tips up under a mayfly. And what about a nice cow in a green meadow? The tropics make a man forget reading, writing, and arithmetic, which my checkbook could confirm. How clever folks are in the north, I marveled. The local hotel's shutting down whole wings was grimly logical; the rapidly decaying local civility gave rise to an ill-tempered poetry as angry folks tried to communicate. At the store, the oranges were from California, the mangoes from Brazil, and the berries from Chile. The bag boy, age eighty, was from Yonkers; the checkout clerk, Cleveland. The entire island was covered with green, rapidly growing plants advancing on seasonal homes with ill-concealed malice.

I hooked a hot fish on the edge of the Intercoastal Waterway. When it went airborne, a cigarette boat full of bathing beauties stopped to watch but left in a roar when the tarpon stopped jumping. Then I was alone with the fish. After two long, straight runs, it let me bring it slowly to the boat. My arms were dead. I hung over the gunwale and removed the fly, then held the great fish by its lower jaw. I could see every detail of its iridescent shape in the pellucid green water, turtle grass and seashells a few feet below. The slow beat of its tail pulsed all the way up through my shoulder, even into my body; its lazy power curled the water. I hung low over the side of the boat until I looked straight into those huge black eyes. I said, "I gotta go." I opened my hand and all the migratory wisdom in that gaze faded to green and the fish was gone. I knew I'd make that plane.

Black Squall

I THINK YOU KNOW when things have come together—a still, over-cast day in July on the Ruby, walking-speed flows over submerged boulders on the Bulkley, early flood tide in the Abaco Marls—the can't-miss feeling that in a significant minority of times blows up in your face, unbearable mosquitos pouring through your weapons-grade Deet, the jetboat settling in on your run as you climb through griz-zly tracks several strides short of having somewhere to fish, the dead Yamaha you forgot to fuel and the wag sitting in front of the console who says, "It was made in Japan. Give it some rice."

I had the good signs, and the bad ones were unimportant. If I had doubts I dismissed them. A huge tide was falling through all the passes, emptying Charlotte Harbor and the Pine Island Sound. Pale dollar-size crabs waving their little appendages were ginning up a protein burst for waiting predators. Example: *tarpon*. Along Johnson Shoals the sharks were in military formation to pick off anything in trouble. Members of the pioneering harbor-pilot Johnsons, namesakes of those shoals, were still around, writing family stories or, recently, repairing my laptop. Great June clouds towered over the pale green Gulf of Mexico, a reminder that with all its problems, with all the times she teed herself up for satire, Florida could still bring the beauti-ful heartbreak, the fecundity and the hope, often misguided. Big bull sharks found canals running through foreclosed neighborhoods while yellow rat snakes raised families in mailboxes that hadn't seen a letter since the last boom. Invading Cuban tree frogs went on surprising you in the bath tub while iguanas, generations from their pet-store origins, slurped down the eggs of migrating warblers. A woman who loved animals all her life, who saved baby rabbits as a girl, who retired from a desk job at Delta, hadn't been seen since she left the condo to give that pesky alligator Wally a Jimmy Dean sausage. Fish and Wildlife hoped to catch Wally and do an autopsy. An F&W officer was sure it would be "interesting."

It was a long evening this time of the year and it was all mine. The gas tank on my skiff was full, rods rigged under the gunwales, floating lines, sink tips and sinkers—black and purple flies on 3/0 hooks. The ice from an unproductive morning still in the cooler, water and the half a sandwich that would do for dinner, when everything in the air meant that something was, as my cracker neighbor liked to say, "fixing to happen." And such a sweet, hopeful breeze, mangrove blossoms, the fragrance of jasmine drifting from backyards as I motored out, the kind of pending fishing that gives you butterflies. Passing the waterside restaurant, a nest of howling tables, cooking smells drifting over the water to my contracting salivary glands. Triumph should be preceded by minor suffering. I thought of Wimpy: "I'd gladly pay you tomorrow for a hamburger today."

Tarpon fishing is about hope. I wondered if many tarpon fishermen had been to Lourdes. Some put tarpon pictures on their skin and file their teeth to cut monofilament during urgent rerigging. But tarpon fishing, especially by yourself, was hard; accelerated aging was a side effect. It could be such a miserable business of hot, dead, tedious days that promising yourself to quit is quite routine until an image of a tarpon taking your fly—such a big fish, such a tiny lure!—enters your thoughts and the trail of suffering begins anew.

Tonight was different: tide, wind, and the state of the migration were . . . *perfect!* I was out of the bayou and running on clear green seas and tall clouds at my customary snail's pace (3200 rpms), a tribute to my days in the Keys long, long ago when my heroes, Harry Snow, George Hommell, and Woody Sexton barely got their boats on a plane, distinguishing themselves from the waterskiers and joyriders. These were the days before Jet Ski operators enlivened the seaside with their arresting imitation of monkeys enjoying sex with footballs.

I could see all the way to the little town of Bokeelia, once headquarters for a vigorous smuggling operation and known then as "Bow-Up-and-I'll-Kill-Ya." There in the long-ago seventies a jolly pot-smuggling acquaintance paid a visit to his rivals and vanished into their hands and memories. Sea turtles were evident in the tide, perhaps eating some of the provender flushing seaward from this splendid estuarine bay, a miniature Chesapeake with its great rivers, the Myakka and the Peace creating an unimaginable biological plenitude, if it can stand the ravages of mankind. I was so pleased to see the turtles, since many of their nests had been lost to a recent hurricane and their oceanic journeys among the shipping lanes were always so perilous. They are among the world's most beautiful and interesting animals, with star maps in their brains and much to teach us.

Fish were rolling in the Pass and blowing up bait with remarkable savagery. Fishing in this deep water required skill, clearly, as some were far better than others at doing it, but eight ounces of lead and a crab missed my wheelhouse by a country mile. First prize for the tarpon tournament this year was an assault rifle. So maybe I was ill suited to the pleasures and rewards of this style of angling, though anyone would have second thoughts when the Hooters boat went past with its array of seminude enthusiasts. They were friendly, vaguely pneumatic, and waved to everyone.

Any boats fishing tonight would be headed southwest, and it was a bit of a parade, no small skiffs like mine, a few bay boats, and the stately old-time Boca Grande tarpon boats built here in the island's bayou, high in front with inside steering, paired fighting chairs aft. In one of these, I caught my first tarpon at age eleven, my father directing the back of the chair while I worried about going over the stern.

My progress down the harbor side of the island brought into view a gated community, private homes giving way to condominiums in a kind of Soviet architectural style. Not long ago, the idea of gated communities would have been unimaginable on an island that pictured itself as having avoided the latest of nouveau Florida; but those days were gone. Now some on Boca Grande would like to require members of the gated communities to enter the town's public spaces through another gate, as though to shelter themselves from affluent riffraff.

Rounding the old phosphate docks, it was clear the tide was already falling hard, boats gathered uptide to drift out of the Pass to the Gulf, run back up, and repeat. I headed around the end of the island and crossed over the north bar and out of the Pass. Here I hoped to see some fish spill over the bar, high in the water where they might succumb to my incredibly backward method, fly-fishing. If I had stayed out there hoisting a crab, my chances would have greatly increased, the Hooters boat endearingly proximate. In a small skiff, this could be tricky: on spring tides, you felt you were fishing and casting in more or less the same place, until you found yourself falling toward a noisy, unmanageable rip, having failed to notice that you'd headed out to sea. *No bueno!*

All across the harbor, miles away, I saw a tall black storm forming, leaning from its stratospheric top toward the south and already on a turbulent move. Because of some effect of backlight, the water around me seemed almost iridescent with the special Gulf of Mexico green. However, I was in the right place and indeed a few tarpon were ambling my way across the bar. Another boat to the west of me seemed to be in a better place; but I noticed immediately the fish felt some bubble of displacement or hull slap and made their way well around his boat. Out of a concern for safety, the poor fellow was fishing in a boat that was pushing away the fish he hoped to catch.

The storm had quickly moved farther south and was now directly east of Pine Island, such a big thing to seem so agile, its top tilted ever more seaward in a huge inclination of inanimate longing. It's easy to see nonhuman things in nature that seem to *want* something.

The boat displacing oncoming fish had moved them toward me and I soon had a chance to cast to rolling, sparkling approaching fish without effect. They saw the fly and were not disturbed by it but were uninterested. I saw several abeam of me traveling slowly, ghosts beneath the surface, easeful movements and delicate surface rolls. I was sure I would catch one even as this school ignored my fly and passed. Meanwhile, I watched the black squall with curiosity; it seemed now to have crossed below Pine Island toward Captiva, and was wider, taller, and blacker than ever, virtually straight south of me, an entity, a being, that had been quite far to the east such a short time ago.

A string of tarpon came in a lazy, meandering line, rolling calmly, smaller forty- to sixty-pound fish. The sea had grown so still that my skiff rested without a ripple or any kind of the displacement that today's pressured fish feel so easily. I had an advantageous shot in front of the lead fish and he swam right past it. So did the next fish, then all the others, though retrieving had pulled my fly away from their zone of visibility anyway. Then, unseen from deep water, a big fish surfaced and snatched the fly, hooked up without my help, and made a burning run into the Gulf. With over a hundred yards of backing out, the tarpon made a long, low jump, the acceleration of which caused the backing to bury on my reel. The fish broke off, was gone, *ping*. This is a kind of postdated operator error and a reliable contributor to self-loathing. I hadn't even seen that fish; I couldn't feel cheated but I could certainly look back to the last fish I'd caught and realize that the backing had not been properly rewound or with sufficient pressure, or it wouldn't have buried and I wouldn't feel like I deserved the punishment I was about to receive from other elements of the natural world. Basically, it was a karmic question.

Having made a westward crossing so that it was now below me, the storm had dropped a black curtain over the entire view to the south and showed every sign of gathering itself to run north up the coast, an ominous U-turn toward all the boats in the Pass and beyond, including mine. It seemed to swell in a black-bellied form that I misunderstood to be some static change of nature when it was simply that it was rushing toward me. I considered trying to run but it was a long way down the Gulf shore before I could try for shelter and I would likely be overtaken. I moved the skiff in close to the beach behind the ruins of an old pier whose abutments had made a small lee, not enough but all I had.

The rain came first, falling then driving. The storm was virtually nighttime dark, I kept my fishing glasses on to protect my eyes from the stinging rain and sea spume that came with a cyclonic wind. The big boats fell north from the Pass and turned bows into the storm. I could see the anglers in the shelter of cabin tops staring out at the uproar while their captains remained at their wheels heading windward, standing up to it while I was reduced in my small craft to hiding behind buttresses that were doing little to stop my storm.

Then it was gone, roaring north up the coast and leaving extraordinarily confused seas in its wake, racing lumps and rips and pyramids extending seaward. Almost dark, I'd have to work my way home, around the south end of Boca Grande, through the inside of the Pass, north up the other side of the island to my inlet, my hurricane hole, my dock, and my dry, quiet house. I should have run the boat as far onto the beach as the motor could drive it and walked home. I thought of that. I could carry the anchor up into the sea grass and hope the boat was still there tomorrow. At worst and as a friend once said of sporting gear about to be lost, "They still make it." But I didn't do that; I headed for the Pass, so nearby, and as soon as I turned into it, I knew I would have problems. The seas were running high and steep and toward the center of the tide, as fast as a train. I drove straight into it and found that they were pushing me where I wanted to go all right, but I could only rise toward the crests of these insistent swells to the very top where they broke, and when the breaking seas tried to come aboard, try to outrun them down the face of the wave—all good, but it was impossible to keep the bow from burying—at which point only a burst of engine could shed the ocean from the foredeck, then back up to the top where a breaker tried to come aboard again, starting another bobsled run down to the buried nose, gun the engine, sluice off the seawater, and so on in a relentless cycle. A single lapse of attention and it would be all over.

Out of the Pass and running the length of the island, things were no better. A few other boats were working their way home, battered but also bigger, and there was less pattern to the seas. I feared being thrown into one wave chain at the wrong angle, and I realized I should think more seriously about swimming. I lifted the dry storage and saw the life jackets and felt I could get ahold of one in a pinch while wondering why I wasn't wearing one already. A bigger bay boat was between me and land, and I felt that they would be in a good position to fish me out of the water. And so I glanced obsessively toward them, four anglers in foul-weather gear. They seemed to be managing as the seas exploded away from their bow, but the next time I looked, they were sinking. The driver applied full power as they foundered; thus they were close to shore before the boat sank entirely. Only the engine cowl and bow pulpit showed above the water. The four anglers went overboard and did everything they could to keep the boat from drifting into pilings. I raised my hands to let them know I was helpless to come to their aid and when I saw the four unvanquished anglers laughing, I realized they assumed I was next.

But I wasn't! As I idled up the inlet, past the fuel docks, a crowd of storm watchers gave me an ovation for my hard-won stardom. This transformed me from a frightened boater to a man home from the sea. What a great feeling!, et cetera, an eternal figure. It was only after I'd washed the boat down—I could scrape the encrusted salt off the console with my fingernails—and taken a warm outdoor shower that I set about undoing the disorder in my reel. I put it on the bench and viewed the buried backing caused by my carelessness. I thought of that brute of a fish and the trough of sea he made landing. I could have been Marlon Brando holding a couple of pigeons. I could've been a contender.

Shrink to Fit

FLY FISHING WHILE OLD

Plus ça change, plus c'est même chose.

LIKE MOST TROUT FISHERMEN my age, normal procedure is to find a place to get into some river and wade, an approach that confers a granular view of all on offer, details of bottom, hydrology, insect life, and general atmosphere. On balance, there are better ways to catch fish; here in the West, floating in a drift boat is probably the most effective and easily freebases ten to twenty miles of river in a day. Now that millennials are making a bit of dough, I often see them go past, when they are not running over me. Things are happening fast for them and their exuberance flows over. The one in the bow shouts, "Shit!" and the one in the stern shouts, "Fuck!" Between the sports, the guide, on the oars, does his best to make sense of this and decode the river as it comes toward them, with an eye to make the most of the opportunities—corners, slicks, glides, tail outs, undercut banks, and troughs. I have no problem picturing trout in these locales but it seems they are flashing past me in a manner disadvantageous to my talents.

I make one of these trips each year and over time I have learned that I am not good at this type of angling. The problem for me, first of all, is that it is going too fast, as it can be even for the millennials, when cascading opportunity causes failures and missed chances. My second inadequacy is actually humiliating and it is that this kind of fishing, during its slow spells, bores me, and so when something important happens, I'm not ready. When staring into the middle-distance wondering, *Will this day never end?* the guide or your companion cries, "Strike!" and it makes you feel like—no matter what else is going on in your life—*a loser*. Earlier in the day, anticipating lunch may have produced a similar collapse, certifying an indelible picture of your age and incompetence but especially your age, which has brought you to this pass.

Long ago, Nat Reed said to me in his usual declamatory style, "No wading staff before your first heart attack." I haven't had a heart attack but I do have a wading staff. I used it for a long time fishing for steelhead, especially early in the season when I was unused to the heavy water. I have since graduated to using a wading staff fishing the rocky freestone rivers near my home. Actually, I use one in easy wading spring creeks, too, since I slid down the bank of one of them and fractured my leg. It is crutchlike. The remaining question is, when will I use something like a wading staff in my own home?

Bamboo czar Glenn Brackett brought Doug Merrick, who built rods for generations, to my house one day to fish. Doug was very old and impaired at that point, hardly able to get around, but we found a pool with a secure gravel bottom and I watched Doug's still-elegant casting stroke and his look of serenity as, without the ability to take another step, he seemed a long way from the days when he and his fellow POWs were placed atop German trains to ward off Allied bombing. He seemed deeply contented to be reunited, to experience something emblematic of the stream of his life.

When Django Reinhardt felt abandoned by luck, he gathered his fishing tackle and was renewed by the sight of the river. One day, on the banks of the Seine, he had a heart attack. It had been difficult to find a doctor and when one *finally* arrived, Django uttered his last words: "You've come *now*, have you?" He died with his wit intact; maybe it was the fishing.

I grew up fishing the rivers of northern Michigan—the Pere Marquette, the Pine, the Boardman, the Black, the Pigeon—rivers I haven't seen in sixty years, but I still like to say those names. Under the instruction I got from my elders, one did not use lead in any form and if those men had heard about tungsten they would have gone mad. Dry flies, wet flies, and streamers were the order of the day. Anything more was tennis without the net. But no lead. Lead was considered to be contrary to the spirit of things. A person with sinkers in his pocket was considered to be something very, very low, perhaps, in the words of one of my uncles, a booger-eating moron. I see a lot of lead these days and it makes me feel old.

The trouble with knowing why you fish is that you may find there are others whom you don't want to fish with. The nature-driven spiritualist does well to avoid the numbers guy. A friend of mine was poling a famous tarpon fisherman when he spotted a rare and beautiful wading bird. When he pointed it out to the renowned angler, he was told, "That is a bird. That is not a tarpon. Let's start paying attention, please." I made the mistake of telling this story to one of the new breed of Keys guides, the kind in board shorts making gang signs behind the permit he just landed. He agreed that it would have been wrong to look at the bird. He said as though speaking to an idiot, "*Obviously* it was no tarpon." What happened to fishing as an immersion in nature?

When successive administrations in Washington approach the condition of a dumpster fire in their gathering grotesquerie, when the head of the Environmental Protection Agency requires an armored car and a soundproof phone booth as a result of his assaults on the natural world, you wonder if, in view of all we hold genuinely sacred, the nation is in steep decline or, at a minimum, you have simply lived too long and have lost the ability to adapt.

It was time to write a few friends who love to fish and ask them how they like being old.

Dear Friends,

I'm working on an essay, about growing old as an angler, based so far on my own insufficiency but I'm hoping you might have a word on the subject, as little as a sentence, or more. If I am disparaging your enduring youthfulness, forgive me. These days you really can't tell. The elder fisherman of yore, in his pipe and crumpled fedora, was happy to give away his age and state; but today's veteran may well have had a facelift, swims laps in a thong, wears a logo ball cap—a timeless figure at once chipper and creaky, who goes on casting and awaiting results. This might be an ideal time to heave yourself off the sofa and toss me a few words from the abyss. I'll be grateful if you do.

As ever,

Tom McGuane

As the following will show, they've had this on their minds.

Dave Grusin

Dave Grusin is a jazz musician and composer. While shaving and watching TV, he noticed he had won an Academy Award. That's Dave. He's been a trout fisherman all his life, since his upbringing in Colorado. He has crossed North America with a fly rod in the front seat of his Austin Healey, a long drive in the long ago, with the top down.

Re: aging on the stream: How many chapters would you like?

John Gierach

I first knew John Gierach as his admiring reader, a state that has only increased with each of his books, starting with the classic *Trout Bum*. He writes in the unadorned, pure American voice of a man who knows what he's talking about. John is not sufficiently delusional to be surprised by anything aging has in mind.

I once said that the solution to growing crowds of fishermen has always been to arrive earlier and hike farther, but that at some point hiking farther and getting older begin to diverge in inconvenient ways. As I write this, two young guys are on the roof sweeping the flues for my wood stoves; a job I once did myself, but that my knees and faulty sense of balance now advise me to hire out. Wading and rock scrambling are now harder for the same reason, although I can still do both, sometimes with the aid of a wading staff. (And more and more I catch myself noting the things I "can still do" as if there were an expiration date attached.) I can't spot small, drab flies on the water as unerringly because my eyes aren't as sharp as they once were, so I lean more toward patterns with big white wings and point out that I could lose sight of a size-18 Blue-Winged Olive at age thirty, too. When did they start making the eyes on hooks so small? I'm less competitive now and can be genuinely happy for a friend who catches more or bigger fish than I do, although I'd just as soon he didn't make a habit of it. I'm also happy with fewer fish and don't feel like I've wasted the day if I'm not out from dawn till dusk. I tend to fish with other geezers who feel the same.

John McPhee

John McPhee is a national treasure, the author of many great books that explain the world to us and somehow manage to combine gravity, faultless prose, good humor, and modesty. I wish everyone wrote like John McPhee.

I fly fish for the chain pickerel, always have, and almost always with yellow Kiwi Muddlers, but now (eighty-seven) I sit down in the canoe. Long, long ago I had a coach who said of English teachers, "They have to sit down to pee." The full range of his remark was lost on me for seventy-some years until my sense of balance became eroded by peripheral neuropathy and I had to sit down to cast, even in heavy and stable Sharpe canoes, throwing the shooting head in the direction of Atlantic salmon. And I regret the contempt, however faint, that I once felt toward fishermen sitting in chairs on the shores of lakes and the banks of rivers. I can no longer wade in currents. If I'm not in a boat, I'm casting from a chair at the edge of the water.

George Anderson

George Anderson, the River Rhino, is the most effective fisherman I have ever known. His drive to catch fish is unparalleled, and he has the skills and technical proficiency to make it all work. I've always enjoyed fishing with George because that's what you're going to do and all you're going to do. Leave male bonding and fine dining at the door; if you fluff a cast, hold your temper when George casts across your line to catch the fish you were trying for. If age keeps degrading his fishing skills, in another thirty years George will only be as good as the best angler you ever fished with.

I have to accept lower expectations than I had when younger and when I could fish a lot better. My inability to walk any distances due to my bad ankles has become a problem for me and affects my ability to wade well now, too. I'm no longer a river rhino, more like a river pussy! Using a wading staff helps a lot and also helps me walking across rocks that never used to slow me down. Failing eyesight and hearing also create problems that I never had before. Fishing dry flies, I just cannot see my fly on the water like I used to, and this causes a lot of missed takes. My hearing has gone downhill a long way, and the hearing aids help, but also pose a problem for me when out in my skiff. I need to wear hearing protectors just to keep the hearing aids from blowing out, and this is a real pain in the ass. But a guy just needs to do what he must to get out on the water and have fun.

Tom Brokaw

Tom and I have lived down the road from each other for at least a couple of decades. He needs no introduction here except to say that he is a garden-variety outdoorsman of the unpretentious sort produced by the American Midwest.

First came the wading staff, then the judgment that slow water over a smooth bottom is likely to hold more fish than the deep pockets around that fast current against the boulder on the far side, followed by the firm grip of the twentysomething guide easing you into the stern chair, tying on the fly, and asking, "Didn't you know my dad? He was in junior high when you graduated from high school." Finally, it is the nodding off in the warm sun while your fly bounces against the current.

Irv Weissman

Dr. Irving Weissman, old friend, native Montanan, lifelong fly fisherman, is a director of the Stanford University Institute of Stem Cell Biology and Regenerative Medicine. He is a world-renowned researcher of stem cell science; he once told me that his early life as a trout fisherman was key to the mental instincts that made him a scientist and a researcher. Irv is great company, a bon vivant, and his interests, including literature, are very wide.

I just came out of the Bob Marshall on the Sun River side. Thirty years ago was our last trip this side. Then I ran down screes, rapidly and safely crossed knee- or thigh-deep rushing water, all with speed and accuracy and confidence. Now at seventy-eight, nearly seventy-nine, I have lost my confidence, and step gingerly with a wading staff, nearly toppling many times as I make my way up a single side of the stream to get to a fishing spot. Am I wobbly because I'm out of practice in my daily life, or is it aging showing itself?

I study the function and evolution of blood and brain, and even muscle stem cells. Individuals compete for niches, and also for reproductive dominance. Several thousand years ago our species probably survived an average of thirty to forty years, still reproductively active, but decreasingly physically dominant, and therefore decreasingly reproductively successful. Natural selection hardly selected for nearly-eighty-year-olds. We are born with a variety of blood-forming stem cells and a variety of brain-forming stem cells and a variety of muscle stem cells. For each of these, the stem cells that win competition for their respective *niches* when we are young are different from the stem cells that win when we are old. Someday we may be able to select for young stem cells of each type to slow down aging, but it won't happen soon. Nevertheless, I am happy that I can still fish, tying my flies on the line much more slowly, getting to the fish a little later than before, and guessing what they might take; and most important, still be able to keep the rhythm of the double-haul cast and watch the fly land where I want. So, muscle and brain long-term memory hasn't gone yet, and at my age, that is what I have accepted and appreciate.

Yvon Chouinard

Yvon is an inspired innovator of outdoor equipment, a renowned mountaineer, and an excellent fisherman. As an innovator, he is unafraid to make mistakes; hence, the huge box of hand-tied, sky-blue flies that was meant to end the search for perfection, now succeeded by an eternal version of the Pheasant Tail Nymph. Yvon is a fierce fighter for the natural world, perhaps the most committed of all. It says a lot about his generous spirit that in the face of the world's war on nature, Yvon still knows how to have fun. Here we have pure YC: he knows ahead of time what's going to happen on the water, prepares correctly, and keeps his sense of humor when it all goes to hell.

I didn't know where Nelson's Spring Creek was, so I drove around aimlessly. Finally, I gave up and drove to Sweetwater Fly Shop and asked a teenage clerk for directions. He sent me thirty-five miles in the wrong direction. I had tied special flies for the occasion and stashed them in a "hook box" in my pants pocket. I searched three times, looking with increasing desperation for that little box. I just couldn't find those specially tied dry midges. Guess what was hatching all day? When I got to dinner I reached into my pocket, and there they were. The exact flies I needed for that hatch. I hate myself.

Fred Torphy

Fred is my cousin. We have fished together since we were boys. On Saturday, I will fly from Montana to his home in Rhode Island and we'll do it again. When we fish, much of what we remember about our long-ago fishing will come back, catching tautog and "choggy" minnows with tarred handlines, making model swordfish boats like the ones our heroes sailed out of Sakonnet Harbor to faraway seas, and refilling our capacity for wonder at each day's tide-pool changes.

> For me, a day that begins with a predawn departure by boat
> to the islands in pursuit of striped bass is of one piece with
> having an early cup of coffee with my fishing friend Tony,
> after biking up to the Commons to fetch a morning paper,
> gardening with grandchildren on a steamy day, strolling down
> to the harbor for a swim, cooking and eating fish stew made
> from the day's catch, all the time wearing the same khaki
> shorts and worn tee shirt in which I started the day.

Nick Lyons

Nick Lyons, a splendid fishing writer himself, has singlehandedly through his publishing made the world know that the angling literature of the Americas has the breadth and importance of any in the world. He is a skilled and exacting angler and a thoroughly cultivated human being. At the time of my inquiry, he had recently lost his wife and son. Nick is undeceived by mortality. I hope, and expect, his spirits to rise.

> It's hard to cast when the pinched nerve in your eighty-six-
> year-old back barely lets you stand without pain or falling,
> and if you do, the damaged rotator cuff in your left shoulder
> renders hopeless your line hand. Happily, the last cataract
> operation provides a ringside seat for the sparest sipping-rise
> hatch.

Carl Hiaasen

In his works, Carl Hiaasen has made and populated a world that never existed before Carl Hiaasen—a world of astonishing invention and comic vision. He's a great fisherman of a kind that once came along with South Florida homeboys, urban, imaginative, and ever aware of the tropical sea at the end of the street.

> The challenge of fly-fishing in my sixties presented itself
> vividly on the bonefish flats of Bimini, where I learned that
> even mild sciatica becomes a breathtaking hindrance when one
> is trying to evade a seven-foot lemon shark.

Huey Lewis

Rocker Huey Lewis lives here in Montana. He is a dedicated trout fisherman who seems to have only one fly rod, an old Winston. I've never heard of such a thing. I, and all our friends, can't figure out why Huey is so unflappable and normal. We're quite sure he's the nicest person we know. He can really fish and if you invite him to do so, he's on the way.

> I'm not extremely old, just old. I'm sixty-eight, and there's
> a list of things I can't do anymore and a much longer list of
> things I can't do as well as I once did. Fly-fishing is on neither
> list. I confess, however, that without magnifying glasses, a
> wading staff, and zipper-front waders (because when Nature
> calls, she will not be put on hold), I'd be a goner. I'd probably
> have to play a lot more golf, and it's on the second list. With
> those three accessories, however, I am better than ever, and
> still (wait for it) learning and improving! I love fly-fishing.

Jimmy Buffett

I must have known Bubba for over forty years because that's how long I've been married to his sister. Our original iteration was as Key West hell-raisers. He is a painstaking lover of fun and adventure and applies his work ethic to all he does without losing the piratical twinkle when he is contemplating his next, often unexpected, move. I have no idea what it will be but I can't wait to find out.

Fishing and aging are two things I have been doing for a long time, and adding up a few "close calls," several bad car wrecks, one airplane crash (or should I say big splash), and a stage fall, I am just glad to be here and still fishing. But one thing I have noticed as a septuagenarian fisherman is reduction in the amount of fishing crap that was part of my life for a long time. I am not saying I am back to a cane pole and a bobber cork, but I think I am doing better.

My love of surfing now outweighs my love of fishing, but I still like my time on the water, if not so much in faraway places. I haven't fished Montana, Belize, the Yucatan, Panama, and God knows where else in a long time. The end of my dock on Peconic Bay in the summer, night fishing for bass with my spaniel Gracie snapping at their tails before we release them, the bass flats of Madaket, and the edge of the Gulf Stream east of Cat Cay, where cautious fish still drive me crazy—those are the spots I care about these days. But if I get the urge to go I head out with my Martin guitar, a nine-weight four-piece fly rod, and a surfboard, just in case. As Mark Twain said, "There is no use in walking five miles to fish when you can depend on being just as unsuccessful near home." Life is still good, and fishing will always be a part of it.

Tom Bailey

Tom Bailey went to my college and behaved so badly that, though he completed his course work, his father had to sue for his diploma. After Tom founded the Janus Fund, our college saw its way to forgiving him. I suspect it was not mutual. I first knew Tom as a Henry's Fork regular, living in his van with his fly rods and jazz records. Tom likes to learn, whether it's economics, fish, or horses. He's a pleasure to fish with because of his infectious happiness when he's standing in running water.

Lately, I've been remembering an evening on Poindexter Slough near Dillon several decades ago, a particularly frustrating evening with an obvious PMD hatch, changing flies like a mad man, sizes, stages (duns, cripples, emergers) while the light lasted and getting pissed. Finally, when I go back to my van in the parking lot, I run into a very old man loading his stuff in a 1948 Willys Jeep. He tells me he has had a great evening, which of course brings me to my knees. He has a small campfire going and invites me to share a drink with him. I pull out my flask of George Dickel and we spend the next hour talking about fishing. Somewhere in that hour he tells me how you become a fisherman: when you begin, you just want to catch a lot of fish; then the Alaska stage where you want to catch a lot of big fish; and when you are a real fisherman you really are satisfied with just one fish that you have found, in a difficult spot, observed the fish, fished for it, perhaps hooked or caught the fish, enjoyed the time on the stream or river in the great light, the interaction, and you *love it*. I have never forgotten that interaction with that old man, brief as it was. As I age, I am more and more like that, maybe because I don't move as well at eighty as I once did, maybe because I am smarter, who knows. I know I enjoy it more.

Skip Herman

Skip Herman is a recovering lawyer with a house on a Montana river. If the Smithsonian ever needs an example of an angling fanatic for future generations to study, they should put Skip in a glass case and suck out all the air. Skip has a lot of fishing opportunities, and he shares them with instinctive generosity.

Nursing home? Home care? No. I am going into an Assisted Fishing Facility. Wheel me out on a platform. Hand me one of the scores of size-18 Blue-Winged Olives, long ago pre-tied to a size 5X tippet. The only issue is whether the monofilament deteriorates in strength and memory before I do.

Guy de la Valdene

Guy and I fished together often in the Keys, usually for tarpon, which have been Guy's passion most of his life. Guy is a thoughtful writer on the things outdoorsmen love.

Age and surgeries should have by now rendered my desire to fish a memory, but they didn't; what has impaired my desire to fish is the unimaginable invasion of anglers on the water who love wearing expensive fishing clothes and hold in their casting hand two thousand dollars' worth of equipment. They do the same thing I have been doing for almost sixty years and like golfers they like to talk about "their day!" I am a salt-water fly fisherman and although I hear from guides and anglers about the traffic jams on big rivers like the Yellowstone, I can only comment on, for example, my last tarpon trip in the Northern Gulf of Mexico. It's a staking-out situation, which can be good if the fish are moving, but most of the time, insanely boring. Nowadays a good day is not referred to as fish "jumped" but as "bites." "That was a good day, we had three bites." Finally, my guide, whom I like very much and have known for ten years, took his phone out of his pocket and talked to his friends, mostly other guides, forty-eight times in a six-hour tide trip. I have retired from tarpon fishing.

Marshall Bloom

Marshall Bloom is a doctor and a scientist, a researcher of the world's dangerous viruses. He has lived in the Bitterroot Valley of Montana for half a century. I first knew him when we long ago had our pot-latches at my house in Livingston, big trading events where packs, flyrods, elk rifles, car parts, and elk jerky were swapped. It was the best low-grade materialism I have ever experienced. Marshall has been a lifelong trout fisherman who understands his responsibility to the environment and acts upon it.

Fly-fishing while aging? Sounds like a nice idea, so what's holding me back? A lack of partners? Well, it is true that now many of my favorite fishing buddies have become either incompatible, incapacitated, or incinerated, but there are still a few. And my son in Seattle has taken to fly-fishing, raising the prospect of coastal cutthroat and steelhead. So it can't be that. A lack of places to fish or fish to catch? Well, it is true that now fishing means dodging rafts that look like PT boats with anglers decked out in regalia resembling Magyar armor, but the fish have never been better and there are still remote native trout streams within a day's drive. So it can't be that, either. What's holding me back? I think it must relate to something that judge from Michigan wrote decades ago about the stages of fly-fishing. I have always felt that the ultimate stage should be when you go from catching to helping the fish. I have enjoyed great trout fishing for almost fifty years, but the trout fishing and trout that future generations will have worry me, as does the shrinking interest in outdoor activities in general. Tying my own flies has given way to teaching middle school kids to tie, and fishing outings have often given way to working on trout conservation. Maybe I am approaching that ultimate stage. But peering through my bifocals at the pile of rods in the corner, perhaps I'll take the three weight down to Teller tomorrow morning. There might be a chance for some fly-fishing while aging after all.

Bo Ivanovic

I met Bo long ago on the Whale River in Labrador and fell for his elegant Spey casting, new then to us duffers, and his discernibly deep commitment to fishing. He has written down every fish he ever caught back to age ten or so. Bo is a Londoner and his insatiable drive to catch fish has mostly been confined to the salmonids. He is one of the few to ever catch a fifty-pound Atlantic salmon and he has fished most of the great rivers where salmon are found. But he loves *all* fishing and to see him, the year he caught his great fish on the Alta in Norway, tear his hair out over a small Montana trout that wouldn't eat is to know the depth of his love for our sport.

> Of course, bloody decrepitude is creeping in like a thief in the night. It steals up on you and then with a roar slaps you in the face. I am just back from Iceland where I fished alone as much as possible to avoid extended hands trying to help me up banks. I felt like Melania swatting away Trump's hand! Last year I was offered a seat in the Underground by a forty-year-old woman. Imagine the lecture I gave her. However, I am not giving up and have taken up shot-putting again and although not the best in the UK in my age group, I'm very near it.

Lefty Kreh

I'm putting Lefty in here as I long intended to do, a kind of Hail and Farewell, as he has just passed away at ninety after a splendid life that began in poverty and included not just fishing everywhere, but the Battle of the Bulge and other clashes with Hitler's Wehrmacht and the deaths of young comrades in arms. At an army germ-warfare lab, anthrax blackened his famous casting arm. Among his remarkable days, he judged a fishing contest in Cuba between Fidel Castro and Ernest Hemingway. Castro, he found, was a delightful, companionable fellow while Hemingway was an utter prick. I met Lefty in the late sixties when his reputation was as an angler, writer, and overseer of the Miami Metropolitan annual fishing tournament, an institution fraught with controversy, which Lefty had to unwind. One disgruntled and world-famous fly fisherman, who may have cheated on a world record, offered to take everything he had, house, car, and bank deposits. Lefty, as the world knows, was a great innovator and a remarkably unselfish fishing companion.

His recent passing encouraged me to remember a recent day in the

Bahamas as we sat in a bonefish skiff in Andros and he discussed the "problems" of aging. I say "problems" because Lefty *liked* problems and working through them. That day, he could not rotate his torso at all and it required peering around awkwardly looking for a bonefish. Once he had one spotted, his casting skills were still remarkable as he rifled the fly to a fish. Lefty was proud of the many knots he had invented and whose strength he tested on a special machine. But that day his biggest fish came off: *a bad knot.* As he looked at the curlicue at the end of his leader, a part of aging seemed to have finally struck him as discouraging, and all he could say was, "I can't believe it."

Maybe that's how we old anglers feel: we can't believe it.